Follow the Lamb

Follow the Lamb

A Pastoral Approach to The Revelation

Douglas D. Webster

CASCADE *Books* · Eugene, Oregon

FOLLOW THE LAMB
A Pastoral Approach to The Revelation

Cascade Books
An Imprint of Wipf and Stock Publishers
199 W. 8th Ave., Suite 3
Eugene, OR 97401

www.wipfandstock.com

ISBN 13: 978-1-62564-799-3

Cataloguing-in-Publication data:

Webster, Douglas D.

    Follow the Lamb: a pastoral approach to the Revelation /
Douglas D. Webster.

    x + 308 pp. ; 23 cm. Includes bibliographical references and indexes.

    ISBN 13: 978-1-62564-799-3

    1. Bible—Revelation—commentaries. 2. Pastoral care. I. Title.

BS2825.3 .W35 2014

Manufactured in the U.S.A.   09/11/2014

for Virginia
my inkling of our future home

Contents

Acknowledgments   *ix*

1   The Canonical Climax   1

2   One Act Drama   12

3   Deep Meaning   31

4   The Jesus I Need to Know   43

5   The Seven Letters   58

6   First Love Witness   65

7   Band of Martyrs   72

8   Urban Fidelity   79

9   Idol Resistant   86

10   Beyond User-Friendly   93

11   Real Mission   99

12   True Riches   106

13   Christ the Center   112

14   The Open Scroll   122

15   Heaven's Perspective on Evil   132

16   Deliverance in Tribulation   145

17   Evil Unleashed   154

18   Witness   165

19   The Measure of the Mission   174

20   The Christmas Story   187

21   The Easter Story   196

22   Filled with Wonder   203

23   Keeping Perspective   212

24   The Wrath of God   222

25   The Beautiful Side of Evil   232

26   Salvation & Judgment   251

27   Millennial Martyrs   261

28   The Second Death   269

29   All Things New   280

30   The Garden City of God   286

    Bibliography   303

Acknowledgments

I AM ESPECIALLY GRATEFUL for the encouragement and editorial counsel of Dale Bruner, Rodney Clapp, Jim Meals, Jeremiah Webster, and Kennerly King.

1

The Canonical Climax

> "If you can't explain it simply,
> you don't understand it well enough."
> —Albert Einstein

THE REVELATION IS NOT a biblical book you master. John's prison epistle masters us. To be swept along by the force of this inspired theological treatise is to be simultaneously humbled and challenged. Recently, I taught the book in northern Ghana to a group of seventy-six pastors and fourteen Christian chiefs. The pastors serve churches throughout this rural and remote region. We met in the small village of Carpenter, where my African brother David Mensah heads up a holistic and fruitful ministry in the northern region.[1] We worked hard, five hours a day for seven days, in the heat. We covered the entire book, but in our last session, I shared with the pastors that I had only given them an introduction, only a taste of the spiritual impact of the Revelation. We agreed that the real work continues as we endeavor to stay in the Spirit and in the rhythm of John's powerful depiction of salvation and judgment.

All the pastors came out of villages steeped in witchcraft and shamanism. For them, the dangers of idolatry are very real. Villagers sacrifice chickens and goats before wooden idols and sacred stones. Their churches wrestle with the occult and demonic taboos. As the followers

---

1. To learn more about the work of David Mensah (PhD, University of St. Michael's College, Toronto) and sustainable evangelistic and humanitarian development in Northern Ghana, go to www.grid-nea.org.

of Christ break away from these customs they are often blamed for disease and drought and anything bad that happens in the villages. Believers are shunned and ridiculed. Their livelihood is threatened. Simple acts of faithfulness are costly. Even Christian chiefs are under pressure to prove their loyalty by complying with ancient taboos. These believers, like the first recipients of the Revelation, know what it is like to suffer for not eating meat offered to idols.

To work through the Revelation with believers who deal with shamans and idol worship was a reminder of what the first-century believers faced in confronting the imperial cult. Ghanian believers have experienced the demonic power of the devil. They know the complexity and dread of evil in ways that Western Christians seldom acknowledge, much less confront. American Christians suffer from idolatry but in ways that are more subtle and seductive. We disciples may not bow before wooden statues but we are in danger of giving ourselves to the gods of success, sports, and sex.

The emerging church in the Muslim–dominated northern region of Ghana resembles the first-century church. She may be relatively small and beleaguered but her witness is strong and her faith is vital. These pastors resonated with the Apostle John's Spirit-led warnings and admonitions. They identified personally with his spiritual direction and his grasp of the Old Testament Scriptures. The pastors impressed me as being emotionally and intellectually present in John's vision of Christ. They were also more open to the apostle's description of evil than we in the West tend to be. Maybe if we had someone living on our street with a reputation for spiritual powers who concocted curses for a fee, we might more readily grasp John's vivid portrayal of the power of evil. These Ghanian pastors were free to concentrate on what John was saying without having to be burdened with the heavy load of false and misleading interpretations that many believers seem to labor under. Instead of being bothered by rapture questions and millennial categories, they were able to enter into the Revelation with fresh ears and receptive hearts. There was no popular *Left Behind* series distorting their perspective. The Revelation's spiraling intensity of worship and judgment made perfect sense to these first-generation believers saved out of spiritual bondage.

A Prison Epistle

"The Apocalypse of John is a work of immense learning, astonishingly meticulous literary artistry, remarkable creative imagination, radical political critique, and profound theology."

—RICHARD BAUCKHAM, *THE CLIMAX OF PROPHECY*[2]

The Revelation builds conviction, inspires worship, and encourages patient endurance. The author was a prophet, poet, and pastor. Tradition has John on the island because he was a political prisoner. The imperial authorities wanted him out of the way, so they exiled him to a mountainous island off the coast of Asia Minor. This veteran ambassador of the gospel, who refused to bow the knee to Caesar, proclaimed the gospel to the world, to the churches of Asia Minor, and then to twenty-one centuries of church history; to every tribe, language, people, and nation. This "revelation of Jesus Christ" is a prison epistle like no other. It is also an extraordinary treatise on Christ and culture. Two thousand years has only deepened its prophetic impact.

Most of us are unaccustomed to the medium that John used to communicate "the word of God and the testimony of Jesus Christ." We come expecting to learn the ABC's of the end times and the Apostle John gives us the fullness and fury of his praying imagination. This Spirit–led prophet-pastor leads us into a vast array of sounds and images drawn from salvation history. We discover that meaning is not found in cleverly devised interpretations, but in God's redemptive story.

Careful study of this prison epistle reveals that John's mind was steeped in prophetic exile texts. His companions for this Spirit-filled experience were Isaiah, Jeremiah, Daniel, Ezekiel, Zechariah, and, most importantly, the risen Christ. The truth of the gospel remains constant: God in Christ is reconciling the world to himself. Salvation is by grace through faith and the atoning sacrifice of the cross of Christ is central to our faith. Evil charges forth, but the Lamb of God prevails. Evil is not the supreme reality. Heaven and hell are real. Salvation and judgment are coming. Jesus is Lord.

John is authorized by the Spirit of God to write to the churches. Twelve times he is told to write what he has seen and heard. Each time the imperative is given, John's holy and demanding work is affirmed. John makes sure we don't take the work of writing for granted. John testified

---

2. Bauckham, *The Climax of Prophecy*, ix.

"to everything he saw—that is, the word of God and the testimony of Jesus Christ."[3] He immersed himself in the Old Testament and the life of Jesus as a biblical theologian. In the Spirit, he is our prophet-pastor and inspired poet. John is not copying down a dream—a verbatim heavenly script; he's crafting a disciple-making manifesto.

Over 500 references to earlier Scripture in the Revelation's 404 verses testify to John's canonical climax. But it is only when we study the layers of parallel texts in Isaiah, Daniel, Ezekiel, and Zechariah that we begin to realize how deeply John's prophecy is steeped in the Old Testament. If John is anything, he is an Old Testament theologian. How fitting that the New Testament should end with such a powerful restatement of God's promises and warnings. John's Spirit-inspired vision is informed from beginning to end by the images, metaphors, numbers, and theology of the ancient prophets. As a writer, John gathered up all this revelation and proclaimed it for the church, not only to the seven churches of Asia Minor, but to every generation of believers in the global church from the Ascension to the second coming.

The apostle's purpose was to strengthen the church against cultural assimilation and spiritual idolatry, not to stimulate end times speculation. He wanted to deepen spirituality and nurture resilient saints. He was not out to heighten fear and scare believers into obedience. The Revelation is a manifesto on living faithfully to the end. It is not a manual charting the chronology of the second coming of Christ. John's prophetic focus was on preparation, not prediction. The Revelation is as necessary for young believers starting out on the path of discipleship as it is for mature believers who have walked with Christ for years. First things first, and a faith that lasts is what John offers not only the first-century church but the church universal.

The Revelation is a sustained attack against idolatry. John explored the complexity of evil in-depth and the simplicity of lifelong faithfulness. He attacked the notion that life could be lived in orbit around the imperial cult. The logic of his prophetic argument applies today to the autonomous individual, to the imperial self. He placed the spirit of the times in tension with the Spirit of Christ. He lifted the believer's gaze to a new horizon—heaven. In the Spirit, his aim was to inspire the believer's faithful presence amidst the harsh realities of evil. We should not be surprised that this biblical book is in sync with the rest of the New Testament. A

3. Rev 1:2.

sensible, straightforward reading of the Revelation reveals a symphony of truth in harmony with not only the Gospels and the Epistles, but with the law and the prophets. John's prison epistle is one long sustained attack against diluted discipleship. His unrelenting focus is on the immediacy of God's presence in the totality of life; nothing escapes the gaze of Christ.

Dispensational Distraction

"Though St. John the Evangelist saw many strange monsters in his vision, he saw no creature so wild as one of his own commentators."

—G. K. CHESTERTON[4]

This may be the devil's favorite book. Believers are confused and intimidated by the Revelation and pastors avoid preaching it because they don't want to stir up controversy. Fanciful interpretations of the rapture and tribulation make faithful preaching difficult. It is an easier book to ignore than to study. As a young Christian I thought that the Revelation was beyond the ability of most Christians to understand—myself included. Many of the preachers I heard made it seem like a complicated end times jigsaw puzzle that required a special expertise to figure it out. Eventually I came to see that John's purpose in writing was not to fuel curiosity or reveal hidden insights into terrorism, oil shortages, and turmoil in the Middle East. There is nothing in his book about modern nuclear warfare. The book was not the crystal ball some made it out to be. John's purpose was not to explore modern history, identify the Antichrist, and make geopolitical prognostications. His mission was to prepare the church for repentance, resistance, and resilience. He wrote to strengthen believers, not scare unbelievers.

In my teens I worked through a 300-page commentary on the Book of Revelation recommended to me by my pastor. The author argued that God had two salvation tracks running parallel to one another, one for Israel and one for the church. The rapture of the church was to take place before the tribulation, followed by the second coming of Christ and the 1,000-year rule of Christ. Armageddon and the final judgment followed the millennial rule. Virtually everything said in the Old Testament about Israel was meant for ethnic Israel. The prophecies of hope, laid out by Isaiah, Jeremiah, Daniel, and Ezekiel, predicted the restoration of a Jewish

4. Chesterton, *Orthodoxy*, 17.

state in Jerusalem and the establishment of a spectacular new temple. One of the interpretive challenges was to know when John was talking about Israel and when he was talking about the church.[5]

Dispensationalists contend that John's letters to the seven churches come before the church is raptured from the world scene. John's heavenly vision, which begins in chapter four, coincides with the church's rapture from the earth and the commencement of Christ's 1,000-year rule.[6] A description of the great tribulation follows. Seven seals are opened, revealing the first phase, followed by seven trumpets blasting judgment in the more intense phase two. Finally, the seven bowls pour out God's wrath in total judgment. In spite of the intensity of judgment and tribulation, people remain adamant in their refusal to turn to God and accept the testimony of Jesus. Two high-powered prophets, Moses and Elijah, literally return to earth to bear witness on the streets of Jerusalem. When

---

5. In the mid-nineteenth century, John Nelson Darby (1800–1882) developed a separatistic ecclesiology (the exclusive Plymouth Brethren) and a literalistic/dualistic eschatology (Dispensationalism). Darby saw himself coming up with a brand new eschatology. He was the inspiration behind Dispensationalism's leading popularizers: C. I. Scofield, Lewis Sperry Chafer, John F. Walvoord, J. Dwight Pentecost, and Charles C. Ryrie. Instead of seeing the continuity of God's grace throughout salvation history, Darby saw discontinuity and a series of new and improved redemptive plans. Darby wrote, "God has always begun by putting His creature in a good position; but the creature invariably abandons the position in which God set it, becoming unfaithful therein. And God, after long forebearance, never, re-establishes it in the position it fell from. It is not according to His ways to patch up a thing which has been spoilt; but he cuts it off, to introduce afterwards something entirely new and far better than what went before." (Darby, "What Is The Church, As It Was At The Beginning? And What Is The Present State?," *Collected Writings*, 87.) Darby held to a fundamental dichotomy between the new covenant promises for Israel fulfilled on earth and the heavenly glory awaiting the church. Darby was a mystic who stressed the believer's heavenly union with Christ. For Darby the "hinge upon which the subject and the understanding of Scripture turns" was the earthly/heavenly dualism and the distinction between Israel and the church (quoted in Henzel, *Darby, Dualism and the Decline of Dispensationalism*, 93). All of the covenant promises to Israel belong exclusively to Israel and do not apply to the church. Darby asserted a dichotomy between covenant and gospel. Darby represents the first modernist controversy. His methods and message instilled confusion and contention among sincere believers and set up fundamentalism for the second wave of confusion in the modernist-fundamentalist controversy of the 1920s. Darby's peculiar hermeneutic and opinionated interpretation of the Bible increased evangelicalism's vulnerability to the onslaught of liberalism.

6. Walvoord, *The Revelation of Jesus Christ*, 101. Walvoord interprets the invitation to John, "Come up here" (Rev 4:1) figuratively. Although "there is no authority for connecting the rapture with this expression, there does seem to be a typical representation of the order of events, namely, the church age first, then the rapture, then the church in heaven" (Walvoord, *Revelation*, 103)..

they are martyred, pictures of their dead bodies are broadcast throughout the world and the world celebrates. But after three and a half days they are brought back to life and they ascend to heaven. During this same period 144,000 Jews respond to the gospel and become converted.

Dispensationalists believe John envisioned the horrendous nature of the tribulation and the battle of Armageddon, but he lacked the modern experience and terminology to describe nuclear weapons and attack helicopters. John improvised by describing armored locusts and a massive two million-man army coming down from the north, presumably from Russia or China. There is also plenty of speculation about the identity of the antichrist, whom Dispensationalists tend to believe is an individual leader. This world leader is Satan's representative on earth, who recovers from a mortal wound and lives to deceive the nations. He is identified by the number 666 and will persuade the masses to reject God. One Canadian friend fell for one of the more ridiculous notions of the Dispensationalists back in the eighties. He was convinced that President Ronald Wilson Reagan was the antichrist, since his three names had six letters each. When Reagan recovered from his near-fatal gunshot wound, my Dispensationalist friend left work one day without telling family or friends, and flew from Toronto to Israel to buy property in Jerusalem. He was certain Christ was coming soon and would set up his kingdom in Jerusalem. He wanted his home near the throne.

Some Dispensationalists believe that the tribulation will end after the 144,000 ethnic Jews accept Christ as their Messiah. This will pave the way for the final conflagration. The battle of Armageddon will bring the forces of good and evil together in the war that will end all wars. Satan and his armies will be defeated and face the final judgment, when the Lord Almighty will sentence everyone whose name is not written in the Book of Life to be cast into the lake of fire—hell. Those whose names are written in the Book of Life will live and reign with Christ forever in a new heaven and a new earth.

John Walvoord claimed that neither the Apostle John nor the first-century church understood the meaning of the prophecy. Although John envisioned the prophecy, he could not know the full meaning of the Revelation. "It is of the nature of prophecy," writes Walvoord, "that it often cannot be understood until the time of the generation which achieves fulfillment."[7] But if the first-century believers were unable to understand

---

7. Ibid., 23.

John's futuristic prophecy, neither can we. Dispensationalists are just as much in the dark today as the first-century church because the prophecy has yet to take place. Walvoord admits that Dispensationalists bring an interpretative scheme to the text.

> The expositor is faced with innumerable hermeneutical deci-
> sions before beginning the task of understanding the peculiar
> contribution of the book of Revelation, an understanding made
> more difficult by the fact that decisions not only color the expo-
> sition of the book itself but also in a sense constitute an interpre-
> tation of all that precedes it in the Scriptures.[8]

The internal coherence of the book and its impact on the early church, together with the canonical shape, literary genre, and theological pur-pose, is lost in favor of interpretative presuppositions brought to the text in advance.[9] The idea that John was reciting a visionary dream, with a detailed step-by-step chronology of a futuristic geopolitical scenario, misses the mark and sidesteps the prophetic message for the church. The restoration of Israel as a nation-state imposes on the book an interpretive scheme that makes most of the book irrelevant for today's church as well as the first-century church.

A chronologically linear, literal, futuristic interpretative approach evades the apostle's strong message against idolatry and compromise. John warned believers against spiritual lethargy, moral complacency and an anemic witness. John's strategic purpose was to prepare first-century believers for intense suffering and a long obedience to the end. He was not speculating on the end times. He was advocating Christ-centered faithfulness for oppressed and persecuted believers. In the Spirit, his prison epistle is a powerful Christ and culture manifesto, crucial for discipleship, and essential for living in a fallen sin-twisted world. The

---

8. Ibid., 7.

9. The Dispensational template interprets the Bible dualistically. Instead of seeing the promises to Israel fulfilled in the church and in the one new humanity created in Christ Jesus, Dispensationalists argue that God has a separate destiny for Israel that in-volves reconstituting the nation, repatriating the land, and restoring the temple. God's promises to ethnic Jews will be fulfilled after the church is raptured, when Israel turns to her Messiah during the great tribulation. This interpretative template calls for two new covenants, one for Israel and one for the church; two different last days, one for Israel and one for the church; Christ's return in two stages, the rapture and the second coming; and two final judgments, the judgment seat of Christ and the final great white throne judgment. This dualism depends on a template imposed on the Bible, rather than a straightforward reading of the biblical text.

Revelation speaks to the church today in the same way as the other New Testament epistles.

The devil rejoices when we evade John's powerful prophetic word. When we use God's word as a modern Rorschach test to reflect our end-times fantasies, the devil is pleased. The Revelation is a significant test case in how the church "correctly handles the word of truth" (2 Tim 2:15). As one pastor shared, "I am both angry and sad. I am angry because my tradition has imposed on the Bible an end times scenario that is not grounded in the Bible. I am sad because what was meant to inspire courage and deepen faith has been used to fuel curiosity and speculation. Needless controversy has kept me from this important biblical book."

Scholastic Abstraction

"Everywhere, knowledge is splintering into intense specialization, guarded by technical languages fewer and fewer of which can be mastered by an individual mind."

—GEORGE STEINER[10]

As a seminary professor I have the deepest regard for the discipline and rigor with which many scholars approach the Revelation. But, ironically, the devil's strategy of negligence and neglect is aided and abetted by some of our best exegetes. Biblical scholarship unwittingly evades the meaning of the text and leaves the text stranded in the first century. Faithful biblical interpretation ought to lead to deep understanding of the text in its original context and in the life of the church today. Careful exegesis requires practical and pastoral application. If our academic effort neglects this essential pastoral task, then the impact of the Revelation is left in the first century. Sadly, good exegesis often remains outside the contemporary congregation, because those who know it best leave it to others to address the contemporary cultural situation and pastoral concerns. The ancient biblical text seldom engages the believer where it counts in the practical outworking of faithful obedience.

The Bible is observed with scholarly detachment as a historical artifact. Some of our most skilled exegetes seem reluctant to bring the message into the twenty-first century. They are experts in the language and culture of the first century but apparently they don't feel it is their place

10. Steiner, *Language and Silence,* 34.

to address the contemporary church. Consequently, their scholarly work rarely impacts the congregation. I suspect that the scholarly exegete will not appreciate this work, because it lacks the scientific approach. There are some notable exceptions by scholars who seek to apply the text to today's church. Craig Keener's *NIV Application Commentary* and Joseph Mangina's *Revelation* serve the pastor well, as does Darrell Johnson in *Discipleship on the Edge* and Eugene Peterson's *Reversed Thunder*. These works address today's church, but they are often deemed "not scholarly enough" in our seminary exegesis courses. One can read a thousand-page commentary on the Revelation with hardly a hint of how the text relates to the twenty-first-century church. But if the text says only what it *said* in the first century and no one seems compelled to speak in the Spirit to the immediate church and contemporary culture, how can believers hope to benefit from the biblical message?

If all we do is debate the book's authorship and date, study the historical context, trace the sources, parse the verbs, describe the style, determine the structure, and then, if there is any time left, mention a few theological implications, we are left empty-handed. We evade the biblical text by confusing research with repentance, by equating the rigors of scholarship with the discipline of surrender. This may be why our enthusiasm for the truth wanes and our creativity in application wanders off. We fail to bring the message home for a church that is unknowingly "wretched, pitiful, poor, blind and naked."[11] I'm afraid no self-respecting scholar in today's evangelical world would ever be as bold as the Prophet John. The apostle is too intense for the contemporary church, so bury his message in a scholarly tome and leave it at that. We disciples have taught ourselves to be polite with the prophetic word. We winsomely hint at the intriguing possibilities that lie buried in John's prophecy. We can afford to be professional rather than prophetic, because the material is safely confined in exegetical courses and commentaries. Imagine the Apostle John showing up at the Society of Biblical Literature to give a paper entitled, "Faithful Witness in a Pagan Culture." Would he gain a hearing? I doubt it, because the Society is not about the essence of the prophetic message and its impact on today's church. The scientific scope of the academy has little to do with what the Holy Spirit seeks to communicate to the church then and now.

11. Rev 3:17.

The Revelation may be the devil's favorite book for the two reasons suggested here. Dispensational distraction and scholarly abstraction have conspired in their different ways to silence the canonical climax. Either way the authorial intent and prophetic impact are evaded. The repeated refrain, "He who has an ear, let him hear what the Spirit says to the churches," falls on deaf ears.[12] In this pastoral approach to the Revelation we will endeavor to understand what the Apostle John said to the first-century church and what he is saying today to the twenty-first century.

12. Rev 2:7.

2

One Act Drama

WE ARE IMPATIENT RECIPIENTS of excessive amounts of information, most of which has little practical or personal impact. Life reduced to digital detail misses the devotional dimensions of prayer and reflection. We prefer watching movies to sitting on the back porch meditating on God's word. Movies are great, but not if they teach us to listen with our eyes and think with our feelings. Taking in the biblical message is becoming more difficult, because we are bored, restless, and overstimulated. The word of God was meant to be engaging, not entertaining. This chapter aims to explore that difference and examine the art of communication in the Revelation.

Our modern habit of scanning doesn't work for Revelation, because it ignores the prophet's creative full-sensory integration of Old Testament Scripture and messianic fulfillment. We skim the text and fail to embrace the message. We need ears to hear what the Spirit says to the churches. John wrote a theological score that was meant to be heard. His writing ministry picked up where Jesus left off. John adds nothing new. He preaches the Bible, expounds Daniel and Isaiah, Ezekiel and Zechariah, but most of all John proclaims Jesus. He writes his salvation symphony from Patmos in harmony with "the word of God and the testimony of Jesus."[1]

1. Rev 1:9.

Poet-Pastor

Some debate whether or not the Revelation was written by the Apostle John, but no one questions whether or not the author was a poet. He wrote with an eye toward the ear. He dipped his stylus in the genres of apocalypse, epistle, and prophecy and created a compelling audible sermon best preached to a worshiping congregation.[2] In less time than it takes to watch a movie, our poet-pastor-prophet offers the hearer a vivid portrait of Christ, a concise critique of the church, and a triumphant vision of redemption. He is an artist painting a picture in metaphor and symbol, invoking adrenaline-rich imagery to awaken all our senses to the stampede of evil and the cry of the saints.

Alternating beats of worship and judgment set the pulsating rhythm for the Revelation. The bugle blasts of judgment announce Exodus-style plagues and the wrath of the Lamb. The stage is finally set for the unrelenting witness of the church. The end of all ends is put off while the drama of salvation is retold in cosmic imagery and the unholy trinity of the dragon, the sea beast, and the land beast exert their domination over "all people, great and small, rich and poor, free and slave." In spite of evil's bluster, the followers of the Lamb prevail. They sing a new song and no lie is on their lips. The angelic word proclaims, "Fallen! Fallen is Babylon the Great," accompanied by the horror of everlasting torment and the great winepress of God's wrath. No one who is squeamish on judgment or soft on evil will find this imagery easy. John describes the final end over and over before taking a closer look at the great prostitute and the great city. Evil is numbered, deciphered, identified, embodied, sexualized, urbanized, stripped, and cannibalized. Her lament is not whimpered by distraught mourners but shouted out with such authority by a mighty angel that all of creation rejoices. Her magic spell is definitively broken forever and the great multitude in heaven resounds with a four-fold thunderous Hallelujah! Hallelujah! Hallelujah! Hallelujah!

But our poet-pastor has not finished portraying the end of evil and the beginning of a new heaven and a new earth. He contrasts the wedding supper of the Lamb and the great supper of God. Worship and judgment remain in spiraling intensity. Satan's power to deceive is checked and the millennial martyrs prevail right up to the end, when Satan takes his last

---

2. Carson, *An Introduction to the New Testament*, 479. Carson writes that the Revelation is "a prophecy cast in an apocalyptic mold and written down in a letter form" (*Introduction*, 479).

stand at the conflagration of Armageddon. John describes the great white throne judgment, the second death, and the Holy City "coming down out of heaven from God, prepared as a bride beautifully dressed for her husband." The prophet's Spirit-inspired literary artistry holds our attention as he unveils the ever fruitful everlasting garden city of *shalom*.

Linguistics on Fire

When I read the Revelation seriously for the first time, I imagined John composing his prophecy in a heightened state of spiritual consciousness. His quill pen was hardly able to keep up with his stream of thought. It simply poured out of him. He was overwhelmed by images, symbols, numbers, battlefields of horror, bloody streets of judgment, and indescribable scenes of worship. I pictured John, like the Apostle Paul, "caught up to paradise" hearing "inexpressible things," but unlike Paul, John was permitted to share what he saw.[3] Writing the Revelation was more or less an other-worldly experience that undoubtedly left John emotionally wiped out and intellectually drained. It was God's content and composition, not his. My impression was that the Revelation was a work of spontaneous spiritual combustion. John must have had a totally unique spiritual and existential experience, a writing experience far different from authoring his Gospel.

I did not envision then what I understand now, that John meticulously crafted a theological manifesto out of a deep understanding of the Old Testament, a thorough grasp of Jesus' teaching, a poetic sensitivity to popular apocalyptic imagery, and a penetrating critique of church and culture. And all of this was done under the powerful inspiration of the Holy Spirit. Why was I inclined to think that intellectual effort, literary mastery, theological depth, artistic creativity, and cultural analysis somehow lessened the spiritual impact of John's work? Instead of exploring the God-ordained synergism between the divine and human, our tendency may be to give the Revelation a gnostic twist.

If the book fell from heaven into John's receptive mind, why not let our imaginations run wild? All we need is an open mind. Interpretation, if we could call it that, is a simply matter of free associating with John's images and visions. Spiritual spontaneity at both ends, in both composition and interpretation, results in an effortless rapture of self-willed

---

3. 2 Cor 12:4.

reflection that claims to hear directly from God. If this were the secret to true interpretation, then an empty mind and vivid dreams might be the way to go. But if John painstakingly labored and prayed over every word, every thought and symbol, then it humbles us to learn that our understanding and application of God's word requires intellectual rigor, careful exegesis, and a labor of love. The Spirit-inspired meaning of the text must be understood as John intended, not as we might imagine.

I believe the first congregations who heard John's one act drama grasped the meaning of the book in one sitting. Like John, they were thoroughly steeped in the Old Testament, familiar with apocalyptic imagery, painfully aware of Roman oppression, and confronted daily by the pressures to compromise the gospel. They knew who John was talking about when he referred to the Nicolaitans and the prophet Jezebel. And it wasn't too hard for them to figure out the unholy trinity or what John meant when he referred to the number of the beast. Their fidelity to Christ was threatened by the imperial cult and an idolatrous culture.

John's theological depth and linguistic mastery produced a work that was not only immediately accessible to its first hearers but inexhaustible to its most ardent students over time.[4] John meticulously crafted a sermon in symbol and song. He embedded layers of metaphor and meaning in dramatic thematic parallels and a patterned series of worship and judgment. He used internal chiastic structures and climactic moments to build intensity. His sequences invariably arrive at an end only to be transcended by new vistas of heaven's glory and earth's evil. Suspense builds as he moves to the final end of all ends and the beginning of a new heaven and a new earth.

John's style fits his purpose. Form follows function. The Prophet John preached a prophetic word of resistance against a watered-down Christianity. His work opposes the church's susceptibility to cultural conformity and accommodation to pagan ways and popular forms of spirituality. His manifesto is an attack on assimilation and idolatry. Above all else he writes to inspire, encourage, and embolden believers to be faithful, to witness in an increasingly hostile culture that seeks to either absorb or annihilate the church. This is why John gave his work such intensity. Every member of every tribe and language and people and

---

4. Bauckham, *The Climax of Propehcy*, 1. "Revelation was evidently designed to convey its message to some significant degree on first hearing, but also progressively to yield fuller meaning to closer acquaintance and assiduous study" (Bauckham, *Climax*, 1).

nation is impacted by this message. The scope of the prophecy is cosmic and eternal. Without exaggeration, it is a matter of life and death, and not just temporal life and physical death, but eternal life and the second death. This message deserves every word of prophetic intensity that John can deliver because the stakes are as high as they can be. If John wanted to communicate in listed propositions he could have done so easily and saved his original hearers and subsequent readers considerable time and effort. But John refused the efficiency model for a more demanding and invigorating approach.[5] He painted his revelation with stories and images, parables and symbols. His prophecy is a true work of art—art that is intrinsic to its message. There is no other way to tell this truth other than the way John preached it. The method and the message are one.

The set of literary techniques John used with such skill are different from techniques used by modern preachers. The Prophet John dwells on the immediacy of God's truth, not on tantalizing trivia that may catch our fancy. Prayer is our entrée into John's message. Worship is the context for understanding. A willingness to embrace the whole counsel of God is a prerequisite. John's literary method is described below. Woven together these literary qualities produce a theological masterpiece. These include:

1. Storied truth

2. Prophetic climax

3. Cosmic parables

4. Structural stress

5. Symbols in tension

6. Patterned repetition

7. Numbered meaning

---

5. Boring, *Revelation*, 52. Boring writes, "The language of Revelation is visionary language that deals in pictures rather than propositions. Pictures themselves are important to John as the vehicle of his message. They are not mere illustrations of something that can be said more directly. A picture makes its own statement; it is its own text. It does not communicate what it has to say by being reduced to discursive, propositional language. Just as the case in visiting an art gallery, while commentary and explanation may help one to 'get the picture,' language about the picture can never replace the message communicated in and through the picture itself. . . . Ultimates can best be expressed in pictures, especially word pictures, by the artist, rather than in logical, propositional statements" (*Revelation*, 52).

Storied Truth

The Revelation is a first-person narrative. In a lecture, personal references are an aside, but in John's letter to the seven churches, the personal is at the heart of the story. "I, John, your brother and companion in the suffering and kingdom and patient endurance that are ours in Jesus . . ."[6] John includes *you* and *me* in this narrative ("ours in Jesus"). This story is our story, too. When John writes to the seven churches, he steps back and hides behind Christ. He is not offering his opinions about the churches, he is delivering Christ's message to the churches. What John thinks on his own and by himself is not important here. The autonomous individual self is not the authoritative resource. The message is what Christ reveals, that is what is is crucial. But that does not mean that John is disengaged from the personal impact of this revealed truth. When the scene changes to the centering throne in heaven, John emerges as the subject of direct encounter: "I looked and there before me was a door standing open in heaven." Throughout his prison epistle John speaks in the first person. The literary form itself underscores the personal. He is describing an experience, not laying out a philosophy or an ideology. John's letter clearly teaches many propositional truths, but John proclaims these truths through personal experience, not propositional logic. He is never lecturing or philosophizing; John is always telling his story. The process of unveiling involves his story—our story.

Prophetic Climax

John's personal story is deeply rooted in the history of God's people. He is thoroughly steeped in the metanarrative of salvation history. Everything he says, literally every vision, metaphor, symbol, number, and image, has its roots in the Old Testament. If John was bereft of Old Testament texts on Patmos, you would never know it. There are more Old Testament references in the Revelation than in any other New Testament book.[7] After years of study and memorizing, John was soaked in "the word of God and the testimony of Jesus."[8] But more important than the number of textual allusions is the intentional way that John used the Old Testament.

6. Rev 1:9.

7. Beale, *The Book of Revelation*, 77.

8. Rev 1:9.

He wrote as if he was aware he was bringing the canon of Scripture to its conclusion.

> John was writing what he understood to be a work of prophetic scripture, the climax of prophetic revelation, which gathered up the prophetic meaning of the Old Testament scriptures and disclosed the way in which it was being and was to be fulfilled in the last days. His work therefore presupposes and conveys an extensive interpretation of large parts of the Old Testament prophecy.[9]

Start here → John shaped his genuine visions into literary form by drawing on the rich imagery of the Genesis creation and fall, the Exodus plagues, Isaiah and Ezekiel's visions of the throne of God, and the eschatological blessings. Zechariah provides John with crucial imagery and Daniel "provides a mother lode of material for John."[10] His praying imagination was saturated with the Old Testament. In his mind's eye he saw Isaiah's slain lamb, Daniel's Ancient of Days, and Ezekiel's vision of God's throne. He took over this powerful apocalyptic vision of salvation and judgment and made it his own. John is more than a faithful exegete of the Old Testament. He is an inspired prophet writing the final chapter in God's progressive revelation. With that said, John's prophecy adds no new material that is not already found in the teachings of Jesus. The prophets form an eschatological chorus, conducted by Jesus, with each prophet, including John, singing their individual parts but ending in harmony.

Cosmic Parables

A third feature of the Prophet John's literary artistry is his use of parable. He used indirect discourse built on metaphor and symbol to keep his hearers' attention and reveal the meaning of the kingdom of God. John doesn't come out and say pedantically that the doctrine of redemption is absolutely crucial to the witnessing content and strategy of the church. Instead, he tells the story of the Lamb in cosmic conflict with the dragon. Jesus drew from ordinary daily life to shatter his hearers' pre-existing understanding. His stories about farmers and seeds, servants and masters, and sons and fathers turned everything upside down to reveal a radical new counterculture: the kingdom of God. On the surface, parables may

---

9. Bauckham, *The Climax of Prophecy*, xi.

10. Beale, *Commentary on the New Testament Use of the Old Testament*, 1082–84.

appear to be quaint moral stories designed to make people nicer, but Jesus worked their obvious hiddenness to open up the secrets of the gospel. He used the common stuff of daily life to teach the extraordinary truths and subversive message of the gospel. He challenged his hearers to interpret the metaphors, to look beyond the surface meaning. This is why Jesus says, "Whoever has ears, let them hear."[11]

The Apostle John was tutored in the power of metaphor from the Master, but instead of drawing on ordinary everyday things, John shaped his parables from the extraordinary complexity of the cosmic realm. He drew his metaphors from the stars instead of seeds and monsters instead of masters. He exchanged an agrarian world of wicked tenant farmers for the cosmic war between God and the devil. He transposed Jesus' everyday world into the end of the world. He merged the parabolic style of Jesus with an in-depth understanding of the prophets and brought the message home, not with homey human interest stories, but with horrific scenarios of global war and ecstatic scenes of rhapsodic worship.

Structural Stress

John engineered a literary style and structure that intentionally works to stress the hearer. He runs at us with a structural intensity that aims to break whatever monotony we bring to the text. Instead of a traditional A-Z linear approach, John designed an Alpha to Omega spiraling strategy that moves forward at irregular speeds and backward without notice to capture a fuller picture of either evil or glory. In John's prophecy, earth's forward motion stops on a dime to take in heaven's worship. The shifts in momentum keep the listener on edge and only add to the intensity. This is no pilgrim's progress along a narrow, albeit challenging, path. This is more like a mountain climb in the whirlwind of tribulation and hostile fire. We come up to what appears to be the final end multiple times only for the end of all endings to be delayed and more of heaven to be revealed.[12]

John has structured the Revelation with four series of seven: seven churches, seven seals, seven trumpets, and seven bowls. Within each series there is an internal dynamic that is designed to hold our attention,

---

11. Matt 13:43.

12. There are seven descriptions of the end: Rev 6:12–17; 9:13–21; 11:13; 14:14–20; 16:17–21; 19:17–21; 20:7–10.

such as the chiastic structure of the letters to the seven churches or a 4/3 division within the seven seals and the seven trumpets. The phrase "in the Spirit" comes at strategic points indicating a major transition, but never in a pedantic fashion.[13] The four divisions are as follows: the inaugural vision of the risen Christ and the seven letters to the churches,[14] the inaugural vision of heaven and sequence of judgments,[15] the vision of the prostitute and the great city,[16] and the vision of the bride of Christ and the new Jerusalem.[17] There is an intervening transitional section describing the movement from the fall of Babylon to the Holy City coming down out of heaven.[18] The hearer is reminded at these strategic points that the whole vision is "in the Spirit."[19]

The force of this one act, sixty-minute drama builds from the centering throne, the opening of the seals, the sealing of the 144,000, the great multitude of worshipers in heaven, the trumpet blasts of judgment on earth and the silencing of the seven thunders. We have reached the center of the book and something of the heart of his message. The same angel described in the prologue gives John the scroll and says, "Take it and eat it."[20] This is the same scroll that the Lamb took "from the right hand of him who sat on the throne."[21]

The progression of revelation from *God* → *Jesus Christ* → *Angel* → *John* → *Servants* is recapitulated at the center of the drama. The key application for John and for all those who hear this message is *witness*. "You must prophesy again about many people, nations, languages and kings."[22] To further intensify the message, John graphically portrays the power and the pain of witnessing for Christ and his kingdom. The content of

13. Rev 1:10; 4:2; 17:3; 21:10.

14. Rev 1:13–20.

15. Rev 4:1–16:21.

16. Rev 17:1–19:10.

17. Rev 21:9–22:9.

18. Rev 19:11–21:8.

19. Bauckham, *The Climax of Prophecy*, 3–6.

20. Rev 10:9.

21. Rev 5:7. See Bauckham: "It is not until chapter 10 that the main content of the prophetic revelation John communicates in his book is given to him. All that has preceded is preparatory—necessary to the understanding of this revelation, but not itself the revelation. Recognizing this is a vital, though neglected, key to understanding the book of Revelation" (*The Theology of the Book of Revelation*, 84).

22. Rev 10:11.

the scroll illustrates how the followers of the Lamb are going to be faithful witnesses right up to the end.[23]

> The new revelation is that their faithful witness and death is to be instrumental in the conversion of the nations of the world. . . . Two individuals here represent the church in its faithful witness to the world. Their story must be taken neither literally nor even as an allegory, as though the sequence of events in this story were supposed to correspond to a sequence of events in the church's history. The story is more like a parable, which dramatizes the nature and the result of the church's witness.[24]

Symbols in Tension

John keeps the listener attentive with a constant contrast of positive and negative symbols and images. He ignores the pedantic charge of mixed metaphors as he paints his paradoxes in the rarefied acoustics of apocalyptic prophecy. There are positive tensions: the Lion and the Lamb, blood-washed robes as white as snow, the 144,000 from all the tribes of Israel and the great multitude in white robes, and the wife of the Lamb and the Holy City. But the negative tensions tend to dominate our attention. The stampede of evil designed to cause humanity to run to God for mercy only hardens human hearts. The power of evil is personified in the king of the abyss, whose aliases are the great dragon, the devil, and Satan.[25] The ancient serpent is set in contrast to the Lamb.

Evil forms an unholy trinity in contrast to the Holy Trinity of Father, Son, and Holy Spirit. The evil consortium of the dragon, the beast of the sea, and the beast of the earth appear transcendent, but the Lamb, together with the 144,000, sing a new song of redemption and triumph. The power of evil rages but evil ends up in the great winepress of God's wrath. The great city of Babylon and the great prostitute contrast with the Holy City and the bride of the Lamb. Babylon's funeral dirge is in

---

23. Rev 11:1–13.

24. Bauckham, *The Theology of the Book of Revelation*, 84.

25. In Hebrew, "Satan" means "adversary." Other titles include the devil, the evil one, or the tempter. Satan is a high angelic being who rebelled against God. Allusions to Satan may be found in Isaiah 14:12–14 and Ezekiel 28:11–16. Satan is called the "god of this age" and is blamed for blinding the minds of unbelievers (2 Cor 4:4). Jesus called him "the prince of this world" (John 14:30), and John said that "the whole world is under the control of the evil one" (1 John 5:19).

antiphonal tension with the great multitude singing the hallelujah chorus. However, the contrast between evil and righteousness prevails even
after the final judgment. Evil has been condemned and obliterated, but
the magnificence of the Holy City is contrasted with the evil that is no
longer allowed.[26]

Patterned Repetition

Another feature John uses to integrate and intensify his work is a pattern
of repeated phrases. These repetitions often occur in a slightly altered
form to create a complex interlocking pattern, weaving John's drama into
a single message. With each repetition these word clusters and variations
on a theme alert the listener to a pattern of intricate cross-referencing.
These patterned cues aid both understanding and momentum, helping to
network the entire text and create a sense of immediacy. John alerted his
hearers to transitions by using the phrase "after this" seven times.[27]

The prologue is linked to John's vision of the heavenly throne with
the phrase: "who is, and who was, and who is to come."[28] And the prologue
is connected to the epilogue with the repetition of "I am the Alpha and
the Omega."[29] God's self-description in the epilogue, "I am the Root and
Offspring of David, and the bright Morning Star," recalls the letter to the
church in Thyatira and heaven's throne vision.[30] John's self-description
unites the beginning—"I, John, your brother and companion . . . "—with
the end: "I, John, am the one who heard and saw these things."[31]

John used particular phrases more than once for audible effect.
Repetition "is a skillfully deployed compositional device" to help the
hearer get the message. "One reason we can be sure of this is that such
phrases almost never recur in precisely the same form." Richard Bauckham continues, "The author seems to have taken deliberate care to avoid
the obviousness of precise repetition, while at the same time creating
phrases which closely allude to each other."[32] Slightly altered phrases can
be cues that the texts relate to one another. John writes that he was on

26. Rev 21:27; 22:15.

27. Rev 1:19; 4:1; 7:1, 9; 15:5; 18:1; 19:1.

28. Rev 1:4, 8; 4:8.

29. Rev 1:8; 21:6; 22:13.

30. Rev 22:16; 2:28; 5:5; see 2 Pet 1:19.

31. Rev 1:9; 22:8.

32. Bauckham, *The Climax of Prophecy*, 22.

the island of Patmos, "because of the word of God and the testimony of Jesus," but later, in his description of the prevailing millennial martyrs he writes, "I saw the souls of those who had been beheaded because of their testimony about Jesus and because of the word of God."[33] Another example of slightly altered wording in related passages is found in John's description of the four living creatures worshiping God. Their "speaking never ceases, day and night, 'Holy, holy, holy, is the Lord God Almighty,'" just as the worshipers of the beast "never cease speaking, day and night."[34]

Paying attention to these small nuances helps connect related passages in subtle ways. Compare the praying saints, who are told to "wait a little longer," (χρόνον μικρόν, "time-short") with Satan's release "for a short time" (μικρόν χρόνον, "short-time").[35] This appears to be John's way of underscoring the correspondence between these two times. Another example is the description of the great multitude who have come out of the great tribulation. The text concludes with the line, "And God will wipe away every tear from their eyes," which relates to the description of the Holy City coming down out of heaven and God's promise that "He will wipe every tear from their eyes."[36] John wrote his one act drama with audible sensitivity. He expected the listener to hear these patterns and pick up on these corresponding passages. He wove his meaning with artistic care.

Numbered Meaning

John used numbers symbolically, similarly to the way mathematicians use them: to help explain the intelligibility of the universe. John's math implies the sovereign control of God and the completeness of the gospel story: "Nothing is haphazard or accidental."[37] The mathematical nature of the universe from, beehives to butterfly wings, is overwhelming. When we have numbered something, devised an equation, mapped a distance, measured the volume, and analyzed discrete units, we feel we have come closer to touching reality and accounting for it. We should not be surprised that John chose to tell the story of salvation history using numbers.

33. Rev 6:9; 20:4.
34. Rev 4:8; 14:11.
35. Rev 6:11; 20:3.
36. Rev 7:17; 21:4.
37. Beale, *Revelation*, 60.

In addition to specific numbers and ordered series, John created some not-so-obvious sequential patterns. There is a clear structural pattern in the seven letters to the churches, the seven seals, the seven trumpets, the seven thunders, and the seven bowls. But John also arranged his material in less obvious numbered patterns, such as the seven Beatitudes,[38] the seven visions of Christ, the seven references to "Jesus Christ," the fourteen (7 x 2) references to "Jesus," and twenty-eight (7 x 4) references to "the Lamb."

The number seven and its multiples signify completeness. The seven features of the one like a son of man—his hair, eyes, feet, voice, right hand, mouth, and face—represent a complete picture of Christ. The seven letters to the churches stand for the universal church, across time and space. The seven ascriptions of praise to the Lamb, "power and wealth and wisdom and strength and honor and glory and praise," indicate complete doxology.[39] The seven seals, trumpets, and bowls represent a complete sequence of revelation, bringing the hearer to a climactic end in each series. The sea beast's seven heads and ten crowns stand for worldwide oppressive power.[40] The twenty-eight products (7 x 4) traded by the merchants of the earth represent all the products in the world economy.

The number seven is also critical in understanding a whole series of numbers used to describe the sovereignly appointed (and relatively brief) time of protection for the persecuted community of believers. This time is represented symbolically in several ways: forty-two months, 1,260 days, a time, times, and half a time.[41] Each reference is to three and half years of persecution, a symbolic duration, that cuts the symbolic number of seven in half. In this case, mercy is more important than completion. God mercifully halves the symbolic number for perfection.

The triple six, 666, the number of the beast, stands for incompleteness.[42] The number corresponds to the sixth seal, the sixth trumpet, and the sixth bowl, and signifies the final judgment of evil and the beast's followers.[43] John used seven to describe the dragon with his seven heads and seven crowns and the beast with his seven heads.[44] G. K. Beale observes

---

38. Rev 1:3; 14:13; 16:15; 19:9; 20:6; 22:7,14.

39. Rev 5:12.

40. Rev 13:1.

41. Rev 11:2, 3; 12:6, 14.

42. Rev 13:18.

43. Rev 6:12; 9:13–19; 16:12–14.

44. Rev 12:3; 13:1; 17:3, 7, 9.

that this is done "to highlight the kingdom of evil's hollow mimicry of the divine."[45] It is likely that John intended 666 to signify an evil parody of the triune God. "The triple repetition of sixes connotes the intensification of incompleteness and failure that is summed up in the beast more than anywhere else among fallen humanity."[46]

The number four stands for the world. The "four living creatures" around the throne of God represent all living things. The "four corners of the earth" and "the four winds of the earth" represent the world in its entirety.[47] Four divisions make up the earth: "every creature in heaven and on earth, and under the earth and on the sea."[48] Earth dwellers are given a fourfold division, "nation, tribe, language and people," and summoned to worship him who made "the heavens, the earth, the sea and the springs of water."[49] Four tribulations afflict the world—conquest, war, scarcity, and death (6:1–8). The trumpets announce judgment on the earth, sea, rivers, and stars, and the first four bowls of wrath are poured out on the land, sea, rivers, and stars.[50] This fourfold judgment, within a series of seven, is repeated three times—with seals, trumpets, and bowls—and presumably would have taken place a fourth time (4 x 7) if the "voices of the seven thunders" had been permitted to speak.[51] By John's calculation, God's judgment is complete and comprehensive. The fourfold repetition of thunder, rumblings, flashes of lightning, and an earthquake stand for the final and universal end of God's judgment.[52] When the blood flows from the great winepress of God's wrath it rises hyperbolically up to "the horses' bridles and flows for a distance of 1,600 stadia."[53] The number signifies not a literal 184 miles, but a figurative number (4 x 4 x 1,000) representing the absolute completeness of God's judgment.

The number three is associated with the triune God. John's opening greeting comes from God, the Seven Spirits, and from Jesus Christ. A threefold temporal formula is used for God, "from him who is, and who

45. Beale, *Revelation*, 64.

46. Ibid., 722.

47. Rev 7:1.

48. Rev 5:13.

49. Rev 14:6–7.

50. Rev 8:7–12; 16:2–9.

51. Rev 10:3–7.

52. Rev 4:5; 8:5; 11:19; 16:18; see Beale, *Revelation*, 61.

53. Rev 14:20.

was, and who is to come."[54] The number seven stands for the completeness of the Holy Spirit, and Jesus Christ is given a threefold description: "the faithful witness, the firstborn from the dead, and the ruler of the kings of the earth."[55] The four living creatures never stop saying: "Holy, holy, holy is the Lord God Almighty, who was, and is, and is to come."[56] "In John's numerology three is the number of God, while four is the number of creation. These come together in Jesus Christ, who unites God and creation in himself, and whose mission to all the nations of the earth is provisionally displayed in the *ekklesia* [the 7 churches]."[57]

The number twelve (3 x 4) signifies the people of God. The triune God, represented by the number three, plus all those drawn from the four corners of the world, represented by the number four, adds up to be the people of God. The vast totality of the people of God is signified by 144,000 (3 x 4 x 1,000 x 12). John adds up 12,000 from each of the 12 tribes to express the enormity and security of the people of God.[58] The woman "clothed with the sun" wears "a crown of twelve stars on her head." Like the twelves tribes of Israel and the twelves apostles, she stands for the people of God. The number twelve is used twelve times in describing the New Jerusalem. The twelve gates are guarded by twelve angels and on the gates are the names of the twelve tribes of Israel. Three gates in each direction: east, north, south, west, reiterate the description of twelve gates. The twelve foundations bear the names of the twelve apostles. The city is laid out as a perfect cube, with its length, width, height and depth, measuring 12,000 (12 x 1,000). The height of the wall is measured at 144 cubits (12 x 12) which alludes to the 144,000, the elect body who are signed, sealed, and delivered. The number signifies perfection. The foundations are adorned with twelve kinds of precious stones, reminiscent of Aaron's breastplate with the twelve jewels representing the twelve tribes of Israel brought before the very presence of God. But now the holy of holies extends in all directions, too vast to be contained by human limitation. The twelve stones recall the Apostle Peter's description: "you also, as living stones, are being built up a spiritual house for a holy priesthood."[59] Each gate is made up of a single pearl, totaling twelve pearls for twelve

54. Rev 1:4, 8; 4:8; 11:17.
55. Rev 1:4–5.
56. Rev 4:8.
57. Mangina, *Revelation*, 55.
58. Rev 7:4–8; 14:1.
59. 1 Pet 2:5.

gates. This series of twelves culminates with the twelve types of fruit on the tree of life, which yields its fruit twelve months a year.[60] Twelve represents the fully realized perfection of the people of God in the presence of God.

The number ten and its multiples signify a complete quota of tribulation or power, such as "ten days" of persecution, an army numbering "twice ten thousand times ten thousand," or a beast with "ten horns."[61] The most famous and the most controversial number in the Revelation is the threefold reference to the one thousand years of protection for the saints.[62] One thousand (10 x 10 x 10) is a figurative number for the ideal church age, extending from Christ's life, death, resurrection, and ascension to Christ's second coming. During that time Satan's influence persists but his power is limited.[63]

Ears to Hear

"Human kind / Cannot bear very much reality"

—T. S. Eliot, Four Quartets

These seven literary strategies—storied truth, prophetic climax, cosmic parables, structural stress, symbols in tension, patterned repetition, and numbered meaning—intensify the message and keep the hearer listening. Prophetic speech is inherently passionate and intense. When eternal issues are at stake and the final judgment is imminent it is difficult to remain professorial and dispassionate. Moral pain invokes a moral seriousness that fits the content of the message. The message John delivers is universally countercultural and disturbing, but at the same time it is compelling and provocative. Even though it is hard to hear, the listener is drawn in and wants to hear what the Spirit is saying through John.

---

60. Rev 22:2.

61. Rev 2:10; 9:16; 12:3; 13:1; 17:7, 12, 16.

62. Rev 20:1–7.

63. Beale, *Revelation*, 995. Beale summarizes his argument thusly: "That this is not a literal chronological number is apparent from: (1) the consistently figurative use of numbers elsewhere in the book, (2) the figurative nature of much of the immediate context ('chain,' 'abyss,' 'dragon,' 'serpent,' 'locked,' 'sealed,' 'beast'), (3) the predominantly figurative tone of the entire book (1:1), (4) the figurative use of '1,000' in the OT [and the NT, see Deut 32:30; Joshua 23:10; Job 9:3; 33:23; Ecclesiastes 7:28; Isaiah 30:17; 2 Peter 3:8], and (5) the use in Jewish and early Christian writings of '1,000' years as a figure for the eternal blessing of the redeemed" (*Revelation*, 995).

Jeanne Boylan is one of the most celebrated criminal sketch artists in America. She has an amazing ability to produce "dead-ringer" sketches of criminal suspects. How does she do it? By listening. Instead of showing traumatized victims hundreds of mug shots of potential suspects or flipping through an art book, asking them to pick out a nose or mouth or eyes, Boylan listens. In lieu of a quick, in and out, impersonal session, Boylan talks with victims for hours. Her aim is to befriend and relax the victim in order to overcome the memory's resistence to revisiting a traumatic image. As a victim of an assault in her twenties, Boylan learned that reporting a crime "was like talking to people with no ears."[64]

To arrive at the truth we have to listen long and hard. We have to get past our defenses and our previously conceived end times scenarios. Many conversations on this book begin with the question, "Are you pre-mil (Christ raptures the church before the tribulation and his one-thousand year rule occurs on earth before the final judgment), post-mil (Christ comes after the kingdom of God has been established on earth for a thousand years), a-mil (the one thousand years is a metaphor for completion and perfection, symbolizing Christ's victory over Satan), or pan-mil (always said with a slight chuckle, to mean everything will pan out in the end)? But beginning with the millennium question corresponds to the sketch artist who wants to produce a satisfactory human likeness of the suspect as quickly as possible. He brings out his flip chart of ears, noses, eyes and chins and in no time he has an image. The eschatological flip chart doesn't work for understanding the Revelation. What is needed are people who listen with ears to hear.

The Layout

Instead of a linear sequence of events in chronological time, John reveals a spiraling intensity of worship and judgment in God's sovereign, grace-filled time. The whole prison epistle, all twenty-two chapters, is a letter to the church—the followers of the Lamb. The prologue and the vision of Christ, along with the seven letters to the churches, form the foundation for what follows. The spiraling intensity of meaning begins with the centering throne of God. It is here where the controlling metaphor of the Lamb is introduced. Christ's redemption is the sole ground for all that develops.

64. Sauer, "Drawing from Experience."

The seven seals are a quick summary of salvation history, covering the human condition, the "impatient" saints who have gone before, and the unrepentant masses who resist the mercy of God. John's repeated description of the end emphasizes God's patience, "not wanting anyone to perish, but everyone to come to repentance."[65] The open seals correspond to the sealing up of the 144,000, the symbolic number of perfection and protection, signifying the church. The great multitude that has come out of the great tribulation corresponds to the 144,000 and identifies believers who are already in heaven, "standing before the throne and in front of the Lamb."[66]

The seven trumpets further intensify the recapitulation of salvation history. The four horses of the apocalypse running wild on earth give way to cosmic plagues that destroy a third of creation. Instead of saints under the altar praying, demonic evil is released from the abyss and evil marches forth like an invincible army. Once again humanity refuses to repent and turn to the mercy of God. Before the seventh trumpet, John reveals the power of Christ's witness, first through himself—the old apostle—and then through the two witnesses who represent the suffering church. Witness and worship prevail in spite of the world's resistance to the gospel.

John delays the description of the third series, the bowls of wrath, in order to expand and deepen our understanding of salvation. He reframes the incarnation, crucifixion, resurrection, and ascension from a cosmic perspective. Christ's coming to earth ignited war in heaven, leading to the defeat of Satan and the continuing struggle on earth between the church and the devil. Like a wounded animal, the devil and his demonic agents fight for the hearts and minds of world. In the midst of this demonic deception the 144,000 continue to sing a new song and practice faithful discipleship. With supernatural help the eternal gospel and the message of judgment is proclaimed "to every nation, tribe, language and people."[67] The finality of judgment is executed as the great winepress of God's wrath, before the seven angels with seven bowls of wrath are even introduced.

The finality of judgment is played out in multiple images of total destruction: the harvest of the earth, the great winepress, the seven bowls of wrath, the battle of Armageddon, and the great supper of God. A loud voice from the throne is heard saying, "It is done!"[68] The great city, Baby-

---

65. 2 Pet 3:9.

66. Rev 7:9.

67. Rev 14:6.

68. Rev 16:17.

lon the Great, signifies human civilization. It is destroyed once and for all. But then, John stops the flow of action to recapitulate human depravity in two ways. He describes the great prostitute and he rehearses the lament that goes up for the fallen city of Babylon. John merges the ugly side of evil and the beautiful side of evil into a holistic analysis of culture that continues to shape Christian understanding of culture. Heaven responds to Babylon's fall with resounding hallelujahs and John completes the picture by describing the heavenly warrior, called Faithful and True, who defeats the combined armies of the beast and the kings of the earth. The wedding supper of the Lamb is set in contrast to the great supper of God. The final judgment is already graphically portrayed before John describes the millennium.

In John's spiraling intensity of salvation and judgment, the final judgment is described in multiple ways. The same holds true for the enduring witness of the church. There are multiple descriptions of God's faithfulness, the sealing of the 144,000, the two witnesses, and the woman clothed with the sun. But the climax to these images of sustained witness comes in the description of God's merciful and missional millennium. Satan is bound and unable to deceive the nations for a thousand years. One thousand symbolizes the perfection of God's mercy and the completeness of the church from Pentecost to the second coming of Christ. Martyred and witnessing saints in heaven and on earth continue to seek Christ's kingdom first and foremost in the fellowship of his suffering and in the power of his resurrection. At the end of the church age all the images of final judgment, including the battle of Armageddon and the great supper of God, come to fulfillment. The great white throne judgment brings to a crescendo all the endings previously described.

Lastly, John describes the new heaven and the new earth "coming down out of heaven." The Holy City, the new Jerusalem, is laid out in biblical images of perfection, beauty, and wholeness. In twelve repeated patterns of twelve, the garden city of God becomes the new and everlasting home to the followers of the Lamb. The epilogue is an antiphonal symphony of promise—"I am coming soon!"—and anticipation: "Come!"

3

Deep Meaning

⤙ Revelation 1:1–8 ⤚

[1:1–8] *The revelation from Jesus Christ, which God gave him to show his servants what must soon take place. He made it known by sending his angel to his servant John, who testifies to everything he saw—that is, the word of God and the testimony of Jesus Christ. Blessed is the one who reads aloud the words of this prophecy, and blessed are those who hear it and take to heart what is written in it, because the time is near.*

John,

To the seven churches in the province of Asia:

Grace and peace to you from him who is, and who was, and who is to come, and from the seven spirits before his throne, and from Jesus Christ, who is the faithful witness, the firstborn from the dead, and the ruler of the kings of the earth.

To him who loves us and has freed us from our sins by his blood, and has made us to be a kingdom and priests to serve his God and Father—to him be glory and power forever and ever! Amen.

"Look, he is coming with the clouds," and "every eye will see him, even those who pierced him"; and all peoples on earth "will mourn because of him." So shall it be! Amen.

"I am the Alpha and the Omega," says the Lord God, "who is, and who was, and who is to come, the Almighty."

DEEP MEANING IS FOUND in the convergence of God's will and human destiny. The Apostle John invites us to experience the will and plan of God with fresh intensity and immediacy. His one act drama lifts the veil and shines the light of the gospel on the world. Creation and redemption converge in the Apostle John's powerful account of "the word of God and the testimony of Jesus." The history of nature and the history of salvation are revelations of the one God, Father, Son, and Holy Spirit. Everything in nature and redemption is moving forward according to plan—"the plan of him who works out everything in conformity with the purpose of his will."[1]

"Without belief in the inner harmony of the world," Albert Einstein observed, "there could be no science."[2] The apostles go further and assert that the God and Father of our Lord Jesus Christ has not only created an inner harmony but an ultimate convergence. The cosmos is not a co-incidence and salvation is not an accident. History is moving forward to its fulfillment. All of life is of God and belongs to God. Creation and redemption converge. "He is before all things, and in him all things hold together," and all things are reconciled through him "by making peace through his blood shed on the cross."[3] The divine purpose—bringing unity to all things in heaven and on earth in Christ—overcomes the great divorce between our fallenness and our fulfillment. In Christ the physical and the spiritual, the temporal and the eternal, the mundane and the devotional, are united. Through the incarnation, God descends into our suffering humanity, joins us on the ash heap, takes up this mean battle with Satan, and goes to the cross. The Lord of glory is crucified, but the cross is not the last word and the resurrection is not a wild card played at the end. There is a beautiful coherence between the life, death, and resurrection of Jesus and the truth of the universe. The power of the resurrection fits with the wonder and meaning of life as we know it, from our understanding of the created order to the justice of the moral order.

The question is this: are we the holy possession of God in Christ, personally chosen by God, predestined for communion with God, adopted into the community of God's people, recipients of God's grace, redeemed by his personal sacrifice on our behalf, and signed, sealed, and delivered by the promised Holy Spirit, *or* are we the accidental product of an impersonal universe, subject to blind chance and random forces,

1. Eph 1:11.
2. Dubay, *The Evidential Power of Beauty*, 40.
3. Col 1:20.

existing in a sphere of energy devoid of promise, plan, purpose, and fulfillment?

The Apostle John proclaims his first line unapologetically: "The revelation from Jesus Christ, which God gave him to show his servants what must soon take place."[4] The gospel is the gift of God revealed through Jesus Christ for the benefit of his servants. This proclamation has specific meaning. Truth is distinctive and defined, substantive and descriptive of what God in his mercy has done, is doing and will do. The truth is all encompassing. The gospel is grandly inclusive of all we are and have. "The revelation from Jesus" is explicit in meaning and universal in scope.

Convergence

On the island of Patmos, the Apostle John experienced the deep meaning of the revelation from Jesus Christ. In the Spirit on the Lord's Day, God revealed to John the convergence of Christ and the destiny of the cosmos. This unveiling of salvation and judgment brings biblical prophecy to a climax. The Revelation is about nothing less than the ultimate convergence of all authority, time, and people.

Start

All Authority

The revelation of Jesus Christ flows from an unbroken and unstoppable current of divine sources. This revelation is given *by* Jesus (subjective genitive), *from* Jesus (genitive of source), and is *about* Jesus (objective genitive). The chain of communication extends from God, "who is, and who was, and who is to come," and from the Holy Spirit, that is, "from the seven spirits before his throne," and from Jesus and his angel to John, and finally from John to us. The message is backed by all the authority and inspiration and empowerment of the triune God. The prophecy is issued out of a unified field theory of divine authority. The Spirit-inspired sources converge: the Old Testament word of God and the New Testament testimony of Jesus are in agreement.

The apostle was called to do what Daniel did. To communicate what "no wise man, enchanter, magician or diviner can explain."[5] No expert, visionary, dreamer, or pundit can deliver the message John was about

4. Rev 1:1.

5. Dan 2:27.

to deliver. In the time of Daniel, the sixth century BC, Nebuchadnezzar wanted his astrologers not only to interpret his dream, but to tell him his dream. He reasoned that it was too easy for his magicians, enchanters, sorcerers, and astrologers to creatively fit whatever he told them. "If you do not tell me what my dream was and interpret it, I will have you cut into pieces . . . "[6] Nebuchadnezzar wanted confirmation that they could interpret the dream. The astrologers responded, "There is not a person on earth who can do what the king asks! No king, however great and mighty, has ever asked such a thing of any magician or enchanter or astrologer. What the king asks is too difficult. No one can reveal it to the king except the gods, and they do not live among human beings."[7] The outraged king ordered everyone killed, including Daniel and his friends. When Daniel heard about the harsh decree, he went to the king and asked for time, "so that he might interpret the dream for him."[8] Then he went to his friends and urged them to "plead for mercy from the God of heaven concerning this mystery."[9] That night the mystery was revealed to Daniel in a vision.

Drawing on the Septuagint version of the Old Testament, John reflected on Daniel's words to Nebuchadnezzar, "There is a God in heaven who reveals (ἀποκαλύπτω) mysteries. . . . [He reveals] what will happen in the days to come."[10] The verb "to reveal" is used five times in the second chapter of Daniel.[11] This unveiling—this opening up and revealing—is not primarily a literary style, but the divine disclosure of destiny. "Apocalyptic" is not used by John in a technical sense, but in a biblical sense. The reason for what he writes, both in content and style, is derived from biblical testimony. Just as Daniel was dependent on the revelation of God, so was John.

All Time

John's apocalyptic symphony transcends a datable time line. He writes within the factual history of Jesus Christ. The actual chronology is encompassed in the life, death, resurrection, ascension, and second coming

6. Dan 2:5.
7. Dan 2:10–11.
8. Dan 2:16.
9. Dan 2:18.
10. Dan 2:28.
11. Dan 2:19, 22, 28–30.

of Christ. John has no interest in connecting the dots in an imaginary end times scenario. He is no further along in understanding the actual time of the end than Jesus claimed to be when he said, "But about that day or hour no one knows, not even the angels in heaven, nor the Son, but only the Father."[12] John was inspired to describe the rhythm of witness and suffering that the church was set to endure through all generations. The spiraling intensity of worship and judgment frames the metanarrative of God's redemption and reckoning.

With the coming of Jesus, the fullness of time had come.[13] Jesus announced, "The time has come. The kingdom of God is near. Repent and believe the good news!"[14] God's great work reached its climax in the coming of Christ and our space-time world was never the same. *Chronos*, the linear flow of time, and *kairos*, God's grace-filled time, intersect in Jesus Christ, who has given time and history a new significance. The one who "was chosen before the creation of the world" has been "revealed in these last times" (*chronos*) for our sake.[15] The coming of Christ becomes the reference point for all of history. The times of ignorance are over.[16] The "revelation of the mystery hidden for long ages past" has been revealed in Jesus Christ.[17] The Revelation brings all of time into focus. Past, present, and future are all immediate to God. The followers of the Lamb live in the real presence of the triune God, before whom all things are immediately present. In the Spirit, John exhorts believers to live with a sense of urgency, in the expectation of "what must soon take place."[18] "If you picture Time as a straight line along which we have to travel," wrote C. S. Lewis, "then you must picture God as the whole page on which the line is drawn."[19] In John's vision of the end everything is coming together—and quickly. Daniel's phrase, "What will happen in the days to come," or "in the latter days," is deliberately transposed to read, "what must soon take place."[20] The once-distant future is now imminent, and the hearers of John's prophecy were meant to live in the immediacy of this prophecy.

12. Mark 13:32.

13. Gal 4:4.

14. Mark 1:15.

15. 1 Pet 1:20.

16. Acts 17:20.

17. Rom 16:25.

18. Rev 1:1.

19. Lewis, *Mere Christianity*, 147.

20. See Dan 8:26; 10:14; 12:9; Rev 1:1.

There is a heightened sense of urgency and intensity that pervades the Revelation. Time is marked by the imminence of Christ's soon return: "Look, he is coming with the clouds . . . "[21] God's sovereignty over time is declared in his name: "I am the Alpha and Omega."[22] He is the beginning and the end and everything in between. The declaration "I am the Alpha and Omega" is a figure of speech called a merism (from the Greek for "part"), a rhetorical device used to encompass polar opposites and everything in between (here and there, life and death, body and soul). If Christ is our beginning point and our end point and all points between these two poles, then nothing lies outside his will and purpose for our lives. Christ is all encompassing. This is true on a personal scale, but the apostle takes the truth deeper and envisions it on a cosmic scale. The descriptive title recalls the name of God in Exodus, "I am who I am," and in Isaiah, "I am the first and the last."[23] Twice the Lord God is described as the one "who is, and who was, and who is to come."[24]

All People

The Revelation is addressed to Christ's servants. "Blessed is the one who reads aloud the words of this prophecy, and blessed are those who hear it and take to heart what is written in it, because the time is near."[25] John addressed his letter "to the seven churches in the province of Asia." These seven historical churches represent the church universal. Seven denotes fullness, totality, and comprehensiveness.[26] All those who are in Christ are included in this description. Their identity is derived from "him who loves us and freed us from our sins by his blood, and has made us to be a kingdom and priests to serve his God and Father."[27]

Although the prophecy is addressed to the church, its truth covers all people everywhere throughout all time. The whole earth and everyone in it is the Lord's. Christ is Lord over the kings of the earth.[28] John

21. Rev 1:7.

22. Rev 1:8.

23. Exod 3:14; Isa 44:6; see 41:4.

24. Rev 1:4, 8.

25. Rev 1:3.

26. The number seven is called a synecdoche, a figure of speech in which the part represents the whole.

27. Rev 1:5–6.

28. Exod 19:6; Ps 89:27.

alludes to Zechariah's prophecy, "They will look on me, the one they have pierced, and they will mourn because of him as one mourns for an only child," but he intentionally alters the wording in two significant ways to include all people.[29] "Every eye" will see the crucified Lord and "all peoples on earth" will mourn because of Christ.[30] Does this "all" refer to the believing community drawn from "every tribe and language and people and nation," or is John referring to all people, including unbelievers?[31] If the latter perspective is in view, then John sets up a striking scene in the prologue that converges the cross of Christ with the throne of Christ. He sees two distinct groups, those who mourn for their sin and praise God for the Lamb who takes away the sin of the world, and those who grieve their eternal loss as if they had lost their firstborn child. The prophecy resonates with the Apostle Paul's Christ hymn,

> Therefore God exalted him to the highest place and gave him the name that is above every name, that at the name of Jesus every knee should bow, in heaven and on earth and under the earth, and every tongue confess that Jesus Christ is Lord, to the glory of God the Father.[32]

All the action described in the prologue issues from the triune God: God the Father, God the Son, and God the Holy Spirit. The Revelation comes from Christ, concerns Christ, and is consummated in Christ. The Lord God Almighty is the source of revelation, the sole sufficient savior, and the superintending sovereign over time and eternity. The Holy Spirit is "the seven spirits before the throne" who along with Christ brings grace and peace. John may have in mind here Isaiah's description of the spirit of the Lord, resting on Christ, "the Spirit of wisdom and of understanding, the Spirit of counsel and of might, the Spirit of knowledge and fear of the Lord."[33] The "seven spirits" represent the fullness of the Holy Spirit working in and through the One who is "the faithful witness, the firstborn from the dead, and the ruler of the kings of the earth."

29. Zech 12:10.
30. Rev 1:7.
31. Rev 5:9.
32. Phil 2:9–11.
33. Isa 11:2.

Creation and History Converge

Three descriptive titles—the faithful witness, the firstborn from the dead, and the ruler of the kings of the earth—underscore the convergence of creation, redemption, and reconciliation. The divine actions of Jesus Christ, prophet, priest, and king, is encompassed by these titles. At the center of this convergence is the cross and resurrection of Jesus. From Genesis to Revelation, the meaning of the cross and the mystery of the atonement unfold under God's sovereign direction. We are prepared for the cross through images, events, allusions, symbols, parables, prophecies, and poetry. Every form, phase, type, and strata of the Bible points to the cross.

Yet the *meaning* of the cross is by no means obvious. The divine necessity is hidden in the course of human affairs. To those who have eyes to see and ears to hear, *history* testifies to the inevitability of the cross and God's revelation declares its meaning. *Salvation is woven into the very fabric of history.* As *history* moved toward the cross, *creation* moves toward the resurrection. Salvation is woven into the very fabric of *nature*, as well. The cross and the resurrection cannot be separated from one another— both are revealed by God, both are space/time historical events, and both are embraced by faith. Moreover, both defy division into physical and spiritual categories. *If the history of God's revelation points to the cross, the nature of God's creation points to the resurrection.*

We are prepared for the resurrection through the "big bang," the language of DNA, the human quest for knowledge, the periodic table, mathematical patterns and formulas, the human capacity for beauty, the anthropic principle of the universe, the incredible complexity of the living cell, and the meaning of the human drama. The divine necessity of the resurrection is hidden in the mystery and complexity of nature. To those who have eyes to see and ears to hear, *creation* testifies to the logical coherence and meaningful power of the resurrection. *God's revelation declares its meaning in the context of nature's wonder and human need. Salvation is woven into the very fabric of creation.* The emptiness of the tomb of Jesus is the ground of *all* meaningfulness. It is the only emptiness that fills history and creation with meaning. The bodily resurrection of Jesus rolls away the stone of nihilism and opens the way to the beauty, complexity, and mystery of life itself.

Faith does not operate in a different realm from sight. Faith is the earnest expectation of sight. In the most real world the two are inseparably linked and inherent in objective reality. "Without faith," wrote the author of Hebrews, "it is impossible to please him, for whoever would draw near to God must believe that he exists and that he rewards those who seek him."[34] Sight does not create that which is seen, nor does faith create that which is believed. The resurrection of Christ is a reputably testified event and history that is believed by faith. If the resurrection of Christ did not actually happen in real time and factual history, the verdict is clear: our faith is useless and we are guilty of bearing false witness. We are still in our sins and we are lost, without hope in the world.

There is order, beauty, meaning, and joy woven into the very nature of creation. Everything points to a complexity that is neither random nor lucky. There is an inherent revelatory quality in all aspects of life. Creation is always beckoning for greater exploration, always inviting us into a deeper experience, always pointing beyond itself, and always bearing testimony not only to its many truths, but to the one and only singular truth, the truth affirmed by Jesus when he said, "I am the way, the truth, and the life, no one comes to the Father but by me."[35] The empty tomb testifies to the world that it is not the product of luck or magic. The world is called into existence by the will and word of God. "By faith we understand that the universe was created by the word of God, so that what is seen was not made out of things that are visible."[36]

The Wedding Feast of the Lamb

The prologue affirms the divine convergence of authority, time, and people. The magnitude of this testimony is both immense and imminent. Everything is coming together in climax and fulfillment. The world is not shallow and superficial after all. Deep meaning is inherent in this world of God's making, redeeming, and reconciling. As we will see, John's most powerful image of convergence is the wedding feast of the Lamb. This redemptive convergence draws us in and invites our anticipation and participation. We disciples are called to cultivate a sacramental view of life, to let God be our Alpha and our Omega through the power of the Lamb of God. Even on this side of eternity life comes together because of the grace and peace of him "who is, and who was, and who is to come."

34. Heb 11:6.
35. John 14:6.
36. Heb 11:3.

We experience earthly convergences as a forecast of the ultimate heavenly convergence—the consummation of the age.

> Since in every breath we take, in every one of our thoughts, in every great and petty experience of our human lives heaven and earth are side by side, greeting each other, attracting and repelling each other and yet belonging to one another, we are, in our existence, of which God is the Creator, a sign and indication, a promise of what ought to happen in creation and to creation—the meeting, the togetherness, the fellowship and, in Jesus Christ, the oneness of Creator and creature.[37]

John dedicates his book "to him who loves us and has freed us from our sins by his blood, and has made us to be a kingdom of priests to serve his God and Father—to him be glory and power for ever and ever! Amen."[38] The immediacy of God's revelation compelled John to write. The eschatological dimension is primary. The imminence of God's sovereign plan for history is the motivation for his work. This means that the "inspiration" for his writing was neither political nor psychological. Roman power and oppression lie in the foreground of John's real-world landscape, but Rome is not the reason for the Revelation. This work is not a political manifesto that uses religion as a medium for resistance and liberation. The prophet's primary audience was not Roman society but the church. John's revolutionary impulse was redemptive, not political in the usual sense. He was no more a threat to the empire than Jesus was to Pilate. John was not out to change the world. He knew nothing of world conquest. It never entered his mind to lead a movement against Rome. John knew firsthand that he lived "in a world permeated by ineradicable injustice."[39]

Nor was John's writing driven by feelings of deprivation or alienation. His tone is confident and strong. He is neither anxious nor resentful. Redemption is his theme, not revenge. The old apostle was neither a powerless victim nor a frustrated warrior in the culture wars. His overriding concern was for the faithfulness of the body of Christ in a hostile culture that threatened to subvert the witness of the church through subtle and overt means. The Apostle John was neither seeking power nor longing to overthrow power. His motive, method, and message were entirely God-centered from start to finish.

37. Barth, *Dogmatics in Outline*, 64.
38. Rev 1:5–6.
39. Volf, *The End of Memory*, 115.

Postmodern Skeptic

Many today have all but given up on the ultimate convergence of time and eternity. For them there is no deep meaning to life or lasting truth thereafter. As we noted at the beginning of this chapter, at least Nebuchadnezzar had the good sense to rage against the pagan outlook. He wanted the truth badly enough to kill for it. The Prophet Daniel, whose prophecy lies beneath John's canvas, praised the God who "reveals deep and hidden things," who "knows what lies in darkness," and who "made known to us the dream of the king."[40]

D. H. Lawrence wrote *Apocalypse* in 1929.[41] He chose to end his literary career writing about what he called "the most detestable" book of the Bible.[42] He mocked its "splendiferous imagery" and its "distasteful" and "pompous unnaturalness." Lawrence claimed that poor, weak, resentful Christians liked the Revelation because of its "grandiose scheme for wiping out and annihilating everybody who wasn't of the elect. . . . From being bottom dogs they were going to be top dogs: in Heaven."[43] In his condemnation of the Revelation, Lawrence echoed Nietzsche's nihilistic conclusions. He claimed John of Patmos was nothing but a weakling who produced a second-rate work for losers.

> For Revelation . . . is the undying will-to-power in man. . . .
> O Christian, you shall reign as a king and set your foot on the
> necks of the old bosses! . . . [Christianity] wants to murder the
> powerful, to seize power itself, the weakling.[44]

Reading D. H. Lawrence on the Revelation reminds me of the "magicians, enchanters, sorcerers and astrologers" in Daniel's day. Lawrence believed that humanity's best hope was to worship the sun and moon and return to the ancient pagan outlook he reveled in:

40. Dan 2:20–23.

41. D. H. Lawrence (1885–1930) was considered a radical visionary in his day, espousing views that have become commonplace in our postmodern age. He advocated unfettered sexuality and a return to pagan spirituality as an antidote to the dehumanizing effects of modernity and materialism. His most famous novel, *Lady Chatterley's Lover* (1928), was considered by some to be pornographic and was not published in its entirety until 1960. Critics have praised the novel for exploring class conflict and the human need for existential fulfillment in spite of social conventions and morality.

42. Lawrence, *Apocalypse and the Writings on Revelation*, 59.

43. Ibid., 63.

44. Ibid.

> What we lack is cosmic life, the sun in us and the moon in us.
> . . . We can only get the sun by a sort of worship: and the same
> the moon. By *going forth* to worship the sun, worship that is felt
> in the blood.[45]

According to Lawrence, truth is nothing more than a mirage on the horizon, an impossibility that ought not to trouble us.

> We always want a "conclusion," and *end*, we always want
> to come, in our mental processes, to a decision, a finality, a
> full-stop. . . . On and on we go, for the mental consciousness
> labors under the illusion that there is somewhere to go to, a
> goal of consciousness. Whereas of course there is no goal.
> Consciousness is an end in itself. We torture ourselves getting
> somewhere, and when we get there it is nowhere, for there is
> nowhere to get to.[46]

D. H. Lawrence articulated a philosophy of life that has become mainstream in our day and stands as the polar opposite of the Apostle John and the Prophet Daniel. His quest for pagan worship and his denial of deep meaning places in bold relief the modern mood and the testimony of the Apostle John. The followers of the Lamb are called to believe and live in the light of great and glorious truths that are now considered strange and absurd by most Westerners.

45. Ibid., 78.
46. Ibid., 93.

4

The Jesus I Need to Know

⁓· Revelation 1:9–20 ·⁓

[1:9–20] *I, John, your brother and companion in the suffering and kingdom and patient endurance that are ours in Jesus, was on the island of Patmos because of the word of God and the testimony of Jesus. On the Lord's Day I was in the Spirit, and I heard behind me a loud voice like a trumpet, which said: "Write on a scroll what you see and send it to the seven churches: to Ephesus, Smyrna, Pergamum, Thyatira, Sardis, Philadelphia and Laodicea."*

I turned around to see the voice that was speaking to me. And when I turned I saw seven golden lampstands, and among the lampstands was someone like a son of man, dressed in a robe reaching down to his feet and with a golden sash around his chest. The hair on his head was white like wool, as white as snow, and his eyes were like blazing fire. His feet were like bronze glowing in a furnace, and his voice was like the sound of rushing waters. In his right hand he held seven stars, and coming out of his mouth was a sharp, double-edged sword. His face was like the sun shining in all its brilliance.

When I saw him, I fell at his feet as though dead. Then he placed his right hand on me and said: "Do not be afraid. I am the First and the Last. I am the Living One; I was dead, and now look, I am alive for ever and ever! And I hold the keys of death and Hades.

Write, therefore, what you have seen: both what is now and what will take place later. The mystery of the seven stars that you saw in my right hand and of the seven golden lampstands is this: The seven stars are the angels of the seven churches, and the seven lampstands are the seven churches."

JOHN INTRODUCES HIMSELF AS our "brother and companion in the suffering and kingdom and patient endurance that are ours in Jesus." He uses the first person singular "I" seven times: "I, John . . . I was in the Spirit . . . I heard behind me . . . I turned around to see . . . I saw . . . When I saw him . . . I fell at his feet as though dead." John's entire being is defined in relationship to the action of God. His engagement is deeply personal. He is leaning into the reality of the revelation of God. "I, John" recalls the similar experience of Daniel:

> I, Daniel, was the only one who saw the vision. . . . I was left alone, gazing at the great vision; I had no strength left, my face turned deathly pale and I was helpless. Then I heard him speaking, and as I listened to him, I fell into a deep sleep, my face to the ground. A hand touched me and set me trembling on my hands and knees.[1]

John writes in the tradition of Daniel and the prophets. He is called to bring biblical prophecy to its climax. He not only shares Daniel's experience, he fulfills Daniel's purpose. John identifies himself humbly by name, not title. Tradition holds that he is the Apostle John, the beloved disciple, but this conclusion is challenged by some scholars, who contend that the differences in literary styles between the Gospel and the Apocalypse are too great to be authored by the same person.[2] However, there are some interesting points in favor of apostolic authorship.

---

1. Dan 10:7–12.

2. R. H. Charles contends that the author was not John the apostle but that the two men knew one another, perhaps "as master and pupil, or as pupils of the same master" (Charles, *Revelation*, vol. 1, xxix). He posits that he author grew up in Galilee, emigrated to Asia Minor, possessed a defective knowledge of Greek, and developed a literary style that was absolutely unique. "While he wrote in Greek he thought in Hebrew and frequently translated Hebrew idioms literally into Greek" (Charles, *Revelation*, vol. 1, xxi). On the basis of 21:14 and 18:20, Charles argues that the author distinguished himself from the apostles and claimed to be a prophet. But it may be important to note that while the author claimed to write prophecy, he never called himself a prophet. He preferred to identify himself as a servant or slave (see 1:1; 19:10; 22:9). Charles calls the author "a great spiritual genius, a man of profound insight and

The fourth Gospel establishes John as the poet-pastor-prophet exemplar. He is a deep thinker who creatively works the images, metaphors, and encounters of the life of Jesus into worship and witness. Many of these images play a strategic role in the Revelation. The Gospel of John introduces Jesus as the living Word, develops the Exodus-Moses motif, emphasizes the metaphor of the Lamb, and reveals that the Son of Man is glorified through suffering. We meet common themes in both the Gospel and the Apocalypse: Shepherd, manna, living water, life and light, and the glory of God.[3] Christians can move from Jesus' upper-room discourse into the Revelation without dissidence or confusion. It is reasonable to believe that the author of the Revelation knew Jesus personally and heard the Master's teaching firsthand.

In any event, John's opening seven-fold self-description encompasses his personal identity and redemptive story. He is our brother in the family of God. His individual "I" does not stand alone. Whether he was by himself on the island of Patmos or in the company of other Christians or exiled prisoners, he was never really alone. In the Spirit, he was in the company of the triune God and the fellowship of believers. Although John was exiled and geographically removed from the seven churches, he remained their companion in the "suffering and kingdom and patient endurance that are ours in Jesus." These three descriptive attributes qualifying John's companionship underscore its costly nature. The fellowship of Christ's suffering and the power of the resurrection go hand in hand.[4] Christ's rule has begun, but the experience of suffering and the need for patient endurance persists. All three attributes of companionship—the suffering and kingdom and patient endurance—are inseparable and stand together. John's self-description underscores the priesthood of all believers.

> To him who loves us and has freed us from our sins by his blood, and has made us to be a kingdom and priests to serve his God and Father—to him be glory and power for ever and ever! Amen.[5]

the widest sympathies" (Charles, *Revelation*, vol. 1, xliv), a commendation with which we can agree. But might we also add that he was a believer with deep humility and that he intentionally chose not to use the title "apostle" to describe himself? (See Charles, *Revelation*, vol. 1, xxi–xliv.)

3. Beale, *Revelation*, 35.

4. Phil 3:10.

5. Rev 1:5–6.

John "was on the island of Patmos because of the word of God and the testimony of Jesus."[6] He refused to give Caesar the credit for his circumstances, even though he was on the island of Patmos because of Rome. In all likelihood John was banished to this rocky thirteen-square-mile island off the coast of modern-day Turkey because he did not support the imperial cult. Instead of dwelling on his plight, he focused on the defining reason for his location—the word of God and the testimony of Jesus. I doubt that John was on a spiritual retreat or a writing sabbatical.[7] It is more likely that the mention of Patmos to the seven churches suggested Rome's heavy-handed political suppression. As Leslie Newbigin explains, the gospel provokes a response:

> Wherever the gospel is preached, new ideologies appear—secular humanism, nationalism, Marxism—movements which offer the vision of a new age, an age freed from all the ills that beset human life, freed from hunger and disease and war—on other terms. . . . Once the gospel is preached and there is a community which lives by the gospel, then the question of the ultimate meaning of history is posed and other messiahs appear. So the crisis of history is deepened.[8]

The reason he was on Rome's watch list was not because he was an outspoken critic of Rome, but because he proclaimed ultimate fidelity and loyalty to the imminent return of the true King of kings and Lord of lords. Jesus is Lord, not Caesar. John's personal experience of this ever-deepening crisis of history was due to the word of God and testimony of Jesus.

The Real Jesus

Shortly after my brother-in-law Paul Long graduated from seminary, he was called to pastor two small rural churches outside of Montgomery,

6. Rev 1:9.

7. Sheets, "Something Old, Something New: Revelation and Empire," 205. Sheets writes, "John was on Patmos 'because of the word of God and the testimony of Jesus' (Rev 1:9). Many interpret this phrase to mean that he was banished to Patmos because of his preaching of the gospel. There is no evidence that Patmos was a penal colony. Considering the fact that John refers to the entire revelation as 'the word of God and the testimony of Jesus' (Rev 1:2) one could conclude that he went to Patmos simply to write the apocalypse" ("Something Old," 205).

8. Newbigin, *The Gospel in a Pluralistic Society*, 122.

Alabama. Behind the pulpit in one of the little churches was a picture of Jesus. The platform was small and the pulpit was only about three feet from the back wall. The large oil painting was mounted directly behind the pulpit. When Paul preached he stood directly in front of Aunt Ruby's painting of Jesus. The painting was bad art: the colors were all wrong— Jesus' eyes and robe were pale blue—and his feet didn't touch the ground. His vacant gaze was eerie. It was definitely a distraction.

On a Sunday visit, after the worship service, I asked Paul if he had thought about removing the picture. He agreed that it was pretty ugly, but he said the church would split if the painting was removed. Ironically, Aunt Ruby didn't even go to the church, but her family did, and I suspect they had a controlling interest in everything that happened in that little country church. When the next pastor came several years later, the first thing he did was take the picture down. And Paul was right: Aunt Ruby's painting of Jesus caused a church split. Her extended family left the church. Our self-styled portraits of Jesus get in the way of "someone like a son of man."[9]

There are seven visions of Christ in the Revelation. Each vision is crafted from what has gone before. John's medium of artistic expression is drawn from the Bible. Every angle is a tradition deeply rooted in Old Testament metaphors, symbols, and experiences. John's revelation is an antidote to the prevailing popularity of the minimal Jesus and the abstract Christ. His thoroughgoing Christ-centered emphasis rejects any hint of Jesus reimagined in our image or of a doctrinaire Christ reduced to a good religious idea.

John's Spirit-inspired vision of Christ is neither defensive nor apologetic. He is not making a case for Christ. He is not arguing for the reasonableness of the incarnation or the resurrection. His orientation is not to defend the Christian faith, but to present the reality of Christ. He does not gain stature through this responsibility. He is humbled to the core of his being. He does not own this vision, as an artist owns her masterpiece. John has no proprietary rights. This is not his intellectual property. He is possessed by the vision. He sees himself as a slave of Christ delivering a message.

The Apostle John's vision of Christ is seven-fold:

1. The vision of "someone like the son of man" is shaped out of seven features. The character of Christ is revealed by his head, eyes, feet, voice,

9. Rev 1:13.

hands, mouth, and face. This is the first and the most complete vision
(1:12–16).

2. In the letters to the seven churches, Christ is introduced to each church
by one aspect of his being. Taken together the churches represent the
fullness of Christ. The remaining visions build upon this foundation
(2:1—3:22).

3. Worship in heaven centers on the Lamb, who was slain. All heaven
sings and shouts, "Worthy is the Lamb, who was slain, to receive power
and wealth and wisdom and strength and honor and glory and praise!"
(5:12).

4. The fourth vision comes at the center of the book and reveals the birth
of Jesus and the advance of the church against a backdrop of cosmic
spiritual conflict. The devil is on the warpath but the bride of Christ,
the church, holds fast to the testimony about Jesus (12:1–17).

5. In the fifth vision, the Lamb is standing on Mount Zion with the
144,000. The number signifies all the true followers of the Lamb. They
are signed, sealed, and delivered (14:1–5).

6. The sixth vision is of the militant Messiah, the conquering Christ, who
is called "Faithful and True." His robe is dipped in blood and he is leading the armies of heaven. He is the "King of kings and Lord of lords"
(19:11–16).

7. The seventh vision is a declaration: "I am the Alpha and the Omega,
the First and the Last, the Beginning and the End" (22:12–16).

⅄ The Christ Vision

John is summoned by a voice like a trumpet—a voice that cannot be
ignored, that must be heard: "I heard behind me a loud voice like a
trumpet."[10] Attention to the matter at hand is instinctive and immediate.
"I turned around to see the voice," writes John. His immediate sensation
was candlelight illuminating an awesome figure. "And when I turned I
saw seven golden lampstands, and among the lampstands was someone
like a son of man." Is there any significance to the fact that the voice is
behind John and that he had to turn around to see the it? The substance
of what John is about to "see" is rooted in Old Testament prophecy. The
truth is behind him and he has to turn around to see the voice. "Turning"

10. Rev 1:10.

is repeated twice for emphasis. Voice and vision come from the past. What John is about to see is based on previous revelations.

There is plenty of talk in today's church of a customized vision uniquely suited for each and every leader and church. But John's vision is neither entrepreneurial nor futuristic. His vision is rooted in salvation history. His mind is saturated with the Old Testament, and images of his biblical heritage, both ancient and original, flood his memory. On a date that can be precisely fixed, February 15, 519 BC, the Prophet Zechariah had a vision of a solid gold lampstand with seven lamps, and two olive trees on either side of it. The lampstand symbolizes the temple of God and light of revelation.[11] The two olive trees signify a continuous supply of oil—they symbolize the Holy Spirit. When Zechariah asked the angel about the lampstand and olive trees, the angel answered obliquely, summarizing the entire prophecy (all eight visions in the Book of Zechariah) in a line: "This is the word of the Lord to Zerubbabel: 'Not by might nor by power, but by my Spirit,' says the Lord Almighty."[12]

John's experience is voice driven, not sight driven. The primary means of revelation is not visual but aural. The juxtaposition of voice and vision recalls the Lord's concern for idolatry at Mount Sinai. The Lord said to Moses, "You have *seen* for yourselves that I have *spoken* to you from heaven."[13] John's vision is more about opening the eyes of his heart than it is about a picture that he could paint.[14] John's vision of Christ invokes a spiritual understanding of God. God defined himself linguistically, not visually. In a visual and visceral sense God remained hidden. Yahweh refused to be reduced to an object that could be worshiped. God reveals himself as the living subject, who is rationally, spiritually, and emotionally comprehensible. The hidden God is present among his people personally, but not materially. Instead of projecting himself in a shrine, Yahweh insisted on a conversation with his people.

The seven lampstands are the seven churches and in their light the Son of Man is revealed. The first thing John sees is the clothing: the priestly uniform is striking. Clothing can be read faster than a resumé. The Son of Man is "dressed in a robe reaching down to his feet and with a golden sash around his chest." Old Testament images of the great high priest fill not only John's mind, but his listeners'. The robe and sash are

11. Exod 25:31–40; Num 8:1–4.

12. Zech 4:6.

13. Exod 20:22.

14. Eph 1:18–19.

as obvious as a surgeon's scrubs or a soldier's uniform. The Son of Man's high-priestly vestments signify his role. The first thing we need from Christ is forgiveness.

> Therefore, since we have a great high priest who has ascended into heaven, Jesus the Son of God, let us hold firmly to the faith we profess. For we do not have a high priest who is unable to empathize with our weaknesses, but we have one who has been tempted in every way, just as we are—yet he did not sin. Let us then approach God's throne of grace with confidence, so that we may receive mercy and find grace to help us in our time of need.[15]

As important as the priestly office may be, it is the character of the Son of Man that John finds most impressive. Seven character-defining features stand out. The hair on his head was white like wool, as white as snow. His eyes were like blazing fire. His feet were like bronze glowing in a furnace. His voice was like the sound of rushing water. In his right hand he held seven stars, and coming out of his mouth was a sharp, double-edged sword. His face was like the sun shining in all its brilliance. John's vision of the Son of Man plays to theological and literary imagination. He invokes meaning through metaphor. Our inspired poet-pastor merges Daniel's vision of the Ancient of Days with his own firsthand experience of the Son of Man. John's style is more parabolic than pictorial. Each image on his canvas comes with a canonical history designed to proclaim the truth of God.

John's idol-busting image of Christ uses metaphor to reveal the truth. From start to finish light dominates the image. Seven golden lampstands flicker in the presence of an incandescent brightness. Remember, it is John who turns and hears the voice and sees the vision. His Gospel begins, "In him was life, and that life was the light of all people. The light shines in the darkness, and the darkness has not overcome it."[16] Daniel described the Ancient of Days: "His clothing was as white as snow; the hair of his head was white like wool."[17] White hair projects wisdom, a crown of splendor obtained by righteousness.[18] But even more importantly, white signifies forgiveness. "Though your sins are like scarlet, they

15. Heb 4:14–16.
16. John 1:4–5.
17. Dan 7:9.
18. Prov 16:31.

shall be as white as snow."[19] White is the color of blood-washed linen, made pure by the blood of the Lamb. The first character-defining truth is this: Christ is our forgiveness.

The penetrating gaze of fire-blazing eyes purifies. Christ sees us better than we see ourselves. Every idol is the object of a thousand human stares, but without a trace of any recognition. We look and look at the object of our admiration but he or she or it cannot even see what we see. The idol sees nothing and knows nothing. "Their eyes are plastered over so they cannot see, and their minds closed so they cannot understand."[20] In an age of celebrity, idolized images demand our attention. We are captivated by the daily viewing of media images of famous personalities that cannot recognize us in return. But Christ's penetrating, purifying eyes see us completely. "Search me, God, know my heart; test me and know my anxious thoughts. See, if there is an offensive way in me, and lead me in the way everlasting."[21]

Christ's golden-bronze feet glow in intensity. The strength of iron and the tenacity of copper is forged in a furnace of perpetual energy. He is the unmoved mover with absolute freedom of mobility—always swift and strong. Like Nebuchadnezzar's ninety-foot-tall golden image, today's idols are spectacular, but as Daniel saw in his vision, at their base they are nothing but clay. Modern-day Nebuchadnezzars strut and strategize, but in the end they are no match for the rock that "was cut out, but not with human hands."[22] The rock pulverizes the clay and smashes every pretense raised up against God.

His voice is like white-water thunder as it roars through the canyon. No utterance compares to his voice. No power on heaven or earth can silence his voice. "Nations are in uproar, kingdoms fall; he lifts his voice, the earth melts."[23] "The voice of the Lord is over the waters; the God of glory thunders, the Lord thunders over the mighty waters. The voice of the Lord is powerful; the voice of the Lord is majestic. The voice of the Lord breaks the cedars."[24] Idols neither see, nor hear, nor speak. Yet people speak up for their idols and they speak to their idols. They say,

19. Isa 1:18.
20. Isa 44:18.
21. Ps 139:23–24.
22. Dan 2:34.
23. Ps 46:6.
24. Ps 29:3–4.

"Save me! You are my god!"[25] Many people seem to prefer it that way. But the voice of the Son of Man is as bold and bright as the brilliance of his appearance.

In his right hand he holds seven stars. The much-publicized spiritual power of the stars in John's day, and the natural power of the atom in our day, is trumped by a metaphor. The one who is all about forgiveness and purity, strength and security, holds the stars in his right hand. He runs the universe. "The Son is the image of the invisible God, the firstborn over all creation. For in him all things were created: things in heaven and on earth, visible and invisible, whether thrones or powers or rulers or authorities; all things have been created through him and for him. He is before all things, and in him all things hold together."[26] The breadth of his hand spans galaxies and the words from his mouth sustain the universe. He has the power to split atoms and save souls, to set the course of the planets and discern the motives of the heart. Christ rules! "By faith we understand that the universe was formed at God's command."[27]

Coming out of his mouth is a double-edged sword. The weapon of choice in the war of words is the word of God. In Isaiah, the Spirit of wisdom and understanding is linked to this sword: "He will strike the earth with the rod of his mouth; with the breath of his lips he will slay the wicked."[28] The sword signifies the wisdom of God that cuts through the rhetoric, the propaganda, the sales pitches, and the gossip. In Hebrews we read,

> For the word of God is alive and active. Sharper than any double-edged sword, it penetrates even to dividing soul and spirit, joints and marrow; it judges the thoughts and attitudes of the heart. Nothing in all creation is hidden from God's sight. Everything is uncovered and laid bare before the eyes of him to whom we must give an account.[29]

His face is like the sun shining in all its brilliance. All things are revealed in the brilliance of the true Light of the World. As Isaiah the prophet said, "The people walking in darkness have seen a great light; on those living

25. Isa 44:9, 17.
26. Col 1:15–17.
27. Heb 11:3.
28. Isa 11:2, 4.
29. Heb 4:12–13.

in the land of deep darkness a light has dawned."[30] This seventh attribute is emphasized in the prologue of the fourth Gospel: "In him was life, and that life was the light of all people. The light shines in the darkness, and the darkness has not overcome it. . . . The true light that gives light to everyone was coming into the world."[31] The last impression is of blessing and *shalom*: "The Lord make his face shine on you and be gracious to you; the Lord turn his face toward you and give you peace."[32]

To further deepen our understanding of Christ, John has arranged these metaphors in a chiastic structure, using a crisscrossing pattern to draw out their meaning. The style is named after the Greek letter *chi* that is formed in the shape of a cross [χ]. Instead of listing these features, John uses poetic symmetry to place each attribute of Christ in a dynamic relationship.

(1) Hair		(7) Face	Encounter & Benevolence
(2) Eyes	(4) Voice	(6) Mouth	Relationship & Communication
(3) Feet		(5) Hand	Capability & Action

Competing Images of Power

John's vision of "someone like a son of man" invokes competing images of power. Richard Bauckham sees in the Revelation "a set of Christian prophetic counter-images which impress on its readers a different vision of the world." Bauckham writes, "The visual power of the book effects a kind of purging of the Christian imagination, refurbishing it with alternative visions of how the world is and will be."[33] John intended this vision of Christ to protect Christians from the seductive power of images that pervade culture. Like the early church, we live in a culture of competing images of power. There are innumerable celebrities and immortality symbols that vie for our attention. How does the truth of Christ stack up against Hollywood stars, sports heroes, newsmakers, tycoons, and politicians? Popular pastors articulate a Nebuchadnezzar philosophy of life. They preach success and prosperity through dynamic imagining. If

30. Isa 9:2.

31. John 1:4–5

32. Num 6:24–25.

33. Bauckham, *The Theology of the Book of Revelation*, 17.

they are right, Nebuchadnezzar should be our hero.[34] He was the ancient prototype of this philosophy of life. When Nebuchadnezzar dreamed his dreams he was the most powerful human being on the planet. He foreshadowed Nietzsche's sentiment, "If there is a God, how can I bear not to be that God?"[35]

Emperor Domitian

If John wrote the Revelation in the late 90s, the most powerful human figure on the scene was the Roman emperor Domitian. In his youth Domitian was described as modest, graceful, tall, and handsome, but in old age he had "a protruding belly, spindle legs, and a bald head."[36] Ironically, he authored a book called "On the Care of the Hair." Like the Caesars before him, he lived in dread of betrayal and assassination and freely indulged his sexual passions. Early in his reign he was an able administrator and presided over a building boom in Rome. He spent $22 million on a gold-plated roof and doors for the Temple of Jupiter, Juno, and Minera, and built an enormous palace for himself.[37] He filled Rome with statues of himself and required officials to address him as "Our Lord and God." He banished philosophers because they encouraged rebellion and astrologers because they predicted his death. "In 93 Domitian executed some Christians for refusing to offer sacrifices before his image; according to tradition these included his nephew Flavius Clemens."[38] In his later years, Domitian's paranoia turned to madness. Many aristocrats and senators were either exiled or killed, because he feared their rebellion. When Domitian ordered the death of his personal secretary, members of the imperial household, including his wife, rose up and killed him.

Historian Will Durant paints a picture of the Caesars, including Domitian, as tragic figures, who gave "peace to the Empire, but terror to Rome" and to themselves. Durant writes,

> Behind the adulteries and the murders an administrative organization had formed which provided, through all this period, a high order of provincial government. The emperors themselves

---

34. Ibid., 56.
35. Ferguson, *Daniel*, 71.
36. Durant, *Caesar and Christ*, 289.
37. Ibid., 290.
38. Ibid., 292.

were the chief victims of their power. . . . Nearly all of them were unhappy, surrounded by conspiracy, dishonesty, and intrigue, trying to govern a world from the anarchy of a home. They indulged their appetites because they knew how brief was their omnipotence; they lived in the daily horror of men condemned to an early and sudden death. They went under because they were above the law; they became less than men because power had made them gods.[39]

Steve Jobs

A contemporary personality who captures peoples' imaginations is Steve Jobs. The late genius behind Apple "stands as the ultimate icon of inventiveness, imagination, and sustained innovation."[40] Jobs devoted his life to innovating not only new products but reimagining an ancient philosophy of life. He offered the iconic apple as the forbidden fruit. He countered the biblical message of the fall of man. In the post-Christian myth, Jobs flips the story. It is God who lies and the devil who speaks truth when the serpent says, "For God knows that when you eat of it your eyes will be opened, and you will be like God, knowing good and evil."[41] The bitten apple is a trademark symbol of defiance. Seamless connectivity between the Internet and a device stands as a kind of transcendent goal, a form of salvation. The gospel according to Apple morphs into a philosophy of life that preaches solidarity through technology. The mesmerizing myth of wholeness through very cool, sexy devices misses the reality of what that technology is doing to the self. Steve Jobs married Eastern spirituality with Western materialism, the result being that innovative products become the essence of salvation. Like the Tower of Babel, Apple's iPhones, iPads, and iPods shape our identity: they make us who we are. We are saved from being "scattered over the face of the earth" by these ingenious devices. "This is the gospel of a secular age," writes Andy Crouch. "It has the great virtue of being based only on what we can all perceive—it requires neither revelation nor dogma. And it promises nothing it cannot deliver—since all that is promised is the opportunity to live your own unique life, a hope that is manifestly realizable since it is offered by one who has so spectacularly succeeded by following his

39. Ibid., 293.

40. Isaacson, *Steve Jobs*, xxi.

41. Gen 3:5.

own 'inner voice, heart and intuition.'" Jobs was able to "to articulate a
perfectly secular form of hope." He was "the perfect evangelist because he
had no competing source of hope."[42]

Admirers or Followers

John's vision of Christ begins and ends on a note of humility. His description of "someone like a son of man" is meant to be neither vague nor
generic, but rather humble and submissive. He knows he cannot exhaust
the mystery, so he doesn't even try. He cannot contain, control, package,
or manipulate the vision. The vision controls him, he doesn't control it.
"When I saw him," John writes, "I fell at his feet as though dead. Then
he placed his right hand on me and said: 'Do not be afraid.'" It is significant that John begins and ends his vision of the Son of Man with a self-
description. His "I" statements are wrapped around his understanding of
Christ. This vision undermines all the "strategies of self-salvation built on
human effort" whether they be guilt induced or self-indulging.[43] This vision removes the pride and the fear that gets in the way of truly following
the Lord Jesus Christ.

Falling at Christ's feet "as though dead" is so un-American. We
declare our independence and defend our personal autonomy, but John
surrenders adoringly to the Alpha and the Omega. Christ is not a means
to an end. Christ is the beginning and the end and all points in between.
Like John, all believers need the fellowship and empowerment of the
right hand of God placed upon us. We need to hear the word of the gospel: "Do not be afraid. I am the First and the Last. I am the Living One; I
was dead, and now look, I am alive for ever and ever! And I hold the keys
of death and Hades."[44] The Son of Man's three-fold "I Am" statements
define who we are and to whom we belong. Our self-description is placed
in orbit around the Son. The Jesus I need to know is not a reflection of
my thoughts and feelings. I am a reflection of his glory and wisdom. John
feels no claim to fame because of this experience. He is an inspired servant, not a creative genius.

We disciples are flickering flames of candlelight amidst the Son in all
his brilliance. The shadows cast by the mere candlelight of churches will

42. Crouch, "Steve Jobs: The Secular Prophet."
43. Keller, *Center Church*, 66.
44. Rev 1:18.

eventually be engulfed by Son-light. But until then, candlelight is God's choice to illuminate the Son of Man's blazing glory. God's plan makes no sense to the world, but the strategy fits perfectly with what we know of salvation history. No one ever imagined that a priestly robed Alpha and Omega would merge Isaiah's Suffering Servant and Daniel's Ancient of Days. But the paradox is crucial to the meaning of salvation. The priestly robe and sash are worn by none other than God himself. He who knew no sin became sin for us. The one who offers up the sacrifice for us is in fact the sacrifice himself. The paradox of the incarnation is expressed in this vision of the apocalyptic Son of Man, who is both the great high priest and the First and the Last.

The vision of Christ is made up of seven parts. No single attribute or short list of attributes can stand alone. We cannot pick and choose this or that in the description of Christ that we like or don't like. To worship Christ is to worship Christ in his totality. The seven-fold essence of Christ means that the purity, power, and passion of the living Lord Jesus belong together. It doesn't work to want God's strength without God's holiness or to take comfort in his forgiveness without responding obediently to his Word. John is not only comforted, but commissioned. It is impossible to see what he sees and remain uninvolved. Responsibility follows revelation. Everything John does flows from this vision; without it he has nothing to write. This is what should impress us about one another: that we become like John—so filled with the work and word of Christ that we do not follow our own agenda, but instead follow the plan and purpose of Christ. John is not making things up, inventing as he goes. His goal is to represent the testimony of Jesus in word and deed. John's vision is more experiential than pictorial. This vision of Christ cannot be artistically rendered on canvas or in stone. It can only be lived. John's vision of Christ casts out fear, inspires courage, and fills the church with meaning.

5

The Seven Letters

⌐· Revelation 2:1—3:22 ·⌐

[2:1—3:22] *"To the angel of the church in Ephesus write . . . To the angel of the church in Smyrna write . . . To the angel of the church in Pergamum write . . . To the angel of the church in Thyatira write . . . To the angel of the church in Sardis write . . . To the angel of the church in Philadelphia write . . . To the angel of the church in Laodicea write . . . "*

THE APOSTLE JOHN WAS commissioned to write "to the angel" in each of the seven churches.[1] He writes to each church *in* the city, not *of* the city. God intended for these churches to be *in* the world but not *of* the world. "Strictly speaking there can be no 'American church' or 'Canadian church,' any more than there could be a church composed of 'German Christians' in the 1930s. There is only the Christian community as it is gathered in these particular geographical and cultural settings."[2] Each letter is addressed to Christians living in a particular time and place. True spirituality is always rooted in a local culture and requires engagement and discernment. The gospel is both affirming and antithetical to its host culture, requiring both intentional contextualization and, at the same time, resistance to being assimilated and seduced by its powers. If we

1. Rev 1:4, 11.

2. Mangina, *Revelation*, 55–56.

58

want to follow the Lamb we have to believe that "the Jesus way wedded to the Jesus truth brings about the Jesus life." Eugene Peterson warns against "the undiscriminating way in which so many of us embrace and adopt the very ways and means that Jesus rejected, taking up with the world in ways suggested by the promises of the devil: assurances of power and influence, domination and success."[3]

Apparently each of the churches has a heavenly guardian angel to which the letter is addressed. The message is mediated through a heavenly representative rather than a single pastoral leader or bishop. By addressing each letter to its respective church's guardian angel, John emphasized not only the writing's divine authority, but its equally shared accountability for every member in the congregation. No one in the church was in charge of the letter or in control of its contents: all sat under its authority. Mediating the message through the guardian angel implies its heavenly authority and its eschatological significance. Any suggestion of local autonomy or of competition between churches is dismissed. The churches are not the product of either entrepreneurial vision-casting or a charismatic personality. The concerns expressed in these letters bring us back to what the church is all about in the first place.

Each letter is personal, practical, and specifically meant for that particular body of believers, but all seven letters were to be read by all the churches in the context of the entire prophecy as well. These seven one-minute messages to the churches emphasized shared concerns and mutual accountability. They may be analogous to imperial edicts issued from Caesar's throne. Only in this case, they come from the Living One, who holds the keys of death and Hades and the seven stars in his right hand. The letters may also have an historical precedent in Jeremiah's letter to the exiles.[4] The Prophet Jeremiah and the Apostle John are instructing the people of God, who live in a culture that is hostile to the will of God, to remain faithful and resilient. The Spirit is speaking to the churches, and every believer is admonished to listen carefully and pay close attention to all of the letters as well as to their own.

Each letter begins by drawing from one aspect of the vision of Christ. Christ is introduced to the churches by his attributes. These attributes of Christ are uniquely related to issues identified in the individual letters. Commendation and correction are briefly stated. Each letter ends

3. Peterson, *The Jesus Way*, 4, 10.
4. Jer 29:1–23.

by focusing on one dimension of the reward promised to those who conquer in Christ. In the last four letters, there is a slight alteration in the pattern. The promise of the reward comes before the call to hear what the Spirit says to the churches. Taken together the letters show us the essence of what it is to be the church. The pattern of spiritual direction in each letter is simple to follow: (1) Christ's Identification; (2) Positive Affirmation; (3) Corrective Discipline; (4) Motivating Promise; (5) Evangelical Call to Listen.

The voice of Christ is always compelling, convicting, and affirming. Christ demands our attention. "These are the words of him who holds the seven stars in his right hand, who is the First and the Last, who has the sharp, double-edged sword, whose eyes are like blazing fire, who is the fullness of the Spirit, who is holy and true, and who is the ruler of God's creation." The Apostle John sets before us an agenda and repeats the refrain seven times, "he who has ears to hear let him hear."

Countercultural Truths

"The church is in really bad shape today.
It's almost as bad as it was in the first century."

—RICHARD MOUW[5]

There are three countercultural truths implied in these seven letters. First, our "brother and companion in the suffering and kingdom and patient endurance that is ours in Jesus" was not a paid consultant. Issues of growth, vitality, leadership, and mission are spiritual issues that require spiritual discipline and a prophetic word. When churches are in trouble or in need of correction, the problem is not the lack of business expertise or marketing savvy or social networking; the problem is a failure to be transformed by the truth of God. The prophet says to give yourselves to worship, prayer, and serving the poor; the consultant tells you how to raise funds from people with deep pockets. There is nothing in these seven letters that indicates that churches will grow through effective event planning. The vision that lies behind these letters is an organic church growth strategy. Authentic spirituality is the key.

Second, apart from the church there is no Christian faith. We cannot belong to Christ and not belong to his church. Eugene Peterson

5. Quoted in Galli and Crouch, "The Future of Today's Christianity," 45.

writes, "Attention to the Gospel message is always an act of community, never an exercise in private." Whether we know it or not, we need the church. "Every tendency to privatism and individualism distorts and falsifies the gospel."[6] Pollster George Barna predicts "an unprecedented re-engineering of America's faith" due to widespread disillusionment with vision casting and the megachurch. A new generation of believers "refuse to follow people in ministry leadership positions who cast a personal vision rather than God's."[7] On the basis of current trends, Barna encourages believers to leave the local church and form their own models of spiritual intimacy, accountability, and service. In the future he sees believers "choosing from a proliferation of options, weaving together a set of favored alternatives into a unique tapestry that constitutes the personal 'church' of the individual."[8] Barna shrinks the "church" down to the autonomous individual believer. He challenges believers to embrace the freedom and excitement of doing what they want to do. They should decide for themselves what meets their personal needs. If playing golf on Sunday lowers their stress and helps them reflect more thoughtfully on the Bible, then skipping corporate worship works for them. Barna's reasoning is simple: Who needs the hassles of the local church? The autonomous individual self can be a denomination of one. You can be your own local church.

Barna's approach runs contrary to the New Testament description of the church. Jesus used metaphors and analogies, such as the "little flock" and the vine and the branches, to picture the emerging church.[9] The apostles spoke of God's chosen people and members of God's household.[10] Peter emphasized, "But you are a chosen people, a royal priesthood, a holy nation, a people belonging to God, that you may declare the praises of him who called you out of darkness into his wonderful light. Once you were not a people, but now you are the people of God; once you had not received mercy, but now you have received mercy."[11]

The solidarity of the saints is a New Testament theme. So real was the oneness of this new humanity that the apostles spoke of the church as being one new person. We are members of God's household, joined

6. Peterson, *Reversed Thunder*, 43.

7. Barna, *Revolution*, 14.

8. Ibid., 66.

9. Luke 12:32; John 15.

10. Col 3:12; Eph 2:19.

11. 1 Pet 2:9–10.

together to become a holy temple. We used to be foreigners and strangers but now we have immigrated to a new country; we have been adopted into a new family, and we belong to a holy temple in the Lord. The good news is proclaimed and lived through the local church—through the community—rather than through the autonomous individual. In a world of hostility the church is an alternative society, a visible sign of the kingdom of God in a fallen world. God's purpose is that we don't divide along ethnic, cultural, racial, social, gender, and generational lines. Rather, we were meant to be fellow citizens with God's people and members of God's household, built on the foundation provided by the apostles and prophets, with Christ Jesus himself as the chief cornerstone. "The church gathers around the character of Christ, not the characteristics of people."[12]

The third countercultural truth implied in these letters is that we cannot take the church for granted. Just because we have a building—we may even have a sprawling church campus—does not mean we have a church. The location may be ideal, but if Christ has removed the church's "lampstand," then she is, spiritually speaking, nothing more than a dark and empty building. The rebuke contained within in these letters recalls the prophetic critique of false temple religion.

There is a prophetic edge to the seven letters that recalls the ministry of the prophets. When Jeremiah stood at the gate of the temple to proclaim the Lord's message against blatant idolatry and false sacrifice, he took his stand in a long tradition that valued obedience over ritual and humble devotion over religious performance. The Apostle John's seven letters to the churches are in the tradition of the Prophet Jeremiah. Jeremiah's stinging accusation corresponds to Jesus in the temple, when he forcibly drove out "all who were buying and selling" and "overturned the tables of the money changers." "It is written," Jesus said, quoting the prophets Isaiah and Jeremiah, "'My house will be called a house of prayer,' but you are making it a *den of robbers*."[13] Jesus equated the religious crisis of his day with the false temple religion that the prophets had confronted. His words and actions vindicated the work of the prophets through the centuries as they sought to drive out empty religiosity, meaningless ritual, and self-righteousness. The letters to the seven churches stand in this prophetic tradition. The people of God cannot afford to turn a blind eye

---

12. Snodgrass, *Ephesians*, 155.

13. Matt 21:13; Isa 56:7; Jer 7:11.

to subtle forms of soft idolatry and sinful cultural accommodation. If we do, Christ promises to blow out the candles and remove our lampstand.

Whoever Has Ears

"I was finding myself vocationally at home in the mysteries of worship and baptism and Eucharist in my Ephesus-Smyrna-Pergamum-Thyatira-Sardis-Philadelphia-Laodicea congregation."

—Eugene Peterson[14]

The seven letters are God's sit-up-and-take-notice, no-nonsense, pay-close-attention spiritual direction to the churches. The risen Lord Jesus speaks to the churches through the prophet-pastor John. Each letter is bold and succinct: no beating around the bush, no long-winded analysis. Each church is different; no two churches are alike, a fact that should silence those who say, "All churches are alike. Every church has problems."

The image of the risen Christ walking in the midst of the churches is both encouraging and sad. I picture Christ warmly embraced by the suffering churches of Smyrna and Philadelphia—beleaguered believers know they need Christ. They depend upon his word and the fellowship of believers to make it through another week. Persecuted disciples celebrate Christ's presence and worship the Lord. I picture Jesus receiving a cool reception at successful congregations like Thyatira and independently minded Laodicea. In these more nominal churches, Christ receives a mixed reception.

The first thing we are impressed with is that Christ knows us: "I know your deeds . . . your afflictions . . . your difficult place . . . your love and faith and service." Christ knows everything about us. Simply knowing that Christ knows should help us listen better. The seven churches focus our attention:

> The First Church of Ephesus
>
> The Suffering Church of Smyrna
>
> Pergamum Hills Fellowship Church
>
> City Church of Thyatira
>
> Sardis Community Church

14. Peterson, *The Pastor*, 22.

Philadelphia Christian Church

Cathedral Church of Laodicea

The positive thrust of these seven letters can be stated in a word: the seven spirit disciplines of the Christ-centered church include love, courage, faithfulness, holiness, authenticity, steadfastness, and humility. There is nothing overly complicated here, nothing new. The One "who is, and who was, and who is to come" is still looking for these same attributes in today's church. A church doesn't need theater seating and special lighting, but she does need these qualities. The secret of a vital church is no mystery. The strategy is the same as it always has been, because "Jesus Christ is the same yesterday and today and forever."[15] What was important then is important today.

15. Heb 13:8.

6

First Love Witness

⌒· Revelation 2:1–7 ·⌒

[2:1–7] *"To the angel of the church in Ephesus write: These are the words of him who holds the seven stars in his right hand and walks among the seven golden lampstands. I know your deeds, your hard work and your persever- ance. I know that you cannot tolerate wicked people, that you have tested those who claim to be apostles but are not, and have found them false. You have persevered and have endured hardships for my name, and have not grown weary.*

Yet I hold this against you: You have forsaken the love you had at first. Consider how far you have fallen! Repent and do the things you did at first. If you do not repent, I will come to you and remove your lampstand from its place. But you have this in your favor: You hate the practices of the Nicolaitans, which I also hate.

Whoever has ears, let them hear what the Spirit says to the churches. To those who are victorious, I will give the right to eat from the tree of life, which is in the paradise of God."

FIRST-TIME VISITORS TO OUR churches may have an inkling of how Jesus felt walking in the midst of these seven churches in Asia Minor. Jesus Christ is right there. His on-site awareness of the churches assures the va- lidity of his commendation and the wisdom of his correction. The Spirit of Christ knows the churches inside out. The living Lord Jesus is in the midst of The First Church of Ephesus. He wasn't kidding when he said, "Surely I am with you always, to the very end of the age."[1]

In each letter to the seven churches, the character of Christ is described before the work of the church is commended and corrected. The sovereign Lord encourages The First Church of Ephesus for her deeds, hard work, and perseverance. The church is recognized for her vigilance against wickedness, her defense of the truth, and for her vital faith. What's left, you ask? What church would not be pleased with this commendation? "Its members were busy in their service, patient in their suffering, and orthodox in their belief. What more could be asked of them?"[2] With this much going for The First Church it is hard to imagine a correction. The congregation is diligent, persevering, doctrinally strong, perceptive, courageous, and is still going strong after all these years. Who wouldn't love to belong to a church with such a strong reputation for faithfulness?

"Yet," Christ says, "I have this against you: You have forsaken your first love." Hidden in their strengths, which were many, was a weakness that was deadly. In every way but one they were healthy. Like an athlete in perfect shape, except for the fact that his heart is diseased and at any moment he could collapse and die, Ephesus had everything but the most important thing: they had lost their first love for Christ. What they lacked was a true passion for God. It was not enough for them to be known by their deeds. They needed to be known for their devotion to God. Defending the faith is important, but it's never a substitute for loving God. The mark of the church is love. "By this all people will know that you are my disciples, if you love one another."[3] Loving the Lord Jesus is always first and foremost, and everything else follows from this central commitment.

Without this love we are susceptible to pride and fruitlessness. We begin to calculate what we have done for God. Hidden in our strengths will be a life-threatening weakness. "Every virtue carries within itself the seeds of its own destruction."[4] We will be tempted to create a climate of suspicion, and as a result we will be known more for what we are against than who we are for. The First Church of Ephesus was known for guarding the apostolic message, but they had lost the passion to bear witness to the love of Christ.

1. Matt 28:20.
2. Stott, *What Christ Thinks of the Church*, 21.
3. John 13:35.
4. Mounce, *Revelation*, 88.

Greg Beale argues that the loss of their first love meant that they were no longer diligent in witnessing of Christ's love to the outside world. They may not have lost their Christlike love for one another, but they had lost their passion to share the gospel with the culture around them. "The idea is that they no longer expressed their former zealous love for Jesus by witnessing to him in the world."[5] This conclusion is consistent with the picture of Christ holding the seven stars and walking among the lampstands. Christ's passion for the world was meant to be reflected in the church's passion for the world. For the congregation at Ephesus to do the things they did at first meant returning to a lively witnessing faith. If a congregation loses her first love, not only will her ability to witness be diminished, but her compassion for one another and her vital experience of worship will eventually suffer. We can defend the truth out of an ingrained habit of religion. We can persevere out of discipline and determination. We can even root out heresy with intellectual rigor and vigilance. But we cannot worship and witness faithfully out of anything but an abiding love for Jesus Christ.

Jesus warned that love is the first thing to go when persecution, apostasy, and wickedness increase. The most unloving thing a church can do is eliminate the gospel of Jesus Christ. In his final sermon before the cross, Jesus said, "the love of most will grow cold, but whoever stands firm to the end will be saved." And proof of fervent love and the strength to stand firm is preaching the gospel of the kingdom "in the whole world as a testimony to all the nations, and then the end will come."[6] The most unloving thing a church can do is eliminate the gospel of Jesus Christ. The gospel is primarily what Christ does for us, not what the church does for others. True, the church of Christ is empowered to love and serve others. But if we remove the gospel witness from the church by denying the reality of the incarnation, or the efficacy of the atoning sacrifice of Christ, or the truth of Jesus' bodily resurrection, we have essentially cut out the heart of the gospel. We have destroyed the foundation for love's good works. We have reduced love to giving people what we think they need.

That said, fidelity to doctrine is not the issue for The First Church of Ephesus: forsaking their first love is. Surely it is the height of sacrilege to believe in the atoning work of Christ on the cross and then refuse to love the very people for whom Christ died! "Believing without loving turns

---

5. Beale, *Revelation*, 230.

6. Matt 24:12–14.

the best of creeds into a weapon of oppression," Eugene Peterson writes. "A community that believes but does not love or marginalizes love, regardless of its belief system or doctrinal orthodoxy or 'vision statement,' soon, very soon, becomes a 'synagogue of Satan' (Rev. 2:9)."[7] To be told that your love has grown cold—that your effective, faithful, and persevering work is inadequate—is tough to swallow. The very congregation that is in deep need of serious heartfelt repentance may have trouble coming to terms with this diagnosis. This church must be convinced that Christ himself is delivering the rebuke.

First Love Discipleship

"Jesus Christ produced mainly three effects—hatred, terror, adoration. There was no trace of people expressing mild approval."

—C. S. LEWIS[8]

For the chastened church the place to begin is with humility and prayer: "Search me, O God, and know my heart; test me and know my anxious thoughts. See if there is any offensive way in me, and lead me in the way everlasting."[9] Discernment is critical. The church's abandonment of its first love for Christ has little to do with existential intensity or personal fervor. To compare this loss to the intensity of romantic love, especially at the beginning of a relationship, is probably misleading. The solution is not to be found in "mountaintop" spiritual experiences or in heightened emotionalism. Greater rhetorical fervor and flair will do nothing to solve this loss. We cannot feel or talk our way out of this rebuke. Correction comes through genuine change and transformation. The gospel is good news to those who live in fear of judgment and death, who long to be released from the burden of guilt and shame, and who struggle with unfulfilled existential longings. The gospel is compelling for those who seek the beauty of God's truth and love.[10]

Our devotion to Christ is only sentimental and superficial if it is not of the love that practices the ethic of Jesus. Joseph Mangina writes, "Our orthodoxy will not save us, our traditions will not save us, our

7. Peterson, *Christ Plays in Ten Thousand Places*, 261.

8. Lewis, *God In The Dock*, 158.

9. Ps 139:23–24.

10. Lewis, *God in the Dock*, 114–15.

soup kitchens and our social programs will not save us; what will save the church is Christ, whose self-giving cannot but call forth a similar response on the part of his people."[11] The danger for the faithful is that they might forget that they are sinners saved by grace. They begin to ignore the love of God in Christ and reduce the faith to practices, rituals, doctrines, and traditions. Without a compelling passion to share the love of Christ with others, our future as a church is in jeopardy. Christ's prescription is emphatic: "Remember the height from which you have fallen! Repent and do the things you did at first." The Apostle Paul describes the meaning of first love this way: "For Christ's love compels us, because we are convinced that one died for all, and therefore all died. And he died for all, that those who live should no longer live for themselves but for him who died for them and was raised again. So from now on we regard no one from a worldly point of view."[12]

New Commandment Love

The world has trouble recognizing the love of Christ, and even many Christians struggle to embrace this love. The world's idea of love, says Kierkegaard, is "group-selfishness." The world condemns *me-only self-love* as selfish, but when selfishness forms a group of other selfish people the world calls it love. The world demands that selfish people give up a measure of selfishness in order to enjoy the privileges of group selfishness. This kind of love sacrifices the relationship with God and "locks God out or at most takes him along for the sake of appearance."[13] The disciples in the upper room did not know it at the time, but Jesus was preaching first love discipleship. He said, "A new command I give you: Love one another. As I have loved you, so you must love one another. By this everyone will know that you are my disciples, if you love one another."[14] Jesus sets forth the new agenda for his disciples. This new commandment is the concrete reality shaping the Christian life. This is what it means for the disciple to follow Jesus in the time between the "already" and the "not yet." John defined the meaning of this love. "This is love: not that we loved God, but that he loved us and sent his Son as an atoning sacrifice for our sins. Dear

11. Mangina, *Revelation*, 59.
12. 2 Cor 5:14–16.
13. Kierkegaard, *Works of Love*, 123.
14. John 13:34–35.

friends, since God so loved us, we also ought to love one another." We see the inseparable relationship between the divine atonement and the praxis of discipleship.

People have always loved one another. There is love between husbands and wives, parents and children. There is love between friends. In carnal affection, even adulterers and adulteresses love one another, and criminals can be said to love one another. But this new commandment calls us to love the way Christ loves us. This love is not based on common sense self-interest but on costly grace and the principle of the cross ("my life for yours"). New commandment love is consistent with the new covenant and the Great Commission. This heart-scripted love communicates to the world that we belong to the Lord Jesus. "By this everyone will know that you are my disciples, if you love another."

The Apostle Paul prayed for the church in Ephesus to have the power, together with all the saints, to grasp the multidimensional character of God's love. The key to interpreting what Paul meant by the width, length, height, and depth of God's love may be found in the spacial analogies Paul used in his letter. The *width* stands for the inclusiveness of God's love and grace that encompasses all people. Jew and Gentile alike are included in the breadth of God's love. The *length* recalls the spacial analogy of "near" and "far." God has gone to great lengths to bring Gentiles into his fellowship and to break down the dividing wall of hostility. "But now in Christ Jesus," Paul wrote, "you who once were far away have been brought near by the blood of Christ."[15] The *height* suggests the distance between being dead in our transgressions and sins and being raised up with Christ and seated in the heavenly realms. This vertical dimension captures well the height of God's love. The *depth* suggests the extent to which God will go to redeem us from our depravity and despair. As death camp survivor Corrie ten Boom said so well, "No pit is so deep, but that God's love is not deeper still."[16] The Apostle Paul's four-dimensional love is what the Apostle John meant by first love.

Fruitfulness

To be victorious requires hearing what the Spirit says to the churches. The triune God sets the terms of victory. We might like to choose other ways

15. Eph 2:13.
16. Ten Boom, *The Hiding Place*, 8.

and different means, but Christ determines what we must do in response to his love and grace. Christ has determined that our response to his love must reflect his love. If we are not a people of the good news then the message of God's love is wasted on us. Only those who love Christ with an undying love, a first love, will be able to eat of the tree of life. Christ's promise to The First Church of Ephesus evokes the last descriptive image of the new heaven and the new earth: the tree of life. In the middle of the Holy City, there was a river of life flowing from the throne of God and of the Lamb. On each side of the river stood the tree of life, "bearing twelve crops of fruit, yielding its fruit every month."[17] The tree of life signifies perpetual fruitfulness and the everlasting removal of the curse. The message to the church in Ephesus and to us is this: love now, the way you have been loved by Christ, and you will live and love forever.

17. Rev 22:1–2.

7

Band of Martyrs

⌐· Revelation 2:8–11 ·⌐

[2:8–11] *"To the angel of the church in Smyrna write: These are the words of him who is the First and the Last, who died and came to life again. I know your afflictions and your poverty—yet you are rich! I know about the slander of those who say they are Jews and are not, but are a synagogue of Satan. Do not be afraid of what you are about to suffer. I tell you, the devil will put some of you in prison to test you, and you will suffer persecution for ten days. Be faithful, even to the point of death, and I will give you life as your victor's crown.*

Whoever has ears, let them hear what the Spirit says to the churches. Those who are victorious will not be hurt at all by the second death."

THE CRUCIFIED AND RISEN Lord Jesus commends The Suffering Church of Smyrna without qualification. He is "the First and the Last, who died and came to life again." His self-description underscores his benefit for a suffering church. Having conquered "the second death," the risen Christ can affirm, "I know your afflictions and your poverty—yet you are rich!" There is no hint of correction. He has only positive things to say about the church in Smyrna.

Christians in Smyrna faced persecution from all sides. It was government sponsored and provoked by religious hostility. They were persecuted by the Roman government because they did not honor the cult of the emperor, and they were persecuted by the Jews because they were judged to be blasphemers. The Romans charged them with atheism and the Jews condemned them for idolatry. The imperial cult permeated every aspect of culture. Emperor Domitian expected his subjects to honor him with the title "Our Lord and our God." Christians who refused to participate "were seen as politically disloyal and unpatriotic" and faced punishment according to Roman law.[1] The Jewish synagogue in Smyrna was an established religion that was recognized and approved by Rome. For political and religious reasons the Jews saw the church as a destabilizing and heretical threat to their special status. It was to their advantage to distance themselves from Christians and to distinguish themselves as the "true Jews." Persecution began with economic penalties and privations, but escalated to imprisonment and even death. Christians were excluded from the trade guilds and ostracized from society. The false accusations and slander coming from the "synagogue of Satan" proved effective in declaring war against the followers of the Lamb.

The Suffering Church of Smyrna reminds believers of the persecuted church throughout the world. Persecution of Christians is a matter of policy in North Korea, Vietnam, China, Burma, Saudi Arabia, and Iran. Religious extremists carry out hate crimes against Christians in Nigeria and Iraq without government interference. Terrorist groups such as al-Shabab in Somalia and the Taliban in Afghanistan target Christians for death. Paul Marshall identifies three causes for the systematic persecution of Christians: "First is the hunger for total political control, exhibited by the Communist and post-Communist regimes. The second is the desire by some to preserve Hindu or Buddhist privilege, as is evident in South Asia. The third is radical Islam's urge for religious dominance, which at present is generating an expanding global crisis."[2]

Polycarp, a native of Smyrna, was an early Christian martyr. According to Tertullian and Irenaeus he was appointed by John himself as Smyrna's lead pastor. On February 2, 156, Polycarp was ordered by the Roman proconsul to swear by the genius of Caesar and revile Christ. He refused, saying that he had served Christ for eighty-six years, adding, "How can I blaspheme my King who saved me?" Tradition records Polycarp's prayer before he was burned at the stake: "O Lord, Almighty

1. Beale, *Revelation*, 241.
2. Marshall et al., *Persecuted*, 7–9.

God, the Father of your beloved Son Jesus Christ, through whom we have come to know you . . . I thank you for counting me worthy this day and hour of sharing the cup of Christ among the number of your martyrs."[3]

Christ's affirmation begins with a word of consolation. The crucified and risen Lord Jesus addresses the suffering church. Jesus has been in their situation. He has experienced the full extent of persecution, even death on a cross, and now he lives to reassure his followers that there is life after death. The crucified Christ reminds the believing community that suffering is limited. "You will suffer persecution for ten days." Ten days: not ten twenty-four-hour days, but a controlled, designated period of time, after which Christ will put an end to the suffering. This is not to minimize the suffering but to relativize it, as the Apostle Paul did when he said, "I consider that our present sufferings are not worth comparing with the glory that will be revealed in us."[4]

Christ's affirmation also serves as a challenge. Don't be fearful, be faithful. Under the pressure and persistence of persecution the believers at Smyrna were vulnerable to fear. Their passion for Christ resulted in privations, increased afflictions, and persistent persecution. Over time the spirit begins to wane, courage softens, and fear builds. But the risen Christ looked at these Smyrna believers another way. The poorest church among the seven was the wealthiest and the weakest church was the strongest. The only church that received no correction was the suffering church. The most persecuted church was the most promising church. The church at Smyrna is a reminder to us that Christ measures wealth not in dollars but in courageous, resilient faith.

The Fellowship of His Suffering

"The world condemned persecutes;
the world reconciled suffers persecution."

—AUGUSTINE[5]

Many of us read the Apostle John's letter to Smyrna in the safety and security of our suburban homes and multimillion-dollar sanctuaries, in a land that is blessed with religious freedom and tolerance. Many of

---

3. Stott, *What Christ Thinks of the Church*, 32–33.

4. Rom 8:18.

5. Augustine, Sermon 96:8, quoted in Bruner, *The Gospel of John*, 909.

our brothers and sisters in Christ around the world and in our broken cities hear these words differently. Millions of believers endure religious repression and terrorism. After years of the Taliban's brutal repression of the church, there is a new openness to the gospel in Afghanistan. Algerian Christians have had to face a reign of terror from the Islamic Salvation Front. Militant Muslims have marched through towns slitting the throats of those who reject Islamic fundamentalism. Christians are second-class citizens and routinely discriminated against in Bangladesh, Cyprus, Egypt, Turkey, and Syria. In many countries evangelism is against the law. In Pakistan and Nigeria, Christians are subject to mob violence, and in southern Sudan they continue to be victims of genocide. "A time is coming," Jesus warned, "when anyone who kills you will think he is offering a service to God."[6] Many in the body of Christ hear the words of Jesus with a sense of immediacy and intensity that those of us in the Western church do not feel or understand. "If the world hates you, keep in mind that it hated me first. . . . Remember the words I spoke to you: 'No servant is greater than his master.' If they persecuted me, they will persecute you also."[7] Dietrich Bonhoeffer wrote, "Suffering is the badge of true discipleship."[8]

In *Their Blood Cries Out*, Paul Marshall tells the story of persecution against Christians in the modern world.[9] He documents the worldwide plague of religious persecution and calls for an international lament. He is critical of Western Christianity's "peace at any price" and our focus on self-esteem and outward success while shutting out the worldwide body of Christ. Our brothers and sisters in Christ are in the throes of persecution and we are debating worship styles, self-help strategies, and our emotional well-being. Jesus did not promise the church peace and prosperity; he promised peace in the midst of persecution and suffering. He warned, "Woe to you when all people speak well of you, for that is how their fathers treated the false prophets."[10]

"Since all the beatitudes describe what every Christian disciple is intended to be," writes John Stott, "we conclude that the condition of being despised and rejected, slandered and persecuted, is as much a normal

---

6. John 16:2.

7. John 15:20.

8. Bonhoeffer, *The Cost of Discipleship*, 100.

9. Marshall, *Their Blood Cries Out*.

10. Luke 6:26.

mark of Christian discipleship as being pure in heart or merciful."[11] "The fellowship of the beatitudes is the fellowship of the Crucified. With him it has lost all, and with him it has found all."[12] The Apostle Paul put it simply when he said, "Everyone who wants to live a godly life in Christ Jesus will be persecuted."[13] The old paganisms and the new messianisms fight against the church with everything they have.

The Path to the Cross

The scandal of the cross is that the one who healed the sick, loved the outcast, and transformed the sinner should die a hideously cruel death at the hands of Rome. What kind of world do we live in that sentences holy and compassionate men and women to die? Jesus exposes the fact that the political and religious authorities are not always on the side of righteousness. Greed, pride, and hate often control the power brokers of society.

Jesus' message clearly had political impact, yet he was completely different from the Zealots and decidedly less dangerous. He resisted violence, rejected popular support, and flatly denied that his kingdom was of the world.[14] He neither defended the political status quo nor encouraged revolution. From a political point of view, Jesus did not have to die. It is true that the Jewish Sanhedrin feared for their social privilege and political influence, but this fear alone was not sufficient to account for his death.[15] The political impact of Jesus does not lead inevitably to the cross. Pilate did not have to kill Jesus. Politically speaking, Jesus could have walked away a free man instead of being nailed to the cross. Part of the scandal of the cross is that God's purposes are accomplished and his word is fulfilled in the midst of political ambiguity and seemingly accidental circumstances.

Dr. Paul Carlson was a medical missionary in the Republic of Congo in the 1960s. Carlson had been falsely accused by the rebel Simbas of being a major in the American military, a mercenary, instead of a missionary doctor. On November 24, as Belgian paratroopers were landing in

11. Stott, *The Christian Counter Culture*, 53.

12. Bonhoeffer, *The Cost of Discipleship*, 127.

13. 2 Tim 3:12.

14. Luke 9:54–55; John 2:24; 6:15; 18:10–11, 36.

15. John 11:48.

Stanleyville, Carlson, along with a number of other hostages, were led by their Simba guards out into the middle of the street while guns were firing all around the area. In the mad confusion some of the hostages were hit. Some ran for the nearest protection. A small group ran to the shelter of a house and clambered over the porch wall. One of the hostages leaped over the wall and reached back. He had his fingers on Paul's sweater when a young Simba came around the corner and fired off five shots, instantly killing Paul Carlson. A second or two later, he would have been on the other side of the wall. His body was graphically shown throughout the world in the glossy pages of *Life* magazine.

The full-page spread of Carlson's dead body raised a lot of questions in my thirteen-year-old mind. The courageous doctor seemed to me more a victim of tragic circumstances than an ambassador for Christ who gave his life for the gospel. Since then, I have come to see that the Christian's cross, like Jesus' cross, must be interpreted on two levels. On the one level, confusion and ambiguity surround the meaning and interpretation of our lives. From this perspective, Dr. Carlson's death was nothing more than meaningless circumstances leading to a tragedy that may have easily been averted. But what may appear to be a tragic, accidental moment is in fact an orchestrated movement in the sovereign plan of God. In so many ways, Paul Carlson died like his Lord.

On the one hand, Jesus appears as a victim of circumstances—a friend betrays him, popular sentiment turns against him, a ruler concerned only with political expediency hears his case, and his disciples abandon him. But on the other hand, Jesus dies in accord with Old Testament prophecy as the lamb who was slain from the foundation of the world.[16] There is an inevitability about his death that lies outside historical circumstance and human arrangement. It is impossible to adequately understand the suffering and death of Jesus apart from God's interpretation of the event. God infuses the cross with meaning from three primary sources: the history of God's revelation to Israel, Jesus' self-disclosure, and the apostolic witness. There is a tremendous redemptive purpose arising out of the muddle of historical circumstances. This glorious purpose is not the product of human imagination and wishful thinking. It is the fulfillment of God's eternal plan of redemption. The real scandal of the cross lies in the fact that God in Christ, the Savior of the world, was crucified.

16. Luke 24:25–27; 1 Pet 1:20; Rev 13:8.

Ten Days of Purpose

We should marvel at the risen Christ's simple and straightforward spiritual direction to The Suffering Church of Smyrna. We normally expect and pray that God will remove suffering, but instead Christ gave the church a rationale for enduring suffering. Talk of afflictions, poverty, slander, imprisonment, and persecution is not the language of faith that we are accustomed to. We run from these words, let alone from their reality. But he who is "the First and the Last, who died and came to life again" uses this vocabulary freely. It is the descriptive language of the Christian life. Ten stands for a complete, thorough, and comprehensive period of suffering. We might wish that this was a literal number rather than a symbolic number that can stretch into forty years of hardship and suffering as in the case of the Prophet Jeremiah or believers in North Korea. There is nothing safely limited about a thorough testing, especially when the devil is involved. But no matter what happens, what is "ten days" compared to eternal life? The victor's crown is a metaphor for eternal life, rewarded to those who remain faithful, "even to the point of death."[17] No matter how severe the persecution, "those who are victorious will not be hurt at all by the second death."[18] The Suffering Church of Smyrna deserved to be encouraged. The words of Jesus echo in this promise: "Do not be afraid of those who kill the body but cannot kill the soul. Rather, be afraid of the One who can destroy both soul and body in hell."[19]

---

17. Rev 2:10; see 2 Tim 4:8; Jas 1:12; 1 Pet 5:4.
18. Rev 2:11.
19. Matt 10:28.

8

Urban Fidelity

[2:12–17] *"To the angel of the church in Pergamum write: These are the words of him who has the sharp, double-edged sword. I know where you live—where Satan has his throne. Yet you remain true to my name. You did not renounce your faith in me, not even in the days of Antipas, my faithful witness, who was put to death in your city—where Satan lives.*

Nevertheless, I have a few things against you: There are some among you who hold to the teaching of Balaam, who taught Balak to entice the Israelites to sin so that they ate food sacrificed to idols and committed sexual immorality. Likewise, you also have those who hold to the teaching of the Nicolaitans. Repent therefore! Otherwise, I will soon come to you and will fight against them with the sword of my mouth.

Whoever has ears, let them hear what the Spirit says to the churches. To those who are victorious, I will give some of the hidden manna. I will also give each of them a white stone with a new name written on it, known only to the one who receives it."

PERGAMUM HILLS FELLOWSHIP CHURCH is addressed by the Christ "who has the sharp, double-edged sword." The highlighted attribute is well suited to the church's experience and need. "I know where you live— where Satan has his throne. Yet you remain true to my name." It is hard to imagine a church's location described in a more ominous way than the place where Satan has his throne. Churches are usually proud of their location and extol the virtues of their city. When churches are searching for a new pastor they often promote their city like the local chamber of commerce. The typical American spin on Pergamum might have been that it was a beautiful, prosperous city of nearly 200,000. It was home to the cult of Askelepios, the god of healing, and known for its magnificent spa. The temple of Zeus, with its huge altar, dominated the city. A replica of this altar is on display today in Berlin. The city was also famous for its library, containing several hundred thousand volumes. Parchment was invented in Pergamum and derives its name from the city. By all counts, Pergamum was a great city. "One imagines Pergamum as being a city of extraordinary presence, combining political importance with cultural and religious power."[1]

We should not be surprised that Christ sees the city from a different perspective. Pergamum is a thriving center of evil. To remain "true to my name" meant that believers were faithful in belief and practice. The "name" represents everything about Christ. Christ does not ask his faithful followers in Pergamum to move away; he asks them to remain faithful. That is what they have done, and they have done it for a long time—ever since the days of Antipas, the only named disciple in the whole book. The opposition that killed Antipas was still in place and Pergamum remained inhabited by Satan. No believer would have downplayed the danger involved in following Christ in Pergamum. But strength in the past did not automatically mean strength for the future.

The costly love of the gospel fills Christ's followers with God's kingdom purpose, but it does so while their eyes are wide open to the power of Satan's throne. Pergamum is a great city; New York is a great city; Hong Kong is a great city—but Christians cannot be enamored with the greatness of the city or naive to its very real spiritual dangers. The Bible is unimpressed by population size and secular calculations of power. Greatness in the eyes of the world is not greatness in the eyes of God. A strong case can be made for the strategic importance of the city. If we want to reach the world for Christ we need to reach the city. The Internet, travel, and all forms of media bring the city to the world and the world to the city. Recently, a photographer set out to photograph children from all 167 countries of the world. He didn't have to leave New York City, because all

---

1. Mangina, *Revelation*, 61–62.

167 countries can be found in the city. Tim Keller is surely right when he says, "All current signs lead us to believe that the world order of the twenty-first century will be global, multicultural, and urban."[2] But commensurate with the city's strategic value is its spiritual danger. Many good things can be said about the city, but the Apostle John begins with a chilling description of the city as "the throne of Satan."

"The Bible has a far darker vision of reality than any secular critic."

—TIMOTHY KELLER[3]

Christ's letter to Pergamum Hills Fellowship Church offers a penetrating correction. "Nevertheless, I have a few things against you: You have people there who hold to the teaching of Balaam. . . . You also have those who hold to the teaching of the Nicolaitans." The church was unaware of the serious theological crisis it was facing. Instead of a direct confrontation with the imperial cult or the worship of Aesculapius (the god of healing), it experienced an internal threat, which jeopardized its identity in Christ.

In Western culture we pride ourselves on being positive and affirming. There is little room for prophetic critique. Richard Rohr writes, "The best criticism of the bad is the practice of the better."[4] If John were writing today to a church in Perth, Australia or Peoria, Illinois instead of to Pergamum Hills Fellowship Church, would he change his style and soften his straightforward spiritual direction? I doubt it. Christ's letter to Pergamum ignores any obfuscation or positive spin and cuts to the heart of the manner: "I have a few things against you." John states the critique briefly. The church was susceptible to false teaching from two sources: Balaam and the Nicolaitans. The names were a dead giveaway. "Balaam" is Hebrew for "devourer" or "conqueror of the people." "Nicolaitan" is Greek for the same thing. The congregation in Pergamum was familiar with the Old Testament account of Balaam.[5] Balaam was an internationally known spiritist, living near the Euphrates in Mesopotamia. Balak, king of Moab, was willing to pay well for Balaam's services to thwart Israel's invasion of Moab. The Bible devotes a long account to

2. Keller, *Center Church*, 158.
3. Ibid., 131.
4. Rohr, *Falling Upward*, 124.
5. Num 22:1–25:3; 31:8, 16.

this incident. As Balaam traveled to Moab on the back of his donkey, his way was blocked by the angel of the Lord. Balaam, the reputed expert on the spirit world, was unable to see what his dumb donkey could see. His donkey got the message, but he didn't. Three times his donkey stopped dead in its tracks and Balaam beat his donkey. Finally, "the Lord opened the donkey's mouth, and she said to Balaam, 'What have I done to you to make you beat me these three times?'" In the New Testament, the Apostle Peter described the situation this way: "Balaam, who loved the wages of wickedness . . . was rebuked for his wrongdoing by a donkey— a beast without speech—who spoke with a man's voice and restrained the prophet's madness."[6]

The story of the talking donkey and a pagan spiritist underscores the power of God to protect and to bless. God's purposes prevail in spite of enemy armies and demonic forces. The priestly blessing holds: "The Lord bless you and keep you; the Lord make his face shine upon you and be gracious to you; the Lord turn his face toward you and give you peace."[7] Israel in the wilderness is like the church in the world. The promises of God cast out fear and anxiety. "You, dear children, are from God and have overcome them, because the one who is in you is greater than the one who is in the world."[8] Jesus said, "In this world you will have trouble. But take heart! I have overcome the world."[9]

Although Israel enjoyed God's remarkable protection from those who wanted to cause them harm, their stubborn hearts persisted in finding ways to reject God. What the king of Moab could not achieve through a curse, he gained by following Balaam's plan of seduction.[10] The story recounts Israel's spiritual and sexual indulgence with the people of Moab.[11] Scholars believe that the reference to "Balaamites and Nicolaitans" signified a seductive but deadly compromise of the gospel of grace. "Saved by grace" became twisted to mean the freedom to do as one pleased. Jude refers to "godless men, who change the grace of God into a license for immorality and deny Jesus Christ our only Sovereign and Lord."[12] The temptation in Pergamum likely involved participating in idolatrous prac-

6. 2 Pet 2:16.
7. Num 6:24–26.
8. 1 John 4:4.
9. John 16:33.
10. Num 31:16.
11. Num 25:1–3.
12. Jude 1:4.

tices sponsored by professional associations and intermarriage outside the faith or sexual immorality—all in the name of Christian liberty.

Nicolaitan Sympathizers

The urban challenge confronting believers in Pergamum was relatively subtle and deceptive. It is similar to the challenge facing urban Christians today. Believers are pressured to accommodate to the spirit of the times in two critical areas: the workplace and sexuality. Instead of an outright in-your-face challenge, Christians are enticed to compromise their faith in Christ. They enter idolatry through the back door. The process is often slow and incremental, impacting priorities, eroding convictions, inculcating habits, and privatizing the faith, all of which work against being true to the name of Christ. The modern equivalent to eating food sacrificed to idols requires discernment. To make it out to be a mystery—to render the nature of the problem obscure or to imply that it is anachronistic—only serves to reinforce the danger of compromise and accommodation in today's church.

Eating food sacrificed to idols is a metaphor for cultural involvement that endangers the soul. The problem can be subtle because it is a step or two removed from actually entering a pagan shrine and bowing before Zeus. But the temptation is serious because it fuels drives and priorities that counter the rule of Christ. An otherwise normal necessity, food, took on spiritual significance in the first century because of its association with idols. In our cultural situation, there are many things that, although neutral in themselves, take on spiritual significance because of how they are used in our culture. Money, marketing, drinking, sports, shopping, family, children, work, cars, and education are among the things that can become the dynamic equivalent to food offered to idols. These objects are no longer neutral when they assume a kind of spiritual power over the believer and subvert the lordship of Christ. They are no longer inconsequential when they drive a lifestyle that compromises the gospel of Christ.

Paul addressed this concern in his letter to the church in Corinth. Some believers were compromising the integrity and witness of the gospel by socializing at the festivals held in the pagan temple. They defended their practice by saying, "An idol is nothing at all in the world," or, "There is no God but one."[13] Paul conceded that in theory they are right. An idol is nothing and "there is but one God, the Father, from whom all things came and for whom we live; and there is but one Lord, Jesus Christ, through whom all things came and through whom we live."[14] However, some of the Corinthian believers boasted that this knowledge gave them a spiritual immunity from the influences and pressures of paganism.

When the immortality symbols of the culture determine the believer's self-worth and significance, then the danger of idolatry is very real. The gods of business do not require that we pay homage at a shrine, but they can require extreme devotion, displacing all other priorities. The gods of fashion do not have holy days, but they transform the narcissistic "me" into an idol to be adorned and adored. The gods of sport give meaning and escape to my intolerably boring life. Idolatry in our culture is a far greater concern than we often acknowledge. Tim Keller writes,

> The biblical concept of idolatry is an extremely sophisticated idea, integrating intellectual, psychological, social, cultural, and spiritual categories. There are personal idols, such as romantic love and family, or money, power, and achievement; or access to particular social circles; or the emotional dependence of others on you; or health, fitness, and physical beauty. Many look to these things for hope, meaning, and fulfillment that only God can provide.[15]

Balaam's advice to the Moabites was, "Don't curse the Israelites, seduce them. Get them to have sex with your daughters and you'll have them." The same demonic strategy appears to be working in the Western church today. Heterosexual promiscuity and homosexual practice have robbed the church of a passionate witness. Self-professing sincere Christians see little wrong with pre-marital sex. We are in the grips of a full-scale spiritual crisis, but few want to acknowledge the sinful compromise. From Sunday to Sunday preachers assuage the guilty consciences of Nicolaitan sympathizers by quoting Romans: "There is now no condemnation for those who are in Christ Jesus."[16] Believers are sent out into the world with grace as an excuse to pursue their selfish dreams without the dire warning that "if your right eye causes you to stumble, gouge it out and

13. 1 Cor 8:4.

14. 1 Cor 8:6.

15. Keller, *Counterfeit Gods*, xix.

16. Rom 8:1.

throw it away," or the clear prohibition, "You cannot serve both God and Money."[17]

Correction is uncomplicated, but by no means easy. "Repent therefore!" The difficulty lies not in biblical interpretation. The commands of God are clear and straightforward, but the pressure to compromise the truth of God is great. Nevertheless Christ is emphatic. The faithful, fruitful church is true to Christ even when it is not politically correct, professionally expedient, personally convenient, or religiously popular to do so. Christ's letter to Pergamum Hills Fellowship Church emphasizes the importance of the word of God from start to finish. The only way to witness "where Satan lives" is by depending on the One who has the sharp double-edged sword, who fights with the sword of his mouth and who offers the hidden manna of God's truth.

New Name

"Uphold my name," says Christ, "and I will give a new name—a true and lasting and eternal identity which cannot be taken away." The new name written on a white stone and the hidden manna symbolize the promised blessing of being in the very presence of God. Not only are we on a first-name basis —the fellowship is that intimate—but the name we are known by has been given to us personally by the Lord. As the Prophet Isaiah wrote, "You will be called by a new name that the mouth of the Lord will bestow."[18] To remain true to the name of Christ means that "whatever [we] do, whether in word or deed, [we] do it all in the name of the Lord Jesus, giving thanks to God the Father through him."[19]

---

17. Matt 5:29; 6:24.
18. Isa 62:2; see Rev 3:12; 14:1; 22:4.
19. Col 3:17.

9

Idol Resistant

⌣· Revelation 2:18–29 ·⌣

[2:18–29] *"To the angel of the church of Thyatira write: These are the words of the Son of God, whose eyes are like blazing fire and whose feet are like burnished bronze. I know your deeds, your love and faith, your service and perseverance, and that you are now doing more than you did at first.*

Nevertheless, I have this against you: You tolerate that woman Jezebel, who calls herself a prophet. By her teaching she misleads my servants into sexual immorality and the eating of food sacrificed to idols. I have given her time to repent of her immorality, but she is unwilling. So I will cast her on a bed of suffering, and I will make those who commit adultery with her suffer intensely, unless they repent of her ways. I will strike her children dead. Then all the churches will know that I am he who searches hearts and minds, and I will repay each of you according to your deeds. Now I say to the rest of you in Thyatira, to you who do not hold to her teaching and have not learned Satan's so-called deep secrets, 'I will not impose any other burden on you, except to hold on to what you have until I come.'

To those who are victorious and do my will to the end, I will give authority over the nations—they 'will rule them with an iron scepter and will dash them to pieces like pottery'—just as I received authority from my Father. I will also give them the morning star. Whoever has ears, let them hear what the Spirit says to the churches."

IF A PHYSICIAN TELLS you that you are in good health except for the tumor in your lung, you will quickly forget the good news. I imagine Christ's commendation was quickly eclipsed by the focus on the Jezebel controversy. Although John was directed to highlight their deeds, love, faith, service, and perseverance, he pointed to a troubling spot on the X-ray. Was City Church of Thyatira surprised by Christ's verdict, "Nevertheless, I have something against you"? I doubt it. Deep down they probably felt the pressure of compromise. John wasn't delivering breaking news. Yet their instinctive reaction was probably more defensive than discerning. We all are inclined to write off our spiritual problems as a minor nuisances. They may have been tempted to say, "What does this old pastor on Patmos know about living in the real world of Thyatira anyway?"

Christ's blazing eyes and unshakable stance qualify him to commend and correct: "I know your deeds, your love and faith, your service and perseverance, and that you are now doing more than you did at first." "Isn't that enough?" we ask. City Church of Thyatira appeared to have it all together, in every way but one. Christ says, "Nevertheless, I have this against you: You tolerate that woman Jezebel, who calls herself a prophet. By her teaching she misleads my servants into sexual immorality and the eating of food sacrificed to idols." Did the church pride itself on its open-mindedness and outreach? Were they a "welcoming" church? What may be surprising to many is how seriously Jesus takes this danger. In language reminiscent of the harshest psalms, God was ready to do battle against his church. Christ was prepared to come down hard on this congregation if they were unwilling to root out their self-indulgent, self-serving religion.

Like the ancient City Church of Thyatira we are reluctant to challenge the popular voices who preach the gospel of the self. This trend is so powerful and pervasive that Christians often feel powerless to challenge it. When we live in a world that caters to an overly indulged self, we don't grow deeper, we shrink. "Too much of the good life ends up being toxic, deforming us spiritually."[1] The irony here is that we don't want to be confronted by our distorted definition of the good life: my latte ritual, my state-of-the-art gourmet kitchen in my starter castle, my children (successful student-athletes), my oversized SUV, my addiction to Apple products. How dare anyone imply that I have a bloated little restless soul!

Doctors can point to X-rays, blood tests, and EKGs to make a medical diagnoses. They have hard evidence. But when it comes to exposing

1. Goetz, *Death by Suburb*, 9.

our everyday idolatries and their impact on our souls we doubt the prophet's verdict. Who is to say that my eighty-hour work week and oversized credit card debt are convicting evidence? The problem is not the lack of evidence; the problem is that we are blind to the blatant evidence before us. We have become like our idols, spiritually deaf and dumb. We have hard hearts and soft minds.

Modern-Day Baalism

"If sincerity were the same thing as faithfulness,
then all would be well."[2]

—JAMES DAVISON HUNTER

The name Jezebel has a history that stands for spiritual pluralism. She convinced her husband Ahab, Israel's king during the days of Elijah, "to serve Baal and worship him."[3] Baal was the top Canaanite god, responsible for fertility in humans, animals, and crops. Baal is pictured as a mighty god, who presides over a pantheon of other local gods. He carries lightning bolts and rides a bull. Ritual prostitution of both sexes and other sensuous practices accompanied Baal worship. Baalism was a threat to the people of God because it drew them into idolatry and immorality. I imagine no one attending City Church was into Baal worship *per se*—no one was teaching Baalism in a Bible study. John's Spirit-led charge was that under the pretense of being open minded and tolerant, believers were promoting ideas and practices that subverted the word of God. Jezebel was his potent metaphor for distorting and compromising the faith and practice of the body of Christ.

One story in particular captures the ethos of the Jezebel problem. Israel's King Ahab coveted a piece of property adjacent to his palace that was owned by a man named Naboth. The king wanted to plant a garden near his palace. He offered Naboth a great real estate deal for his vineyard, but Naboth refused to sell. The land had belonged to his family for generations and he did not want to give it up at any price. Ahab went home "sullen and angry." He laid around sulking, refusing to eat, prompting his wife Jezebel to ask him what was wrong. He told her about Naboth's refusal to sell and she exclaimed, "Is this how you act as king

2. Hunter, *To Change the World*, 212.
3. 1 Kgs 16:31.

over Israel? Get up and eat! Cheer up. I'll get you the vineyard of Naboth the Jezreelite."[4]

Jezebel launched her devious strategy. She wrote official letters in Ahab's name arranging for Naboth to be falsely accused in public of blasphemy and treason. The plot worked and led to Naboth's swift execution. But when Ahab went down to take possession of Naboth's vineyard, the king was confronted by the Prophet Elijah, who made it clear that God was not fooled. There was judgment to be paid because Ahab had sold himself to do evil in the eyes of the Lord. Like Elijah, John was directed by the Lord to deliver a prophetic message. He confronted the believers in Thyatira over an alternative form of popular spirituality. In all likelihood, this appealing new spirituality was taught right alongside faithful biblical exposition.

We know that one nagging issue that troubled the early church was the common practice of paying homage to the gods of local trade unions, professional guilds, and commercial institutions. Thyatira was a thriving economic hub for the textile and metalwork industries. Richard Bauckham concludes:

> It appears that the Thyatiran prophetess, who was encouraging her followers to participate without qualms of conscience in the thriving commercial life of the city, was so to speak, the local representative of the harlot of Babylon within the church at Thyatira. Through her the seductive power of Rome's alliance of commerce and idolatrous religion was penetrating the church.[5]

"Jezebel," whoever he or she was, may have argued that honoring the patron deities and revering the imperial cult was acceptable practice. Jesus' words, "give back to Caesar what is Caesar's," may have been twisted in support of this compromise.[6] Another possibility was "Jezebel's" insistence that Christians who participated in the pagan festivals sponsored by these trade guilds could not be harmed. They were protected spiritually from even the deep things of Satan. The Jezebel pitch may have been that it is all about grace.

In our culture we do a poor job of identifying our idols. Today's biblical scholars are confident in their assessment of what transpired in the first century. They reach back 2,000 years and describe the tension

---

4. 1 Kgs 21:7.

5. Bauckham, *The Climax of Prophecy*, 378.

6. Matt 22:21.

between pagan culture and the church. They explain John's concern to defend fidelity to Christ in the face of cultural pressure to bow the knee to Caesar and pay homage to the local trade-guild deities. They have no problem identifying the pervasive political, spiritual, and commercial interests of the great city of Babylon with the Roman Empire. But when it comes to the twenty-first century, scholars are reluctant to pass judgment. Consequently, our "Jezebels" and workplace gods remain unidentified.

John's prophecy alerts believers to the dangers of compromise in the marketplace and in relationships. These idols are not in the shape of a pagan deity, but in the form of pagan commitments. We disciples are not asked to bow before a bronze statute, but we are asked to sacrifice our families on the altar of pagan priorities and passions. Many believers struggle with living in two worlds. They feel the constant pressure to give in to a consumer society's norms on sexuality, finance, ambition, sports, and truth. The Baalism that threatens the church today is our receptivity to a live-and-let-live pluralism and our reverence for the imperial self. These twin, interfacing dangers undermine our passion for Christ and our witness.

Two popular "Jezebels" on the scene today are Oprah and Joel Osteen. Their popularity within the church leads many Christians into moral compromise and caters to the cult of self. Both powerhouse entrepreneurs engage in positive humanitarian causes, but their fundamental message is that spirituality is what you achieve for yourself. Oprah's trademark slogan, "Live Your Best Life," and Osteen's famous tagline, "Your Best Life Now," celebrate personal success. Seated on the throne in their modern-ancient gospel is the self. You are your own redemption. You decide whether you are going to mount up on eagles' wings and be successful. Oprah and Osteen believe that their personal "I" represents the American "we." If they can find success, we all can find success by following their example.

Oprah's Jesus-less God and Osteen's Bible-less Jesus allow for the "flexodoxy" necessary to mass market salvation. Oprah's new spirituality is "the nondogmatic dogma that encourages an ambiguous theism alongside an exuberant consumerism."[7] Osteen's spirituality is therapeutic deism, seasoned with iconic references to the Bible and Jesus in service of the American Dream. The power of positive thinking replaces prayers of confession. A material and emotional makeover serves in lieu of Chris-

---

7. Lofton, *Oprah*, 49.

tian conversion. The new holy spirit is whatever is really great about yourself. Feelings don't trump truth: feelings are the truth. You have to be true to your dreams if you are going to be true to yourself. The most pernicious aspect of these "Jezebels" may be the inability of the church to know how to respond to these alternative "gospels." Well-meaning Christians are into Oprah's pop spirituality and Joel Osteen's prosperity gospel. They watch their shows, read their books, follow their advice, and believe in their promises while the church stands idly by, lending tacit approval by saying nothing.

We fail to understand the devil's seductive approach. We are repulsed by the ugly side of evil, but spiritualize the American Dream and fall for it. When the devil promotes a vision of something new and better we are hooked. Eugene Peterson asks, "Do we realize how almost exactly the Baal culture of Canaan is reproduced in American church culture? Baal religion is about what makes you feel good. Baal worship is a total immersion in what I can get out of it. And of course, it was incredibly successful."[8]

John delivered Christ's pronouncement of judgment. He boldly warned against "Jezebel" tolerance and Baalistic idolatry. The Son of God with eyes like blazing fire promised to cast all those who had compromised "on a bed of suffering" until they repented. This hard-line approach is foreign to us. We hesitate to think in these bold terms and evade the pointed cultural critique. We usually preach in vague generalities, garnering our constituency without offending lost souls. Our usual method is winsomely polite. We seek to win people over rather than warn them. We are not in the habit of calling for repentance and identifying our idols.

Iron Scepter

Some people in the City Church of Thyatira were too far gone to want to be restored. They were sold on this new, more open-minded theology. Jezebel's supporters were dismissive and critical of the old apostle. Consequently, Christ warns that he will split the congregation—judgment is certain. The Sovereign Lord says, "I will strike her children dead. Then all the churches will know that I am he who searches hearts and minds, and I will repay each of you according to your deeds." But to those who remained faithful, Christ says, "Now I say to the rest of you in Thyatira,

8. Peterson, "Spirituality for All the Wrong Reasons," 45.

to you who do not hold to her teaching and have not learned Satan's so-called deep secrets, 'I will not impose any other burden on you, except to hold on to what you have until I come.'"

Faithfulness is never complicated in the Revelation. Authentic discipleship is always straightforward. Obedience may be costly, but it is not shrouded in mystery. To follow the Lamb means what it has always meant. Nothing has changed. Jesus said it clearly: "Come to me, all you who are weary and burdened, and I will give you rest. Take my yoke upon you and learn from me, for I am gentle and humble in heart, and you will find rest for your souls. For my yoke is easy and my burden is light."[9]

Given the reluctance of many to replicate the Apostle John's ministry in the American church, we may want to reconsider the reward Christ promises. If we are squeamish about bold warnings and dire judgments, we may not want the responsibility that comes with ruling "[the nations] with an iron scepter" or dashing "them to pieces like pottery."[10] To rule and reign with Christ is not for the fainthearted, and it is certainly not for those who believe in themselves.

9. Matt 11:28–30.
10. Ps 2:9.

10

Beyond User Friendly

∽· Revelation 3:1–6 ·∼

[3:1–6] *"To the angel of the church in Sardis write: These are the words of him who holds the seven spirits of God and the seven stars. I know your deeds; you have a reputation of being alive, but you are dead. Wake up! Strengthen what remains and is about to die, for I have found your deeds unfinished in the sight of my God. Remember, therefore, what you have received and heard; hold it fast, and repent. But if you do not wake up, I will come like a thief, and you will not know at what time I will come to you.*

Yet you have a few people in Sardis who have not soiled their clothes. They will walk with me, dressed in white, for they are worthy. Those who are victorious will, like them, be dressed in white. I will never blot out the name of that person from the book of life, but will acknowledge that name before my Father and his angels. Whoever has ears, let them hear what the Spirit says to the churches."

THE RISEN LORD IS introduced to Sardis Community Church by what he holds in his hands, Seven Spirits and seven stars. Jesus Christ has a firm grip on the seven-fold fullness of the Spirit and the seven-fold comprehensiveness of the church. Christ misses nothing. His insight is complete and comprehensive. Undoubtedly the believers did not like what they heard: "I know your deeds; you have a reputation of being alive, but you are dead."

In the popular imagination, Sardis Community Church is always a successful church: an outwardly impressive church with beautiful buildings and an attractive professional staff. A full range of service programs and outreach ministries is displayed on their website. The Sunday morning service is televised and the pastor is a nationally known preacher and author. Sardis has more members than the church at Ephesus and more "ministries" than the church at Pergamum. They were, in fact, the church that other churches aspired to be like. Sardis was the trend-setting church that everyone talked about. But their great reputation did not match with their true reality. They were religiously busy, but spiritually dead. Their budget was huge but their impact for Christ was nil. They played the numbers game but lost their young to the world. In today's language, Christ says, "I see right through your work. You have a reputation for vigor and zest, but you're dead, stone dead."[1]

The gap in Sardis between reputation and reality is no mystery. Discernment is not a matter of opinion or conjecture. The Sardis Community Church "business plan" calls for reaching the culture by appealing to the culture on its own terms. This involves defining a target audience, finding their market niche, and coming up with a game plan that is attractive and meets felt needs. It helps to have a "dream team" of young, edgy, personable, and charismatic leaders. As one Unitarian church ad put it, "Instead of me fitting a religion I found a religion to fit me."

Since we are immersed in a highly competitive, materialistic, secular marketplace, some churches cater to the fact that they live in an image-conscious culture and need to find ways to appeal to the consumer. Sardis Community Church is our prime example for modern church growth theory. It promotes the idea that churches need to keep up with the latest trends in music, communications, technology, architecture, and leadership if they expect to compete effectively in today's marketplace. In our rapidly changing world, churches that don't keep up will be left behind. Can you imagine the prophets concluding that the reason the church was weak and anemic was because the people of God had failed to copy the Canaanites or the Babylonians in attracting a larger audience?

The fatal flaw in the dying church, according to the church growth consultant, is an older generation's paradigm paralysis and marketplace

---

1. Rev 3:1, *The Message*.

insensitivity, rather than biblical disobedience and spiritual weakness. The proposed solution is found in shifting from maintenance mode to marketing mode. Their prescription for a church stuck in the past and muddling through the present is not spiritual transformation—repentance, forgiveness, prayer, and deeper insight into the word of God—but a practical sociological transformation: exciting facilities, market-savvy communication, high-energy programs, and enviable personalities.

The leadership team at SCC knows how to engineer a user-friendly, hipster church. It's not that complicated. People want high-tech communications; in-touch pastoral care; laid-back, easy-flowing, eighteen-minute messages; multiple service times, with a variety of musical genres; just the right combination of anonymity and tender loving care; a creative blend of reverence and irreverence; lightheartedness with a touch of seriousness; great child care; ample parking or subway accessibility; an upbeat, positive, exciting atmosphere; a warm, winsome, engaging pastor who can make you laugh and make you cry; and plenty of options for community service and subsidized adventure trips.

The strength of the SCC lies not in its costly witness or deep communion with God but in its smooth-running organization. Entertainment and evangelism are so intertwined that they are difficult to separate. Professionalism has infiltrated the holy vocation of pastoral ministry to such an extent that pastors often think more like executives, while some executives attending the church, thankfully, think more like pastors. Performance overshadows worship and paid talent replaces the gifts of the Spirit. Leaders have the tough job of discerning the difference between catering to religious consumers and growing strong disciples.[2]

There is a growing inability among Christians to talk about their faith in Christ in any kind of meaningful way, especially outside the bounds of Sunday school, sermons, and small group Bible studies. Sermons are a recital of evangelical platitudes, publicly performed without lasting impact, usually in a style that does not flow from the biblical text. At SCC many are listening to sermons designed for someone else—the seeker or the young Christian. Thousands gather every Sunday to hear what they have heard many times before. There is a large and appreciative market for religious consumers who want to be told familiar truths. The

---

2. Lewis, *Screwtape Letters*, 35. Lewis expresses the devil's philosophy this way: "Once you have made the world an end, and faith a means, you have almost won your man, and it makes very little difference what kind of worldly end he is pursuing" (Lewis, *Screwtape*, 35).

consequence of this kind of preaching is bigger auditoriums filled with strangers who rarely fellowship beyond their familiar cliques. Christian communication has virtually no context outside of the pulpit. Any attempt to bring Jesus up in any kind of meaningful way outside the prescribed bounds of the sermon or Bible study feels like a violation of social etiquette. Christians at SCC talk freely about sports, food, fashion, stocks, celebrities, and politics, but serious talk about the kingdom of God is almost nonexistent. The reason for this may be that many attendees at SCC remain anonymous. They can go to church without ever uttering a word or making meaningful eye contact.

The great irony here is that Christ rebukes the church for its spiritual lethargy and complacency, even though it may be the most active of the seven churches. "Up on your feet!" Christ says to the church. "Take a deep breath! Maybe there's life in you yet. But I wouldn't know it by looking at your busywork; nothing of God's work has been completed. Your condition is desperate."[3] Christ's rebuke of Sardis Community Church challenges believers to evaluate the gap between reputation and reality. The point is not to look at large, successful churches cynically or to judge other churches critically, but to examine our own church honestly.

Sardis is a sad picture of religious hypocrisy and nominal Christianity, "having a form of godliness but denying its power."[4] Christ's corrective for the church in Sardis is simple and straightforward. No one can claim confusion over the diagnosis and prescription. The five staccato imperatives are clear: "Wake up! Strengthen what remains! Remember! Obey! Repent!" Christ commands a straightforward, back-to-basics renewal agenda. If the Apostle John were preaching at Sardis, he might turn to the prophets and preach on Jeremiah chapter seven or the sixth chapter of Micah. He might quote the word of the Lord from Amos, "I can't stand your religious meetings. I'm fed up with your conferences and conventions. I want nothing to do with your religion projects, your pretentious slogans and goals. I'm sick of your fund-raising schemes, your public relations and image making. I've had all I can take of your noisy ego-music. When was the last time you sang to me?"[5]

The consequence for not waking up and fixing their eyes on Jesus was the unexpected coming of Christ. The parable of the thief in the night usually points to the absolute final coming of Christ, but here the coming

3. Rev 3:2–3, *The Message*.

4. 2 Tim 3:5.

5. Amos 5:21–23, *The Message*.

is a conditional threat directed at those who refuse to "wake up!"[6] But even this pending, historical visitation "is connected to the final coming in that both are part of the same inaugurated end-time process."[7] Instead of being so concerned about keeping up with trends and staying relevant, Sardis Community Church needed to focus on pleasing Christ and living faithfully. Between the threat of disciplinary action and the promise of final vindication, there is plenty of work to be done. Not the busywork that many churches feel compelled to perform, but the real work of the gospel, bearing witness to what Christ has done for us. In the eschatological tension between "already" and "not yet," some churches give up too easily. They put off or ignore the very issues that the Spirit of Christ would have them tackle. Sadly, it is our failure to work out our salvation in fear and trembling in such areas as race and money and sex for which we must repent. Sardis Community Church was put on notice for our sake as well as theirs. We must wake up from our spiritual complacency and ask the Lord for the power to be faithful today.

The Book of Life

In this outwardly thriving market-driven church there was a small minority who remained close to Christ. They had not "soiled their clothes." The metaphor alludes to the church's idolatrous relationship with the culture. Only a few had remained faithful. Evidently, in spite of everything— denominational direction, pastoral leadership, outreach programs—this minority group of believers continued to walk with Christ. Their worship in the midst of this trendsetting church was meaningful, their commitment to the word of God faithful, their love for others genuine, and their hope in Christ life changing. The church within the church was Sardis's hope. The popular majority needed to wake up and pay attention to those whose who were taking Jesus seriously. The unreal Christians who thought that keeping Jesus' words was not all that important needed to repent.[8]

The Apostle John used an apt metaphor to describe the faithful believers in Sardis. He said they will be "dressed in white, for they are worthy." White signifies purity and fidelity—nothing elaborate or fancy.

---

6. Matt 24:42–44; 1 Thess 5:2; 2 Pet 3:10.

7. Beale, *Revelation*, 275.

8. Bruner, *The Gospel of John*, 844.

"Clothe yourselves," says the Apostle Paul, "with compassion, kindness, humility, gentleness and patience. Bear with each other and forgive whatever grievances you may have against one another. Forgive as the Lord forgave you. And over all these virtues put on love, which binds them all together in perfect unity."[9]

They will be dressed in white and their names will never be blotted out from the Book of Life.[10] And Christ will present them personally, by name, to the Father and his angels. This heavenly acknowledgment recalls the words of Jesus when he said, "Whoever publicly acknowledges me I will also acknowledge before my Father in heaven. But whoever publicly disowns me I will disown before my Father in heaven." Jesus said this in the context of emphasizing the cost of discipleship, adding, "Do not suppose that I have come to bring peace to the earth. I did not come to bring peace, but a sword."[11] The bottom line for the church at Sardis was "Get real!" Not an easy thing to do in our consumer-oriented society.

9. Col 3:12–14.

10. Luke 10:20; Phil 4:3; Heb 12:23.

11. Matt 10:32–34.

11

Real Mission

[3:7–13] *"To the angel of the church in Philadelphia write: These are the words of him who is holy and true, who holds the key of David. What he opens no one can shut, and what he shuts no one can open. I know your deeds. See, I have placed before you an open door that no one can shut. I know that you have little strength, yet you have kept my word and have not denied my name. I will make those who are of the synagogue of Satan, who claim to be Jews though they are not, but are liars—I will make them come and fall down at your feet and acknowledge that I have loved you. Since you have kept my command to endure patiently, I will also keep you from the hour of trial that is going to come on the whole world to test those who live on the earth.*

I am coming soon. Hold on to what you have, so that no one will take your crown. Those who are victorious I will make pillars in the temple of my God. Never again will they leave it. I will write on them the name of my God and the name of the city of my God, the new Jerusalem, which is coming down out of heaven from my God; and I will also write on them my new name. Whoever has ears, let them hear what the Spirit says to the churches."

THE PHILADELPHIA CHRISTIAN CHURCH, in marked contrast to the church in Sardis, received unqualified praise. The relationship between these two churches is important. Philadelphia's strengths are better understood in the light of Sardis's weaknesses. Believers in Sardis prided themselves on being progressive. With their substantial resources and cutting-edge ministries, they cast a big vision. But as we have seen, their lively reputation concealed a spiritual malady that could only be remedied by decisive spiritual action. SCC thought they were accomplishing God's mission through their own creative and expensive efforts, but all they were doing was building up their own reputation. The Philadelphia Christian Church, on the other hand, knew they were weak, but it was the kind of weakness that Christ could use for his kingdom purposes. The Lord honored their faithfulness and set before them great opportunities.

Christ is identified as the one who holds the key of David. "What he opens, no one can shut; and what he shuts no one can open. I know your deeds. See, I have placed before you an open door that on one can shut." The description harkens back to the prophecy of Isaiah and the promise that Eliakim son of Hilkiah would be given "the key to the house of David; what he opens no one can shut, and what he shuts no one can open."[1] Eliakim, the chief steward in Hezekiah's palace, is used as a type for the exalted Christ who holds the keys to the kingdom and gives them to his followers.[2] The imagery is emotionally charged because the Jewish Christians had been thrown out of the local synagogue. The conflict was over the identity of Jesus. The Jewish synagogue rejected Jesus as the Messiah who was to come, and they felt it was their duty to excommunicate and persecute those who believed Jesus to be the Messiah. Jesus' upper-room warning on the night of his betrayal was realized: "All of this I have told you so that you will not fall away. They will put you out of the synagogue; in fact, that hour is coming when those who kill you will think they are offering a service to God. They will do such things because they have not known the Father or me."[3]

True Jews

The synagogue defended Jewish cultural heritage and ethnicity. The Gentile-inclusive gospel of Jesus Christ was a threat to their existence. But for Christians the identity of the true Jew was no longer a matter of race and

1. Isa 22:20–22.
2. Matt 16:18–19.
3. John 16:1–3.

ritual. As the Apostle Paul explained, "No, a person is a Jew who is one inwardly; and circumcision is circumcision of the heart, by the Spirit, not by the written code."[4] The believers in Philadelphia faithfully witnessed to the truth that was in Christ. Justification was not based on observing the law, "but by faith in Jesus Christ."[5] The true children of Abraham received Christ, who was not only the Messiah to the Jews, but the Savior of the world. They proclaimed the gospel to Jew and Gentile inclusively.[6]

The gospel of Jesus Christ proved highly offensive to the Jewish community in Philadelphia, just as the exclusive truth claim of Christ proves highly offensive in the world today.[7] One of the most famous and most controversial lines of the gospel is Jesus' one-liner: "I am the way and the truth and the life. No one comes to the Father except through me."[8] Within weeks of the upper-room experience, Peter said to the Jewish religious leaders, "Salvation is found in no one else, for there is no other name given under heaven by which we must be saved."[9] In Philadelphia, the Jewish synagogue thought they were fighting for the integrity of their religion. Today, the world fights for ideological pluralism and opposes the exclusive truth claim of the gospel. Neither Jewish Christians in Philadelphia nor Christians throughout the world proclaim Christ, the

---

4. Rom 2:29.

5. Gal 2:16.

6. Gal 3:26–29.

7. Elaine Pagels in *Revelations*, 54–65, argues that John of Patmos attacks the syncretistic inroads of early Gentile Christianity. The heresy that was condemned as the "synagogue of Satan" was none other than the gospel preached by the Apostle Paul (Gal 3:28). Pagels speculates that John defended the ethnic purity and ritual practice of Jews who accepted Jesus as their Messiah and condemned "Gentile followers of Jesus converted through Paul's teaching" (Pagels, *Revelations*, 54). When John writes, "you have tested those who claim to be apostles but are not, and have found them false" (Rev 2:2), he is referring to "the maverick called Paul of Tarsus" who "came out of nowhere and began to preach a 'gospel' quite different from what was taught in James' and Peter's circle" (Pagels, *Revelations*, 55). Pagels promotes a speculative theory that pits John against Paul and slanders them both; John for his alleged racial exclusivity and Paul for his morally compromising religious syncretism. According to Pagels, John was distressed by "the greatest identity theft of all time." The perpetrators of this deception were Gentile believers who falsely claimed to be the true Israel and the rightful heirs "to the legacy of God's people." In an Orwellian twist of historiography, Pagels writes, "Nor did John foresee that Paul's 'gospel' which adapted Jesus' message for Gentiles, would soon overflow the movement to create, in effect, a new religion" (Pagels, *Revelations*, 65).

8. John 14:6.

9. Acts 4:12.

Savior of the world, out of pride or privilege. Jesus declared, "I am the way and the truth and the life" to bring comfort, not condemnation.

Christ's letter to the church in Philadelphia does not handle the situation diplomatically. He calls the Jews liars because they claim "to be Jews though they are not" and he calls them members of the "synagogue of Satan." Two things should be kept in mind. First, this beleaguered congregation did not have the power or the weapons of the world to wage against the Jewish synagogue; Christ never meant for this harsh assessment to become grounds for attacking Jews. In Philadelphia, the believers were socially ostracized nothings. The condemnation leveled at "liars" and the "synagogue of Satan" brought a measure of comfort. The letter answered the self-doubt and second questioning that attacked the confidence of the believing community. Christ reassured the Philadelphia Christian Church of their gospel identity. In spite of the painful persecution they endured, their identity as the people of God was secure. In a similar situation, the Apostle Paul used strong language to expose "enemies of the cross of Christ" whose "god is their stomach, and their glory is in their shame."[10] Paul said this not about outright hedonists, but about religious people who scrupulously followed ritual food laws but rejected the grace of Christ. The second concern to keep in mind is that opposition to the gospel always invokes Jesus' teaching on loving the enemy. It would have been disingenuous to deny the persecution. The persecution was real and Christians can expect that wherever the gospel is preached and practiced there will always be serious opposition. The measure of an authentic witness can be determined, at least in part, by the hostility that it provokes against the church. Against the hate, the followers of the Lamb are called to "love your enemies and pray for those who persecute you, that you may be children of your Father in heaven."[11]

Life would be easier if George Bernard Shaw's famous line were true: "There is only one religion in the world, though there are a hundred versions of it." The world wants to believe Mahatma Gandhi's verdict, "Religions are different roads converging to the same point. What does it matter if we take different roads so long as we reach the same goal? Wherein is the cause for quarreling?"[12] Sardis Community Church may have been tempted to lower the walls of hostility by scaling back on the

---

10. Phil 3:18–19.

11. Matt 5:44–45.

12. Gandhi, quoted in Burch, *Alternative Goals in Religion*, 111.

exclusive truth claim of the gospel, but not the Philadelphia Christian Church.

Believers in Philadelphia didn't believe in a vague, undefinable higher power, but in the living God who revealed himself by name and in history. They shared the incredible good news that there is one way to God, not through self-effort or self-exploration, but through Jesus Christ. True spirituality was not found in tribal deities, cultural faiths, speculative philosophies, and mystery religions. Believers in Philadelphia had strengths that truly counted and weaknesses that accentuated their dependence on the Lord. "I know that you have little strength, yet you have kept my word and have not denied my name." What Sardis thought it was earning and achieving through its hard work, Philadelphia was receiving in its weakness as a gift from the Lord. The key to evangelism and God's kingdom purposes depended on what God opened up.

An Open Door

Because of their faithfulness, Christ blessed this congregation with an open door of opportunity. Ironically, it was the outwardly weak but inwardly strong church that Christ commissioned for ministry, reaffirming the ancient prophecy: "'Not by might nor by power, but by my Spirit,' says the Lord Almighty."[13] The Philadelphia Christian Church aspired to be "deeper and truer" rather than "bigger and better." Sardis Community Church reasoned that by avoiding tensions with the world they would become more popular and consequently more successful. The household of faith in Philadelphia knew there was no way around the real tensions produced by the truth of the gospel. They accepted their weakness, their economic privations and social ostracism, and embraced their God-given mission by sharing the gospel with others, especially their Jewish brothers and sisters.

As the battle raged in Philadelphia over the identity of the people of God, Christ promised in no uncertain terms that the church would win that battle. The very people who claimed to be the people of God, yet refused to receive Christ as the Anointed One, would be forced to recognize Jesus as Lord. "Christ will continue to empower his church to witness by opening the door of salvation for the unbelieving Jews in their

13. Zech 4:6.

community."[14] Christ's promise is in keeping with the prophecy of Isaiah and the glory of Zion, when all the nations will gather to recognize what God has done:

> Your gates will always stand open. . . . The children of your op-
> pressors will come bowing before you; all who despise you will
> bow down at your feet and will call you the City of the Lord,
> Zion of the Holy One of Israel. Although you have been for-
> saken and hated, with no one traveling through, I will make you
> the everlasting pride and the joy of all generations. . . . Then you
> will know that I, the Lord, am your Savior, your Redeemer, the
> Mighty One of Jacob.[15]

The promised recognition is followed by the promise of protection: "Since you have kept my command to endure patiently, I will also keep you from the hour of trial that is going to come on the whole world to test those who live on the earth."[16] The promise of everlasting security is reiterated throughout the Revelation.[17] The hour of trial facing the Philadelphia Christian Church is both imminent and eschatological. In the midst of trial and tribulation, the faithful church is comforted by the hope that Christ is coming soon.

Pillars of Strength

The Philadelphia Christian Church has been promised vindication, commended for their patience endurance, and challenged to hold on to what they have. They are almost home, and what a wonderful home it will be.[18] Christ's word to the church was a mixture of challenge and comfort: "Hold on to what you have, so that no one will take your crown" and "whoever overcomes I will make a pillar in the temple of my God." On this side of eternity, Christ didn't promise relief from the struggle, but he did promise eternal security and a lasting identity. His promise to this struggling church assumes the concreteness of brick and

14. Beale, *Revelation*, 286.

15. Isa 60:11, 14–16.

16. Rev 3:10.

17. The following texts affirm the security of believers: the 144,000 in Revelation 7:1–11; 14:1–5; the measuring of the temple of God, 11:1–3; the woman protected in the wilderness, 12:6, 13–17; and the millennial martyrs, 20:4–6.

18. John 14:1–3.

mortar—the monumental weight of impressive columns. "I will make them pillars in the temple of my God." Christ's faithful followers would be identified by a new name. They would belong to the new city coming down out of heaven. Their strength and solidarity rested in their union with Christ, not in church buildings. Early Christians had a sense of place and a feeling of being at home—not in a facility, but in the family of God. There was no outward temple or tall steeple to symbolize their place, but as they met together there was a powerful presence of the risen Lord Jesus. The early Christians knew that "the Most High does not live in houses made by human hands."[19]

19. Acts 7:48.

12

True Riches

⌁· Revelation 3:14–22 ·⌁

[3:14-22] *"To the angel of the church of Laodicea write: These are the words of the Amen, the faithful and true witness, the ruler of God's creation. I know your deeds, that you are neither cold nor hot. I wish you were either one or the other! So, because you are lukewarm—neither hot nor cold—I am about to spit you out of my mouth. You say, 'I am rich; I have acquired wealth and do not need a thing.' But you do not realize that you are wretched, pitiful, poor, blind and naked. I counsel you to buy from me gold refined in the fire, so you can become rich; and white clothes to wear, so you can cover your shameful nakedness; and salve to put on your eyes, so you can see.*

Those whom I love I rebuke and discipline. So be earnest, and repent. Here I am! I stand at the door and knock. If anyone hears my voice and opens the door, I will come in and eat with them, and they with me.

To those who are victorious, I will give the right to sit with me on my throne, just as I was victorious and sat down with my Father on his throne. Whoever has ears, let them hear what the Spirit says to the churches."

THE ONLY WAY THAT Christ's rebuke can be effectively heard is if the messenger hides behind Christ. There is a good reason why some pulpits are made out of solid oak and raised up. For years I wore a black Geneva robe when I preached. The robe signified humility, not status. It was a sign of submission to the word of God. The raised pulpit did not elevate my ego, it lifted up the word of God. Every time I put on my robe I prayed that I would be faithful and obedient to the gospel of Christ. This is what I mean when I say the pastor hides behind Christ. We need some protection and the congregation needs to know that the authority lies not in us, but in "the words of the Amen, the faithful and true witness, the ruler of God's creation." Throughout these seven one-minute messages to the churches, the authoritative "I" belongs to Christ, not to the Apostle John. Only Christ knows, truly knows, everything about us: our deeds, our afflictions, our enemies, our love, our sins.

Given the strength of character behind each of these letters, it must have been difficult for churches to turn a deaf ear. Christ's penetrating eyes, thunderous voice, unshakable stance, and sovereign power made resistance unthinkable. But I imagine that if any church was tempted to rebel, it was the smug, self-sufficient, self-satisfied congregation of Laodicea. They had to be shocked by Christ's assessment. Instead of being congratulated and praised, they heard the risen Christ say,

> I know you inside and out, and find little to my liking. You're not cold, you're not hot—far better to be either cold or hot! You're stale. You're stagnant. You make me want to vomit. You brag, "I'm rich, I've got it made, I need nothing from anyone," oblivious that in fact you're a pitiful, blind beggar, threadbare and homeless.[1]

There was a gap between how they saw themselves and how Christ saw them. They prided themselves on being the Cathedral Church, but Christ saw them as "wretched, pitiful, poor, blind and naked." Their ministry was ineffective, their witness innocuous, and their lifestyle idolatrous.[2] They may have had plenty of emotional zeal, but they lacked wholehearted commitment to Christ. Believers in Laodicea blended into the urban-suburban culture so completely that their lifestyle left no distinguishing marks of true faith in Christ. There was no hint of authentic discipleship, since they limited their religious orthodoxy to Sundays. They gave themselves to making money, indulging their children, climbing the ladder of success, dressing in fashion, serving on church boards, following their sports teams, eating healthy, working out, and having fun. They knew

1. Rev 3:15–17, *The Message*.
2. Beale, *Revelation*, 303.

enough of the Bible to debate doctrine. They paid their taxes to the state and their tithes to the church. They gave to maintain excellent child care, beautiful buildings, and a professional staff.

Of all seven churches, the Cathedral Church of Laodicea may best capture the ethos of the wealthy American church. The sins of the previous churches—the loss of first love, indifference to heretical teaching, tolerance of immorality and apathy—culminate here in this bland, lukewarm spirituality and cultural superiority. Christ's rebuke doesn't even bother to focus on the surrounding pagan culture. Christ's critique is leveled at Christianity without Christ. The wealthy church in Laodicea was doing everything in its power to be a successful church. But their expenditure of emotional energy and material resources to meet the high expectations of affluent, self-focused people diverted resources from global missions and social justice concerns. Their market-driven strategies appealed to time-pressured, family-focused, career-centered spiritual consumers, but preempted serious considerations of what it means to follow the Lord Jesus.

Money is a serious issue in churches endeavoring to minister in upscale communities, whether they be in the affluent suburbs of Denver or midtown Manhattan. The cost of building and staffing a church in a major urban center can be staggering. Funding can easily become the absorbing preoccupation of the leadership. The Laodicean liability is faced by any church that exists in a culture where money is the driving force and focus of attention. In *Death by Suburb*, David Goetz captures the ethos of the church in Laodicea when he describes the dangers of an affluent culture. Modern American life tends to produce "spiritual cripples," who live too large materially to nurture their own bloated little souls. The constant quest for security, efficiency, excitement, and pleasure leaves believers with a smorgasbord of spiritual activities but little spiritual growth. "The drive to succeed, to make one's children succeed, overpowers the best intentions to live more reflectively, no matter the piety. Should it be any surprise that the true life in Christ never germinates?"[3] For all practical purposes the Cathedral Church of Laodicea was enmeshed in a self-indulgent idolatrous culture.

Coveting was probably more important than the covenant at the church of Laodicea. Professing Christians were painfully self-conscious

3. Goetz, *Death by Suburb*, 9.

nd insecure in their effort to obtain status and the approval of others.[4] Spirituality tended to be reduced to programs and meetings. There was little encouragement to identify with the deep suffering of the world or to "enter into a relationship with someone of raw emotional and physical need."[5] Friendship was transactional. Relationships were based on a cost-benefit analysis. There was a kind of caste system in the church, where members of a given social class stuck together. The Laodicean church confused the good life with the Christian life; they exchanged patient endurance for passive acceptance; they chose prosperity over persecution and self-expression over self-denial. They talked about God without knowing God and catered to the self at the expense of the soul.

A spirit of defiance and superiority is implied in their self-confidence. "You say, 'I am rich; I have acquired wealth and do not need a thing.' But," Christ adds, "you do not realize that you are wretched, pitiful, poor, blind and naked." The Laodicean pursuit of excellence impacted church operations from top to bottom. There was a Fortune 500 flair to the Cathedral's pastor. He was a winsome and charismatic executive. He exuded warmth and success, with a gift for inspiring people and catering to their sense of self-importance. He had a great sense of humor and knew what subjects to avoid. The leadership was adept at running an institution successfully, but inept at making disciples. Their pride and self-confidence stemmed from their wealth, which they looked to for protection and empowerment. Their independence recalls Ephraim's boast, "I am very rich; I have become wealthy. With all my wealth they will not find in me any iniquity or sin."[6]

The prescribed correction employs the language of the marketplace and is as radical as it is simple. Christ says, "I counsel you to buy from me gold refined in the fire, so you can become rich." Pastor John Stott says, "I can never read this verse without being strangely moved. He is the great God of the expanding universe. . . . He is the creator and sustainer of all things, the Lord Almighty. He has the right to issue orders for us to obey. He prefers to give advice which we need to heed. He could command; he chooses to counsel. He respects the freedom with which he has ennobled us."[7]

4. Ibid., 71.
5. Ibid., 115.
6. Hos 12:8.
7. Stott, *What Christ Thinks of the Church*, 119.

Christ was willing to make a deal with the Laodiceans. "Buy from me gold refined in the fire." In effect, Christ said, "If you want to transact business, do business with me." But what a strange sales pitch, because it has already been established that the believers were "wretched, pitful, poor, blind and naked." They have nothing to give in exchange for this "gold refined by fire"—this pure gold. The "buy-in" is a matter of pure grace. They must come to the place of acknowledging that they have nothing and that Christ has everything they need. The Apostle Paul said it so well: "For you know the grace of our Lord Jesus Christ, that though he was rich, yet for your sake he became poor, so that you through his poverty might become rich."[8]

The correction was radical, because it meant changing everything, but it also meant Christ loved them: "Those whom I love I rebuke and discipline." To the commercially sophisticated Laodiceans Christ offered not only a new currency ("gold refined in the fire"), but a new "white-robed" identity. Instead of going around spiritually naked in their Brooks Brothers suits and Nordstrom's outfits, they could clothe themselves in the righteousness of Christ. Instead of trusting in the famous Laodicean glossy black wool industry, the believers could trust in the resources of the Lamb who was slain for their salvation.[9] As God's chosen people, holy and dearly loved, they could clothe themselves "with compassion, kindness, humility, gentleness and patience."[10] And in addition to this new currency and their brand-new identity, Christ offered them a new vision. Instead of an entrepreneurial vision of material success and social status, Christ promised a healing vision of love and wisdom. Laodicea's famous product line of eye salve may have been medicinally effective, but it did nothing to restore spiritual sight. Only Christ's anointing was able to restore true sight to the blind.

Christ offered a different kind of wealth, measured not in dollars but in devotion. He offered liberation from the soul-deadening effects of money, sex, and power. But the big question remained: would the Cathedral Church of Laodicea "buy in" to the risen Christ's investment offer? There was nothing complicated or mysterious about the offer. It was up to them. The bottom line was simple: "Be earnest, and repent." "A 'zeal' or

8. 2 Cor 8:9.
9. Beale, *Revelation*, 307.
10. Col 3:12.

eagerness to get right with God must replace the 'lukewarm' spirituality that characterized the church."[11]

Table Fellowship

To the status-conscious Laodiceans Christ offered simple table fellowship: "Here I am! I stand at the door and knock. If anyone hears my voice and opens the door, I will come in and eat with them, and they with me." Fellowship in the world is often based on self-importance, but Jesus' fellowship is based on self-sacrifice. The principle of the exchanged life, my life for yours, remains the hallmark of Jesus' table grace; the principle of the expendable life, your life for mine, is frequently the force behind the world's social status. But the principle of the cross, my life for yours, empowers Christian hospitality. With a simple invitation Jesus intended to transform the Cathedral Church of Laodicea into a genuine household of faith.

Taken together we have the seven Spirit disciplines of churches: love, courage, faithfulness, holiness, authenticity, steadfastness, and humility. The Apostle John's inspired vision of Christ and the churches offers a deeper understand of God's priorities and values. Success and failure, strength and weakness—these are measured very differently in Christ's assessment. We see the danger of worldly strengths obscuring real weaknesses and we see the blessing of true weakness opening up exciting ministry opportunities. There is more at stake in the life and testimony of these churches than we realize. Christ doesn't put up with excuses, such as "Look on the bright side," or "Think positive!" or "They mean well." There is no turning a blind eye to sin or pretending things are better than they are. There is nothing casual or lighthearted about this analysis and diagnosis. Christ's passion for the church comes through. There are grave consequences for refusing to respond and glorious promises to those who choose to obey. "He who has an ear, let him hear what the Spirit says to the churches."

11. Osborne, *Revelation*, 211.

13

Christic the Center

⌐· Revelation 4:1–11 ·⌐

[4:1–11] *After this I looked, and there before me was a door standing open in heaven. And the voice I had first heard speaking to me like a trumpet said, "Come up here, and I will show you what must take place after this." At once I was in the Spirit, and there before me was a throne in heaven with someone sitting on it. And the one who sat there had the appearance of jasper and ruby. A rainbow that shone like an emerald encircled the throne. Surrounding the throne were twenty-four other thrones, and seated on them were twenty-four elders. They were dressed in white and had crowns of gold on their heads. From the throne came flashes of lightning, rumblings and peals of thunder. Before the throne, seven lamps were blazing. These are the seven spirits of God. Also before the throne there was what looked like a sea of glass, clear as crystal.*

In the center, around the throne, were four living creatures and they were covered with eyes, in front and in back. The first living creature was like a lion, the second was like an ox, the third had a face like a man, the fourth was like a flying eagle. Each of the four living creatures had six wings and was covered with eyes all around, even under its wings. Day and night they never stop saying: "Holy, holy, holy is the Lord God Almighty, who was, and is, and is to come."

Whenever the living creatures give glory, honor and thanks to him who sits on the throne and who lives for ever and ever, the twenty-four elders fall down before him who sits on the throne and worship him who lives for ever and ever. They lay their crowns before the throne and say: "You are worthy, our Lord and God, to receive glory and honor and power, for you created all things, and by your will they were created and have their being."

THE ONE "WHO HOLDS the seven stars in his right hand and walks among the seven golden lampstands" is in a position to know the churches better than we could ever imagine. King Jesus is quick to commend and encourage, but equally ready to confront and expose. He knows our convictions and our complacency, our courage and our conceit. He wields the "sharp, double-edged sword" and cuts through our excuses and compromises. With eyes like blazing fire he sees everything. He sees the weakness behind the impressive reputation and the emptiness behind the worldly success. He who "is the First and the Last, who died and came to life again," sees the faithfulness of the suffering church. It is he "who holds the key of David" and opens the door of opportunity for the church with "little strength."

Correction is not belabored; it is concise and to the point, delivered in staccato commands of spiritual admonition: Repent! Hold on! Wake up! Remember! "These are the words of the Amen, the faithful and true witness, the ruler of God's creation," "Come to me!" It is to the *church*, and not to the world, that Christ says, "Here I am! I stand at the door and knock. If anyone hears my voice and opens the door, I will come in and eat with them, and they with me." We hasten to add that Christ extends his invitation to all people.[1] Christ is knocking on the door, making himself known within the human conscience and throughout the cosmos.

The Open Heart

The risen Lord Jesus Christ stands outside the church, asking permission to enter a self-satisfied congregation. The picture confirms the humility of the incarnate Son of God who persists in pursuing the church. Are we in danger of interpreting the knock at the door as a bothersome solicitation? John's original hearers would not have thought twice about answering the knock with gracious Eastern hospitality. Each letter closes with

1. Matt 11:28–30.

an eschatological promise. Faithfulness to the end evidences faithfulness from the beginning. Those who endure in Christ will reign with Christ.[2] "To those who are victorious," Christ says, "I will give the right to sit with me on my throne, just as I was victorious and sat down with my Father on his throne."[3] The open door and the throne of God introduce the next vision. In the Spirit, John reminds the churches that their destiny is not determined by the world's political and social forces, but by the sovereign will of God. In the Spirit and in the presence of the Incarnate One we anticipate the convergence of heaven and earth.

The Open Door

Christ invites us into his presence.[4] The voice of invitation, "Here I am," is followed by the voice of revelation, "Come up here, and I will show you what must take place after this." Open the door of your life to Christ and Christ will open the door of revelation. Faith is the earnest expectation of sight. We move from table fellowship to throne worship. John's vision of the seven churches is followed by dramatic worship in heaven. These concurrent realities are inseparable. They belong together and provide the believer with a 20/20 vision of the suffering church and the reigning Christ. "After this" denotes a transition from one vision to another.[5] To suppose that the dramatic rescue of the church from the struggle against evil, known as the rapture, takes place at this point, invents an escape from reality that Christ does not promise and the Bible does not teach.[6] The transitional phrase "after this" introduces the next sequence in John's visionary experience; it does not indicate a displacement of the church

2. 2 Tim 2:12.

3. Rev 3:21.

4. Rev 3:20; 4:1.

5. Rev 4:1; see 7:1, 9;15:5; 18:1; 19:1.

6. Mark Hitchcock, *The End*, 150. Hitchcock, as heir to J. Dwight Pentecost's Dispensational mantle, explains, "While no single verse says Jesus is coming to rapture His saints before the seven-year Tribulation, there are clear statements that He is coming to deliver His people from the coming wrath (1 Thess 1:10; 5:9; Rev 3:10). Thus, it stands to reason that God will use the Rapture to accomplish this promise" (Hitchcock, *The End*, 136). Hitchcock sees "the rapture" in biblical texts that most biblical scholars attribute to the second coming of Christ (e.g., John 14:1–3; Rom 8:19; 1 Cor 1:7–8; 15:51–53; 16:22; Phil 3:20–21; 4:5; Col 3:4; 1 Thess 1:10; 2:19; 4:13–18; 5:9, 23; 2 Thess 2:1, 3; 1 Tim 6:14; 2 Tim 4:1, 8; Titus 2:13; Heb 9:28; Jas 5:7–9; 1 Pet 1:7, 13; 5:4; 1 John 2:28—3:2; Jude 1:21; Rev 3:10).

from the world. Next up is a vision of heaven: "After this, I beheld the open door in heaven."

As the churches struggle to overcome, heaven is pulsating with praise. Worship on earth has its counterpart in heaven. First earth, then heaven: first the struggling churches striving to be faithful, then the blazing glory of God's throne, full of light and sound, color and cantata. Christ's invitation and promise to the church at Laodicea introduces John's second Lord's Day vision. The curtain is parted, the shade is raised, the door is opened to the universe next door—the most real world. What transpires in heaven inspires and reassures the church. However, Dispensationalism counters this interpretation. John Walvoord writes, "It seems that the church as the Body of Christ is out of the picture, and saints who come to know the Lord in this period are described as saved Israelites or saved Gentiles, never by terms which are characteristic of the church, the Body of Christ."[7] On the contrary, what transpires in heaven provides inspiration and assurance to the faithful church. In the midst of trial and persecution on earth, the Apostle John offers struggling believers a vision of the awesome worship and sovereign power of God happening concurrently in heaven.

John's vision runs counter to those who pride themselves on being open minded, yet who are in fact close minded to the open door of revelation. Reality proves the naysayers wrong, no matter the era. The open door applies to earth's secrets and heaven's reality. Human civilization has its explorers, but none are greater than the Spirit-inspired Apostle John and his ongoing adventure of God's revelation. In the fifteenth century, the great explorers Vasco da Gama, Columbus, and Magellan discovered the open door of the earth's vast continents and oceans. In the sixteenth century, Copernicus began to open up the mysteries of our galaxy. He discovered that the earth was not fixed in space, but revolved around the sun. In the seventeenth century Kepler studied the laws of planetary motion and Robert Hooke used the microscope to uncover a previously unobserved microuniverse. Creation appears to offer an almost unlimited "open door" experience to human exploration and discovery.

7. Walvoord, *Revelation*, 103. "Though the rapture is mentioned in letters to two of the churches (2:25; 3:11), the rapture as a doctrine is not a part of the prophetic foreview of the book of Revelation. This is in keeping with the fact that the book as a whole is not occupied primarily with God's program for the church. Instead the primary objective is to portray the events leading us to climaxing in the second coming of Christ and the prophetic kingdom and the eternal state which ultimately will follow." (Walvoord, *Revelation*, 103).

"I do not know what I may appear to the world," wrote Isaac Newton in the 1600s, "but to myself I seem to have been only like a boy playing on the seashore, and diverting myself, in now and then finding another pebble or a prettier shell than ordinary, whilst the great ocean of truth lay all undiscovered before me."[8] More than 400 years later, we can claim little more. Albert Einstein said, "The eternal mystery of the world is its comprehensibility."[9] The Apostle John shows us the source of this comprehensibility; the One who is responsible, the Creator of the cosmos, the Author of life. The means of exploration do not depend upon compass or computer, telescope or electron microscope, but on the Spirit of God and the Word of God.

The Centering Throne

John is front and center, standing at attention, fully alert: "before me was a throne in heaven with someone sitting on it." His description unites the vision of "someone like a son of man" in chapter one with this vision of God on the throne in chapter four. A throne centers authority and power. Worship is the centering reality and everything is described in relation to the center. The Apostle John was concerned for believers to get their bearings. Everything in heaven is God centered and oriented around the throne of Christ. We gain our orientation by tracking the little words: "on," "from," "before," and "around."[10] Combine the prepositions with the verbal gravity of "encircled" and "surrounding," and the believer is placed "in the center." The emerald-like rainbow encircles the throne, the twenty-four elders surround the throne, and the seven blazing lamps and the crystal sea of glass are before the throne. Everything is centered in Christ.

"And there before me was a throne in heaven with someone sitting on it." There is a deliberate visual vagueness in the statement that relates back to the first vision of "someone like a son of man."[11] We are not encouraged to draw too fine a distinction between the Father and the Son in the description of God. The high-priestly robe and sash of the vision of the one like a son of man corresponds here to the radiating beauty of

8. Quoted in Boorstin, *The Discoverers*, 404.

9. Quoted in Highfield and Carter, *The Private Lives of Albert Einstein*, 79.

10. Rev 4:2–10.

11. Rev 1:13.

the light reflected from the one who sits on the throne. The supernatural splendor of God is conveyed through the enameled images of jasper, carnelian, and emerald, and the image of the rainbow.[12] The first word sof creation, "and God said, 'Let there be light,'" is John's first impression of heaven. The vision conveys the impression of an encircling brightness around the throne. The light of God's mercy is revealed in a rainbow.[13] John conveys a sense of mystery surrounding the heavenly court. Light is the first act of creation and light is the first symbol of redemption: "In him was life, and that life was of the light of all people."[14] Not surprisingly, light is the first impression of heaven. The refracted light of jasper and ruby recall the high priest's breastplate, adorned with three rows of four precious stones, each one representing one of the tribes.[15]

sardis (carnelian)	topaz	carbuncle
emerald	sapphire	diamond
jacinth	agate	amethyst
beryl	onyx	jasper

Jasper and carnelian are the last and first stones, Benjamin the youngest and Reuben the eldest, and the fourth stone, the emerald, represent Judah.[16] John's readers readily recognized the Exodus breastplate and the Genesis rainbow. The history of God's people is gathered up and centered. The throne stands for atonement and mercy.

The twenty-four elders and the four living creatures form a heavenly worship team. The number twenty-four is a derivative of twelve, with twelve being the symbol of divine government (twelve months in a lunar year; twelve tribes of Israel; twelve apostles; twelve gates in the new Jerusalem; twelve angels at each gate; twelve thousand sealed from each tribe and twelve times twelve, multiplied by a thousand, equals 144,000 to represent the signed, sealed, and delivered believing community). The twenty-four elders represent the entire believing community and the four living creatures represent the created order. The number four is symbolic of the created order. The Bible speaks of the four corners of the earth and the four winds of the heaven.

12. Ezek 1:27–28.
13. Gen 9:16–17.
14. John 1:4.
15. Exod 39:10–14.
16. Exod 28:17–21.

The four creatures are all of the aspects of creation, just as the twenty-four elders are all the facets of faith. "These creatures symbolize a power which is world-wide and manifold in its operation and which holds up and pervades the entire universe, even transcending it. The living creatures are symbolic of creation and the divine immanence. They are what is noblest (lion), strongest (ox), wisest (man), and swiftest (eagle)."[17] They represent "the astonishing vitality and diversity found in creation" and they sing a version of the great hymn of the seraphim in Isaiah:[18]

> Holy, holy, holy is the Lord of hosts;
> the whole earth is full of his glory![19]

> Holy, holy, holy is the Lord God Almighty,
> who was, and is, and is to come![20]

Stretching out before the throne is what looks like a sea of glass, clear as crystal. This "sea" may be reminiscent of the large basin of water—fifteen feet from rim to rim, with a circumference of forty-five feet—used for ceremonial cleansing in Solomon's temple.[21] Some scholars have suggested that the sea signifies a baptismal font.

Humility and Human Flourishing

We long to be at the center. Many people aspire to be at the center of power or finance or pleasure or sport or fashion or entertainment. But our personal experiences of these centers of influence and culture tend to quickly demystify them, and often the height of our aspiration is matched by the depths of our disillusionment. Working at the center is not what we thought it would be. The centering power of Jesus Christ differs from all other centers of power and influence. To be centered in Jesus Christ means that we pay attention to what truly matters. The centering power of Christ brings rest and inspiration into our lives and peace and passion into our souls. In Christ we are at the true center. This "centering" leads to the truest form of humility: the humility that does not humiliate but instead leads to *shalom*. True humility centers life on Christ rather than

17. Ford, *Revelation*, 75.
18. Mangina, *Revelation*, 79.
19. Isa 6:3.
20. Rev 4:8.
21. 1 Kgs 7:23–26.

self. Humility frees us from the often subtle, manipulative, and destructive powers of humiliation and egoism. True humility shapes our self-understanding and strengthens our commitment to God's will. With it, we are finally invested in a center that holds.

"The thrust of this vision is powerfully affirmative; yet the affirmations have an edge to them," writes Joseph Mangina. "To confess that God alone is the Creator, that only he is worthy of our worship, entails the denial that anyone or anything else should occupy the heavenly throne. . . . The throne in heaven has everything to do with earthly thrones. . . . It is the Roman emperor cult that offers a grotesque parody of the true worship of God."[22] The issue of idolatry looms large in Revelation, and here before the centering throne of God we have its greatest opposing argument. Idolatry meets its devastating match in the presence of God. "The vision of 'him who sits on the throne' is, one might say, a powerful display of the impossibility of idolatry."[23] In the Prophets, the critique of idolatry begins at the throne of God. The word of the Lord transports Jeremiah into the very presence of God. The scene in chapters four and five of Revelation parallel Daniel's vision of the Ancient of Days seated on his throne:

> Thrones were set in place, and the Ancient of Days took his seat. His clothing was as white as snow; the hair of his head was white like wool. His throne was flaming with fire, and its wheels were all ablaze. A river of fire was flowing, coming out from before him. Thousands upon thousands attended him; ten thousand times ten thousand stood before him. The court was seated, and the books were opened.[24]

The key to human flourishing is found at the throne of our Creator and Redeemer. To be centered in Christ is to realize our true human potential. Miroslav Volf writes, "Human beings flourish and are truly happy when they center their lives on God, the source of everything that is true, good, and beautiful. As to all created things, they too ought to be loved. But the

---

22. Mangina, *Revelation*, 81.

23. Ibid., 82. Mangina writes in full, "The first commandment of the Decalogue, 'You shall have no other gods before me,' is never quoted in Revelation. Yet the argument can be made it is the most important single passage in the Old Testament for understanding the book. The vision of 'him who sits on the throne' is, one might say, a powerful display of the impossibility of idolatry. . . . Alas, this 'impossible' has proved to be all too possible in the course of church and world history!" (Mangina, *Revelation*, 82).

24. Dan 7:9–10.

only way to properly love them and fully enjoy them is to love them 'in God."[25] Yet it is this fundamental and basic truth that is challenged, not only in the culture but in the church. Instead of Christ on the throne, it appears that the self has been enthroned. The first-century church contended with the idolatry of the imperial cult. Christians were expected to pledge fidelity to Caesar. In the twenty-first century, the church contends with the idolatry of the imperial self.

Most of us struggle with the largeness of the Apostle John's God-centered, Christ-focused, Spirit-empowered worldview—and that's a good thing! We are so easily tempted to reduce everything down to the small world of the self. Give us comfort, convenience, and entertainment and we are happy campers. May it not be so! Coping with stress, realizing one's dreams, and finding happiness are in the minds of some the modern equivalent to salvation. The pressure in our culture is to narrow our vision down to the things we can control. We are tempted to focus on the things that distract us from the important realities of life. A four-dollar Starbucks drink is nice, but not a taste of heaven.

Theologian David Wells writes: "The self is a canvas too narrow, too cramped, to contain the largeness of Christian truth."[26] Miroslav Volf observes that "many today would not care whether they live with or against the grain of reality. They want what they want, and the fact that they want it is a sufficient justification for wanting it. Arguments about their desires fit with a more encompassing account of reality—how they relate to 'human nature,' for instance—are simply beside the point."[27] The church faces a double challenge: convincing both nonbelievers and confessing Christians that human flourishing is centered in Christ. The power of self-rule dominates in both culture and the church. Volf writes, "Maybe the most difficult challenge for Christians is to actually *believe* that God is fundamental to human flourishing . . . to really mean that the presence and activity of the God of love, who can make us love our neighbors as ourselves, is our hope and the hope of the world—that this God is the secret of our flourishing as persons, cultures, and interdependent inhabitants of a single globe."[28]

---

25. Volf, *A Public Faith*, 58.
26. Wells, *No Place For Truth*, 183.
27. Volf, *A Public Faith*, 69.
28. Ibid., 74.

Seek the Center

The worship scene in Revelation is as exuberant as it is exalted. "The scene is marked by a tremendous dynamism, an energy that flows first of all centripetally" toward the throne of God and then centrifugally away from the throne and into the world.[29] The Apostle John's horizon is as broad and as wide angled as it could be. The scope of the heavenly vision is simultaneously personal and cosmic. His Spirit-inspired praying imagination is stretched to the limit. There is nothing narrow and individualistic about this description. John is caught up in something grander and more real than himself. We may be surprised to learn how deeply the heavenly throne of God affirms creation and culture. We too easily forget that "God so loved the world that he gave his one and only Son."[30] The encircling rainbow, the global church (twenty-four elders), the release of energy—"flashes of lightning, rumblings and peals of thunder"—the sea of glass, the four living creatures, and the first two praise anthems emphasize the totality of God's holiness and the worthiness of his sovereignty over all creation. Heaven assures believers, even beleaguered, persecuted ones, that they have the home-court advantage. "Cultures are not foreign countries for the followers of Christ," writes Mirsolav Volf, "but rather their own homelands, the creation of the one God."[31]

29. Mangina, *Revelation*, 75.
30. John 3:16.
31. Volf, *A Public Faith*, 89.

14

The Open Scroll

⌐· Revelation 5:1–14 ·⌐

[5:1–14] *Then I saw the right hand of him who sat on the throne a scroll with writing on both sides and sealed with seven seals. And I saw a mighty angel proclaiming in a loud voice, "Who is worthy to break the seals and open the scroll?" But no one in heaven or on earth or under the earth could open the scroll or even look inside it. I wept and wept because no one was found who was worthy to open the scroll or look inside. Then one of the elders said to me, "Do not weep! See, the Lion of the tribe of Judah, the Root of David, has triumphed. He is able to open the scroll and its seven seals."*

Then I saw a Lamb, looking as if it had been slain, standing at the center before the throne, encircled by the four living creatures and the elders. The Lamb had seven horns and seven eyes, which are the seven spirits of God sent out into all the earth. He went and took the scroll from the right hand of him who sat on the throne. And when he had taken it, the four living creatures and the twenty-four elders fell down before the Lamb. Each one had a harp and they were holding golden bowls full of incense, which are the prayers of God's people. And they sang a new song, saying: "You are worthy to take the scroll and to open its seals, because you were slain, and with your blood you purchased for God members of every tribe and language and people and nation. You have made them to be a kingdom and priests to serve our God, and they will reign on the earth."

Then I looked and heard the voice of many angels, numbering thousands upon thousands, and ten thousand times ten thousand. They encircled the throne and the living creatures and the elders. In a loud voice they were saying: "Worthy is the Lamb, who was slain, to receive power and wealth and wisdom and strength and honor and glory and praise!" Then I heard every creature in heaven and on earth and under the earth and on the sea, and all that is in them, saying: "To him who sits on the throne and to the Lamb be praise and honor and glory and power, for ever and ever!" The four living creatures said, "Amen," and the elders fell down and worshiped.

TRUE WORSHIP LEADS US out of the closed universe of our own making and into the larger world of God's creation and redemption. An open heart to Christ's invitation leads through the open door of revelation in anticipation of the open scroll of redemption. John yearns for the truth that only God can reveal. We are invited into God's natural world: "You created all things, and by your will they were created."[1] Creation is vastly more complex and alive than we could have imagined. And John is about to show that what is true of nature is also true of redemption. There is a scroll in the right hand of the one who sits on the throne, signifying God's revelation. It contains the truth about reality, the end of human civilization, and, more specially, the culmination of salvation history. The scroll is filled to overflowing. It is written on on both sides and sealed with seven seals to insure the secrecy of its decrees. It contains the full account of what God in his sovereign will has determined is the destiny of the world.

Who really cares? John cares! Worship has made him care. He longs to know what God is doing in the world, to know the conclusion to salvation history. The promise to the churches was clear: "He who has an ear, let him hear what the Spirit says to the churches." More than anything else John wants to hear what the Spirit says to the churches. "And I saw a mighty angel proclaiming in a loud voice, 'Who is worthy to break the seals and open the scroll?'" For a moment John despairs, fearing that the question is truly unanswerable, for "no one in heaven or on earth or under the earth could open the scroll or even look inside it."

1. Rev 4:11.

John Weeps

John is overwhelmed by the need to know what is on the scroll. No one responds to the mighty angel's loud request. No one claims to be worthy. "No one in heaven or on earth or under the earth could open the scroll or even look inside it." The situation appears hopeless and John's emotional response is intense. He is overcome with grief. In Isaiah's day the sealed scroll was met with a shrug of indifference, a good excuse for not knowing, but not in John's case.[2] He wept and wept; the truth he longed for appeared tragically unobtainable. John's reaction fits the Apostle Paul's warning, "If only for this life we have hope in Christ, we are to be pitied more than all others."[3] John was overwhelmed by the possibility that no one was worthy to open the scroll and reveal the truth.[4] He contemplates the dire possibility of the absence of truth, the irrationality of hope, and the utter emptiness of nothingness. What if there is no redemption? John weeps: feelings of ecstasy and visions of glory are no comfort if salvation cannot be consummated.

Nietzsche's Will to Power and the Philosophy of the Beast

This is exactly the kind of weeping that Friedrich Nietzsche (1844–1900) despised, because he found such weeping to be an embarrassment to the human animal. Those who weep, Nietzsche argued, fail to face the facts. There is no divine promise. Salvation is a lie. Hope in anything other than the will to power is an illusion. For Nietzsche there never has been a scroll to open; there is only the strong man and his will to power. Nietzsche drove skepticism and cynicism to its fatal and nihilistic conclusion. What other skeptics whisper Nietzsche shouted from the rooftops, and over time he has only gained more attention. Nietzsche had the courage of his convictions, even if those convictions drove him mad. He sought "to think pessimism through to its depths and to liberate it"

2. Isa 29:11–12.

3. 1 Cor 15:19.

4. Mangina, *Revelation*, 85. Mangina writes, "John's weeping reminds us of the tears of other biblical figures, such as Rachel, who 'refuses to be comforted' for her lost children (Jer 31:15; Matt 2:18); Jesus weeping over Jerusalem (Matt 23:37–39) or at Lazarus's tomb (John 11:35); and Mary Magdalene weeping in the garden on Easter morning (John 20:11). 'Blessed are those who mourn, for they will be comforted' (Matt 5:4)" (*Revelation*, 85).

from Christianity, which he believed was an essentially cruel religion that asked people to sacrifice for nothing.[5]

Nietzsche argued that Christianity used the myth of love to foster an illusion. Humanity was falsely educated to believe in something other than the hard fact of exploitation and self-mastery. Nietzsche despised "The innocuous Christian-moral interpretation of our most intimate personal experiences 'for the glory of God' and 'for the salvation of the soul'—this tyranny, this caprice, this rigorous and grandiose stupidity has *educated* the spirit."[6] Nietzsche contended, "In real life it is only a matter of *strong* and *weak* wills."[7] He believed Christianity was created out of fear of "an incurable pessimism"; the avoidance of a deep-down, unteachable, unyielding spiritual fate that "life itself is the will to power."[8] The "cardinal instinct of an organic being," Nietzsche argued, was self-preservation. All talk of motive, purpose, freedom, and morality is meaningless. "I shall repeat a hundred times; we really ought to free ourselves from the seduction of words!"[9]

John's weeping, according to Nietzsche, was utterly pointless. There is no one to open the scroll and no scroll to open. Nietzsche applied the law of the jungle to the human beast. No one weeps when the lion tears apart its prey and no one should weep when the noble dominate the weak. There is no Incarnate One, only the human being who "will have to be an incarnate will to power, it will strive to grow, spread, seize, become predominant."[10] Nietzsche gave narcissism its marching orders. If men— and Nietzsche meant men, because he denigrated women as inferior beings—were true to their instincts, they would reverence superior rank and the hardness of heart born of unfavorable circumstances. "Egoism belongs to the nature of a noble soul."[11] "The noble soul has reverence for itself."[12] For Nietzsche there were only two kinds of people: the exalted and the exploited, the proud and the humble, the powerful and the petty, the hardened and "the doglike people who allow themselves to be

---

5. Nietzsche, *Beyond Good and Evil*, in *Basic Writings*, sec. 56, 258.

6. Ibid., sec. 188, 291.

7. Ibid., sec. 23, 221.

8. Ibid., sec. 13, 211.

9. Ibid., sec. 16, 213.

10. Ibid., sec. 259, 393.

11. Ibid., sec. 265, 405.

12. Ibid., sec.287, 418.

maltreated."[13] Humility was unbecoming to the noble soul. To exploit and dominate was a worthy goal for the man of superior rank and self-made self-worth. Nietzsche complained,

> For two millennia now we have been condemned to the sight of this new type of invalid, "the sinner" . . . everywhere the sinner . . . everywhere dumb torment, extreme fear, the agony of tortured heart, the convulsions of unknown happiness, the cry for "redemption."[14]

Nietzsche despised the Apostle John's weeping. He condemned all such emotion as an "orgy of feeling" without rhyme or reason in a world where all that mattered was the survival of the fittest. He claimed Christianity was "this most ingenious, unscrupulous, and dangerous systematization of all the means for producing orgies of feeling under the cover of holy intentions." He called for "unconditional honest atheism," not as an antithesis to an ideal, but as an "inner consequence" to "the awe-inspiring catastrophe of 2000 years of training in truthfulness that finally forbids itself the *lie involved in belief in God*."[15] Against all weeping, Nietzsche argued that the human animal must accept "a fearful void" and no longer suffer the question of meaning or a reason for suffering.

In the past, the reason for suffering came down to sin and guilt, but having eliminated that "meaning" and the spirituality that made suffering "deeper, more inward, more poisonous, more life-destructive," man no longer wills salvation but nothingness. He can live more like the animal he is, free to follow his instincts and reason—a will to nothingness, "a rebellion against the most fundamental presuppositions of life; but it is and remains a will!"[16] Nietzsche understood that the Lamb signified our need for redemption, our dependent state before God, and our humble approach to the world. He found everything about the Lamb of God utterly intolerable and detestable.

The Lamb of God

Suspense builds as the apostle of love walks through heaven's open door and experiences Christ-centered worship. The mighty angel asks in a loud

13. Ibid., sec. 260, 395.
14. Ibid., sec. 20, 577.
15. Ibid., sec. 27, 596.
16. Ibid., sec. 28, 598–99.

voice, "Who is worthy to break the seals and open the scroll?" In the book of Revelation, the Apostle John's preferred metaphor for Jesus Christ is the Lamb; his shorthand notation for the one who "has freed us from our sins by his blood, and has made us to be a kingdom and priests to serve his God and Father" is the Lamb of God. It is fitting that this metaphor, first used by John the Baptist at the beginning of the New Testament to introduce Jesus' earthly ministry, was used by the Apostle John to focus our attention on the redemption found in Christ alone. When John the Baptist declared, "Look! The Lamb of God, who takes away the sin of the world," he used a metaphor rooted in Genesis.[17]

Abel's sacrifice of the firstborn of his flock was chosen by God over the fruit of Cain's garden.[18] Abraham was commanded by the Lord to offer his firstborn son Isaac on an altar, just the way he would have offered a sacrificial lamb. When they arrived at the site of the sacrifice, Isaac innocently asked, "The fire and the wood are here, but where is the lamb for the burnt offering?" Abraham answered, "God himself will provide the lamb for the burnt offering, my son."[19] This is the first time the word "lamb" is used in the Bible and it is significant. Abraham's faith preaches the cross from the beginning. The metaphor is deeply rooted in salvation history. Faith in the Lamb of God is first introduced here. The Passover lamb was first sacrificed by the Israelites in Egypt and its blood was sprinkled on the doorframes of their homes.[20] By the blood of the lamb God reclaimed a people through whom to bless all the world. The Prophet Isaiah was the first to liken Israel's Suffering Servant to a lamb when he wrote, "He was oppressed and afflicted, yet he did not open his mouth; he was led like a lamb to the slaughter, and as a sheep before its shearers is silent, so he did not open his mouth."[21] Isaiah's picture of a silent, suffering lamb was allowed to acquire meaning through the course of salvation history. The meaning of the metaphor and the significance of the atonement builds slowly, but the purpose of redemption is rooted in salvation history from the beginning. The identity of the One who is the Lamb is well established before the Apostle John applies the metaphor. He waits to introduce the Lamb until after he has given his description of

17. John 1:29.
18. Gen 4:2–5.
19. Gen 22:7–8.
20. Exod 12.
21. Isa 53:7.

the Jesus we need to know.[22] John waits until he has revealed the vision of Christ to the seven churches. He waits until he has introduced the open door and the open scroll.

"Do not weep!" is the elder's uncomplicated spiritual direction. "See, the Lion of the tribe of Judah, the Root of David, has triumphed. He is able to open the scroll and its seven seals." The elder is emphatic with John: "Stop crying! See the Lion of the tribe of Judah." John *hears* lion-like sovereignty, yet *sees* lamb-like sacrifice. "What he hears is strength, what he sees is weakness. What he hears is a conqueror, what he sees is the quintessential victim—the Lamb."[23] He sees the only one in heaven or on earth or under the earth that can set in motion the culmination of salvation history. He sees a Lamb, "looking as if it had been slain, standing in the center of the throne."[24] The seven horns symbolize the all-powerful warrior and king and the seven eyes symbolize all-knowing wisdom—the fullness of the Spirit. "It is quite impossible to conceive a figure embodying the characteristics of the Lion of the tribe of Judah, the Root of David, and the seven-horned Lamb with seven eyes."[25] We should think of John's vision as a theological composition drawn from many sources, including Genesis and Isaiah.[26]

These prophecies unite power and omniscience with self-surrender and sacrifice. "Whatever else this Lamb is, he is not *cute*. He is nothing less than 'the Lamb of God who takes away the sin of the world.'"[27] By designating Jesus as the Lamb twenty-eight times, John keeps the focus on who it is that brings us to the throne of God and the redemption that makes our salvation possible. John's Spirit-inspired vision of the glory of God centers worship on "the Lamb that was slain from the creation of the world."[28] Heaven declares, "Worthy is the Lamb, who was slain, to receive power and wealth and wisdom and strength and honor and glory and praise!" Those who follow the Lord Jesus Christ are included in this metaphor, for their names are written in the Book of Life belonging to the Lamb. They are known by his name and they will overcome evil by the

22. Rev 1:12–20.

23. Mangina, *Revelation*, 87.

24. Rev 5:6.

25. Charles, *Revelation*, 142.

26. Gen 49:9–11; Isa 11:1–3; Jer 23:5–6.

27. Mangina, *Revelation*, 88.

28. Rev 13:8; 14:1.

blood of the Lamb.[29] Those who follow the Lamb keep themselves pure and as the bride of Christ they are invited to the wedding of the Lamb.[30]

The metaphor of the Lamb underscores the meaning of God's great act of redemption. Human weakness and vulnerability is subsumed under the image that underscores the power of God to bring about salvation. John speaks of the throne of the Lamb and the wrath of the Lamb.[31] He uses the image of the lamb theologically, not sentimentally, and any association that the Lamb might have in our imagination with timidity or passivity or ineptitude is dispelled by John's portrayal of the Lamb, who is the Alpha and Omega, the sovereign Lord of history and humanity.[32] "It is almost as if John were saying to us at one point after another, 'Wherever the Old Testament says, 'Lion,' read 'Lamb.' Wherever the Old Testament speaks of the victory of the Messiah or the overthrow of the enemies of God, we are to remember that the gospel recognizes no other way of achieving these ends than the way of the Cross."[33] John insisted on the metaphor of the lamb because it represents the atoning sacrifice of Christ on the cross. Images that connote power, such as the throne and the Book of Life, are linked to the Lamb because they depend upon the sacrifice of the cross. The Lamb of God who takes away the sin of the world is the same Lamb who takes over the world. Yet no worldly militancy or spirit of triumphalism belongs to the followers of the Lamb.[34] We are only and always, as John described himself, brothers and sisters, companions "in the suffering [tribulation] and kingdom and patient endurance that are ours in Jesus."[35]

29. Rev 12:11.

30. Rev 14:4; 19:7.

31. Rev 6:16; 22:1.

32. Rev 1:8.

33. Caird, *A Commentary on the Revelation*, 75.

34. Bauckham, *The Climax of Prophecy*, 183. Bauckham: "It is not likely that John's readers were tempted to zealotism, expecting God-given success for a military uprising against the Roman oppressor. Temptations seem to have been rather in the opposite direction: towards compromise with the imperial cult. . . . John writes about the victory of the Messiah and his people, often in the traditional militaristic imagery of the messianic war. . . . The notion of messianic conquest is reinterpreted. Jesus Christ is the Lion of Judah and the Root of David, but John 'sees' him as the Lamb. Precisely by juxtaposing these contrasting images, John forges a symbol of conquest by sacrificial death, which is essentially a new symbol" (*Climax*, 183).

35. Rev 1:9.

Songs of Praise

The worthiness of the Lamb, "looking as if it had been slain" and signifying redemption, makes all the difference in the world. "The moment the Lamb takes the scroll, John's tears cease. The next sound is not weeping but a great redemption hymn, confident in worldwide salvation: "by your blood you ransomed people for God." There is an outpouring of prayer and praise. Cosmic liturgy is inspired by cosmic rule. Without the power there is no true worship. "A radius of praise is drawn inward to the center and a new song is sung."[36] "The people of God sing. They express exuberance in realizing the majesty of God and the mercy of Christ, the wholeness of reality and their new-found ability to participate in it. . . . When persons of faith become aware of who God is and what he does, they sing. The songs are irrepressible."[37]

John hears five hymns of faith, beginning with a song of ceaseless praise devoted to the being of God: "Holy, holy, holy is the Lord God Almighty, who was, and is, and is to come."[38] The second hymn is a hymn of exaltation, celebrating the creation of God: "You are worthy, our Lord and God, to receive glory and honor and power, for you created all things, and by your will they were created and have their being."[39] The third hymn is sung by the four living creatures and the twenty-four elders. It is a song of redemption, dedicated to the mercy and grace of Christ: "You are worthy to take the scroll and to open its seals, because you were slain, and with your blood you purchased for God persons from every tribe and language and people and nation. You have made them to be a kingdom and priests to serve our God, and they will reign on the earth."[40] The fourth hymn is an angel anthem to the glory of God sung by thousands upon thousands, ten thousand times ten thousand. Together they sing, "Worthy is the Lamb, who was slain, to receive power and wealth and wisdom and strength and honor and glory and praise!"[41] Finally, "every creature in heaven and on earth and under the earth and on the sea, and all that is in them," join in the doxology: "To him who sits

36. Wilcock, *Revelation,* 69.
37. Peterson, *Reversed Thunder,* 66–69.
38. Rev 4:8.
39. Rev 4:11.
40. Rev 5:9–10.
41. Rev 5:12.

on the throne and to the Lamb be praise and honor and glory and power, for ever and ever!"[42]

W. B. Yeats laments the disintegration of civilization in "The Second Coming." He wrote, "The centre cannot hold; / Mere anarchy is loosed upon the world, / The blood-dimmed tide is loosed, and everywhere / The ceremony of innocence is drowned; / The best lack all conviction, while the worst / Are full of passionate intensity."[43] As the seals are opened, Yeats's lament of a fallen world fits John's vision. But for the apostle the question is not "Will the center hold?" but "Will we hold to the center?" John remains on the island of Patmos. His circumstances have not changed, but he is caught up in this powerful, exuberant worship. And the words of the elder resound in his hearing, "Do not weep! See, the Lion of the tribe of Judah, the Root of David, has triumphed."[44]

---

42. Rev 5:13.
43. Yeats, "The Second Coming," 187.
44. Rev 5:5.

15

Heaven's Perspective on Evil

⟶ Revelation 6:1–17 ⟵

[6:1–8] *I watched as the Lamb opened the first of the seven seals. Then I heard one of the four living creatures say in a voice like thunder, "Come!" I looked, and there before me was a white horse! Its rider held a bow, and he was given a crown, and he rode out as a conqueror bent on conquest.*

When the Lamb opened the second seal, I heard the second living creature say, "Come!" Then another horse came out, a fiery red one. Its rider was given power to take peace from the earth and to make people slay each other. To him was given a large sword.

When the Lamb opened the third seal, I heard the third living creature say, "Come!" I looked, and there before me was a black horse! Its rider was holding a pair of scales in his hand. Then I heard what sounded like a voice among the four living creatures, saying, "Two pounds of wheat for a day's wages, and six pounds of barley for a day's wages, and do not damage the oil and the wine!"

When the Lamb opened the fourth seal, I heard the voice of the fourth living creature say, "Come!" I looked, and there before me was a pale horse! Its rider was named Death, and Hades was following close behind him. They were given power over a fourth of the earth to kill by the sword, famine and plague, and by the wild beasts of the earth.

ALL EYES ARE ON the Lamb as he opens the first of seven seals. The scroll signifies what will transpire at the end of history. It is filled to overflowing, "with writing on both sides," and sealed with seven seals to insure its secrecy. The scroll of destiny contains the full account of what God in his sovereign will has determined for the world. History is not haphazard or subject to chance. Humanity's future is not driven by fate, but by the will of God. The process of unsealing does not slowly disclose the revelation within the scroll. All seven seals need to be broken for that to happen. "The opening of the seals one by one is a literary device enabling John to narrate a series of visions which *prepare* for the revelation of the contents of the scroll."[1]

Until now the dominating theme has been worship. John beholds the awesome glory of God. He excites our praying imagination with vivid impressions of the majesty and glory of God on earth and in heaven. The vision of the glorified Son of Man, the letters to the seven churches, and the awesome worship experience set the stage for the opening of the seven seals, the sounding of the seven trumpets, and the pouring out of the seven bowls. The impact of all of this on John himself is overwhelming. He receives this revelation on his knees.[2] The prerequisites for receiving the revelation are clear: a passion for Christ, a love for his church, and a vital experience of worship. Everything that follows is grounded in Christ and his church; everything flows from the triune God, the God of all creation and the Lord of redemption. Nothing overshadows the awesome reality of lion-like sovereignty and lamb-like sacrifice.

What Is Coming Is Already Here

As the Lamb breaks the seals our understanding of reality is deepened. Christ's followers face the future by embracing the truth about the present. Each of the events triggered by the release of the seals prepares the believer for life as we experience it today. Evil has to be understood if it is to be overcome. John's inspired vision begins by exploring the extent and complexity of evil. There appears to be a deep affinity between what the early church experienced in the first century and what the body of Christ experiences in the twenty-first century. John challenges the cultural captivity of the church and explores the meaning of true redemptive

1. Bauckham, *The Theology of the Book of Revelation*, 80.
2. Rev 1:17–18.

cultural engagement. The human dilemma stems from the fact that the entire created order is under God's curse because of human sin. D. A. Carson writes, "The most urgent need of human beings is to be reconciled to God. That is not to deny that such reconciliation entails reconciliation with other human beings, and transformed living in God's fallen creation, in anticipation of the final transformation at the time of the consummation of all things."[3]

The Apostle John witnesses the devastating four-fold impact of evil. Evil charges into our lives leaving destruction and death. We are challenged to pay strict attention. The four horses of the apocalypse symbolize the stampede of evil thundering across the world scene, pounding out pain and producing havoc. With the opening of the seals we are reminded that life hangs in the balance and we are in need of salvation. Despair and devastation run rampant. Conquest, violence, famine, and death come charging at us like a team of wild horses. The truth about the human situation is revealed with a one-word command: "Come!" Likewise, the devastating impact of evil is called out: "Bring it on!" The image of horses pounding the pavement recalls the Lord's admonition to the Prophet Jeremiah, "If you have raced with men on foot and they have worn you out, how can you compete with horses?"[4] Of all people, Christians ought to understand the devastating power of evil. We should not be surprised by the comprehensive scope and painful intensity of evil any more than a doctor is shocked at cancer or a police officer is shocked at crime. We cannot turn a blind eye to the suffering that goes on all around us. We hear the pounding hooves of John's four horses of the apocalypse.

The four horses are called forth "in a voice like thunder" by the four living creatures.[5] These horses are summoned and sent out by the powers emanating from the throne of God. They signify the forces of evil harnessed by the power of God for divine purposes of judgment, enlightenment, and vindication. The imagery corresponds to Zechariah's prophecy and his eighth vision, when the prophet saw four chariots coming out from between two mountains at dawn. Zechariah's first and last visions parallel one another. The scouting party on a reconnaissance mission reports at dusk and four powerful chariots go forth to conquer at dawn.[6] Zechariah envisioned the complacency of an unjust world shattered by

3. Carson, "Three Books on the Bible."

4. Jer 12:5.

5. Rev 4:6; 6:1.

6. Zech 1:8–15; 6:1–8.

"the four spirits of heaven, going out from standing in the presence of the Lord of the whole world."

John's vision develops Zechariah's prophecy. Instead of four chariots, each with a team of horses, John describes four horses. The white horse and crowned rider symbolize conquest. The sword wielding rider on the fiery red horse stands for bloodshed and violence. The rider on the black horse carries a measuring scale signifying scarcity, famine, and economic disparity. The pale horse is ridden by death itself, representing pestilence, disease, plague, and mortality. It is a frightful quartet of misery that is unleashed upon the world. The power of these images conveys a picture of evil that the followers of the Lamb are meant to grasp. Five truths shape our understanding. The first truth about evil is that Christ has conquered evil. "In this world you will have trouble" is true enough. "But take heart!" Jesus says. "I have overcome the world."[7] Evil is numbered, classified, and cataloged. Like a veteran cop or surgeon who says to himself, "I've seen it all," believers should not to be overwhelmed by evil—we have been briefed. The dimensions of evil are defined and understood. Evil is parasitic; it plays off the good. It is a pathogen, robbing health from life. Evil is a malignancy. It is the insanity of a sane mind. Evil is the love of hate and the hate of love. "Nothing that we experience as evil is unnoticed or unacknowledged. . . . Christians do not shut their eyes to the world's cruelty in themselves or others. St. John has trained us to be especially attentive to it, to name it with honesty—no euphemisms, no evasions—and deal with it courageously."[8]

The second truth about evil is that we live with the threat of the stampede of evil coming at us from all directions. The human condition is vulnerable to conquest, violence, scarcity, and disease. This is why we have armies, police, firefighters, and government. We work against the impact of evil through medicine and education. We pass laws that favor gun control, road safety, and building accessibility for the disabled. We try to regulate the economy to minimize scarcities and disparities. Evil is complex and demands constant vigilance, but its immediate and enduring effect ought always to drive us to God. The followers of the Lamb are called upon to mitigate the impact of these wild horses. This is what it means to be salt and light in a dark and decaying world. Christ's disciples seek to curb the lust for war and reverse humanity's destructive ways.

7. John 16:33.

8. Peterson, *Reversed Thunder*, 81.

We seek to overcome famine and starvation, to defend the powerless and comfort the grieving.

3   The third truth is that no matter how righteous we are in Christ, we live under the threat of the stampede of evil. John's four-fold description of judgment corresponds to Ezekiel's prophecy against Jerusalem. The Lord announced that he would send "four dreadful judgments—sword and famine and wild beasts and plague" against Jerusalem.[9] The Lord stressed to Ezekiel that the judgment was inevitable and inescapable: "Son of man, if a country sins against me by being unfaithful and I stretch out my hand against it to cut off its food supply and send famine upon it and kill its people and their animals, even if these three men—Noah, Daniel and Job—were in it, they could save only themselves by their righteousness, declares the Sovereign Lord."[10] Even those who are in Christ and serve him faithfully are subject to evil's impact. Christians are vulnerable to awful car accidents, months of chemotherapy, and the loss of a limb when they step on an improvised explosive device. We live in a fallen, broken, sin-twisted world, and even in Christ we have not been given a free pass when it comes to the painful effects of evil. The common refrain when tragedy strikes is "Why me?" But perhaps we should ask is, "Why not me?"[11] Our evangelism is rooted in empathy for those who suffer the devastating impact of evil. We share in their pain and brokenness. Redemption does not spare us this identity. We are saved out of the world of sin and evil by God's grace, then sent back into it to share the love of Christ. Moreover, we confess that even in Christ we continue to perpetuate evil and suffer its consequences.

4   The fourth truth about evil is that these horses run wild, wreaking havoc in human civilization, but their impact does not cause humankind to turn to God. On the contrary, the stampede of evil only seems to harden human hearts against God. God gives people over to their sinful desires, their shameful lusts, and their depraved minds, but the experience and consequences of evil do not dissuade people from it. God uses evil against evil, like a black belt karate expert who turns his attacker's advances to his own advantage; like a firefighter who sets a backfire to literally fight fire with fire; like a doctor who administers chemotherapy with the hope that the deadly weapon causes more good than harm. The earth is under siege, and the fearful experience of evil should cause people to

9. Ezek 14:21.

10. Ezek 14:13–14.

11. Sittser, *A Grace Disguised*, 108.

turn to God. But it doesn't. In Jeremiah's day, God expressed his wrath against Israel by using Nebuchadnezzar, king of Babylon, to subjugate the Israelites and desecrate the temple because of Judah's disobedience.[12] In the days of Isaiah, God used the conquering Assyrians to punish Israel for its idolatry. The prophets claimed that the foreign enemy was a tool in the hand of God to keep Israel close to God. God used the Babylonians and the Assyrians, wicked as they were, as instruments of divine wrath. But this deployment of evil for divine purposes did not change the fact that the evildoers would face the judgment of God: "Woe to the Assyrian, the rod of my anger, in whose hand is the club of my wrath!"[13]

The fifth truth about evil is that the apocalyptic horses of conquest, revolution, famine, and disease are catalysts for prayer and worship. The followers of the Lamb are vulnerable to suffering just like everyone else. But what embitters and enrages others ought to drive the believer to Christ. Living as we do in an evil and hostile environment, the followers of the Lamb are dependent on the mercies of God. Worship takes place in the real world of sin and evil, suffering and persecution. The nightly news is a contemporary guide to prayer. Prayer ought to raise our soul-searching sensitivity against complicity in evil's advance. Christ's disciples try hard to mitigate the impact of evil. Instead of benefitting from conquest, war, scarcity, and death, the believer seeks to minimize evil and maximize justice.

The Fifth Seal

[6:9–11] *When he opened the fifth seal, I saw under the altar the souls of those who had been slain because of the word of God and the testimony they had maintained. They called out in a loud voice, "How long, Sovereign Lord, holy and true, until you judge the inhabitants of the earth and avenge our blood?" Then each of them was given a white robe, and they were told to wait a little longer, until the full number of their fellow servants and brothers and sisters were killed just as they had been.*

When the fifth seal is broken we are startled by the cry of martyrs, whose "untimely deaths on earth are from God's perspective a sacrifice on the

12. Jer 27.
13. Isa 10:5.

altar of heaven."[14] The fifth seal reveals an extraordinary prayer meeting. The saints who have gone before have been "slain because of the word of God and the testimony they had maintained." They humbly confess their need for God's grace and zealously pray for the salvation and judgment of God. John envisions them "under the altar," not a literal basement under a heavenly altar, but a figurative altar corresponding to the golden altar of incense near the holy of holies.[15] This fifth seal prayer meeting recalls the revival prayers in Exodus, Nehemiah, and Acts.[16] There is "a compassion and zeal for the flourishing of the church and the reaching of the lost." Their prayers yearn "to know God, to see his face, to glimpse his glory."[17]

The faithful saints cry out to the "Sovereign Lord, holy and true," asking how long the horses of judgment and persecution will be allowed to run wild. The answer comes back, "until the number of their fellow servants and brothers who were to be killed as they had been was completed." We are sobered by the fact that time is measured not in conversions, but in martyrdoms. "We are uncomfortable with the response which calls the saints to rest a little longer," writes Miroslav Volf. "God's patience is costly not simply for God, but for the innocent."[18] The "white robe" each martyr is given is a symbol of purity.[19] They are clothed in the righteousness of Christ.

These are the saints who suffered Taliban atrocities in Afghanistan and the crackdown against Christians in Iraq. Some are martyrs from Nigeria, slain by the ruthless Boko Haram. Many are victims of North Korea's brutal regime. Under the altar there are new converts from Sri Lanka, who were targeted and killed by radical Buddhists. Some of the praying saints are from Saudi Arabia and Iran. There are Egyptian and Syrian believers who are praying, "How long?"

Prayer is the link that ties us to the Lord of history. Prayer expresses our shared anticipation of Christ's second coming and our shared community with those who have gone before. Their longing becomes our longing, their hope our hope. They are not dead and buried, but alive and waiting! We may place a premium on personal security and entertainment, but the fifth seal offers the perspective of the martyrs. Their voices

14. Mounce, *Revelation*, 157.

15. Exod 30:1–20; Lev 4:7; see Rev 8:3–5; Heb 9:4.

16. See Exod 33; Nah 1; Acts 4.

17. Keller, *Center Church*, 73.

18. Volf, *Exclusion and Embrace*, 299–300.

19. Rev 1:14; 3:5, 18; 4:4; 7:9, 13; 19:8, 14.

cry out, "O Sovereign Lord, holy and true, how long before you will judge and avenge our blood on those who dwell on the earth?" In the company of the saints who have gone before we confront real life and feel the weight of glory. John's Spirit-inspired vision calls for courage, endurance, and perseverance. When the peace and power of Christ are available, why settle for the survival tactics of the world? Christians believe that there is real hope in a world that is constantly trying to adapt to hopelessness.

The fifth seal is a call to honor the eighth Beatitude: "Blessed are those who are persecuted because of righteousness, for theirs is the kingdom of heaven."[20] The saints who have gone before are praying the psalms just as we are. Their prayers are reminiscent of Asaph's prayer, "Why should the nations say, 'Where is their God?' Let the avenging of the outpoured blood of your servants be known among the nations before our eyes!"[21] They cry out, "When the foundations are being destroyed, what can the righteous do?" The saints respond, "The Lord is in his holy temple; the Lord is in his heavenly throne. He observes everyone on earth; his eyes examine them. The Lord examines the righteous, but the wicked, those who love violence, he hates with a passion. On the wicked he will rain fiery coals and burning sulfur; a scorching wind will be their lot. For the Lord is righteous, he loves justice; upright people will see his face."[22]

The Sixth Seal

[6:12–17] *I watched as he opened the sixth seal. There was a great earthquake. The sun turned black like sackcloth made of goat hair, the whole moon turned blood red, and the stars in the sky fell to earth, as figs drop from a fig tree when shaken by a strong wind. The sky receded like a scroll, rolling up, and every mountain and island was removed from its place.*

Then the kings of the earth, the princes, the generals, the rich, the mighty, and everyone else, both slave and free, hid in caves and among the rocks of the mountains. They called to the mountains and the rocks, "Fall on us and hide us from the face of him who sits on the throne and from the wrath of the Lamb! For the great day of their wrath has come, and who can withstand it?"

20. Matt 5:10.
21. Ps 79:10.
22. Ps 11:3–7.

The sixth seal propels us forward, moving us from the current chaos of evil to the coming cataclysmic undoing of everything. This is the first of seven ends, each of which describes the end of the end. In the prophetic tradition, John describes the end as a finality that is as good as done. The reality of judgment was meant to reassure believers that justice would prevail. The sequence of intensifying endings establishes the truth from which believers can live with courage and hope. In addition to the description of the sixth seal, six more climactic ends will be described.[23]

The prophet describes history coming to its ultimate end. The great earthquake shakes the world loose.[24] The imagery of a blackened sun, a blood-red moon, and stars falling out of heaven like rotting fruit describe a cataclysmic end. Suddenly the sky rolls up like a snapped window shade. Mountains and islands give way. This expectation of final judgment calls believers to be wise advocates and patient defenders of the mercy of God. For we know that "The Lord is not slow in keeping his promises. . . . He is patient . . . not wanting anyone to perish, but everyone to come to repentance."[25]

The Wrath of the Lamb

The wrath of the Lamb is strikingly paradoxical. The wrath of the Lion would make more sense than the "wrath of the Lamb," except for the fact that the wrath of God can only be understood in the light of the cross. No one can stand up to the wrath of the Lamb, but no one needs to unless they adamantly refuse to accept the mercy of God.[26] The Lamb of God who takes away the sin of the world stands eager to redeem. Nevertheless, both the high and mighty and the down and out refuse to receive God's mercy; they would rather die than yield. In words strikingly reminiscent of the humanity's sinful fall, they call to the mountains and rocks to come down on them, to hide them "from the face of him who is seated on the throne, and from the wrath of the Lamb."[27] Their commitment to self-destruction defies all reason.

23. Rev 9:20–21; 11:13; 14:19–20; 16:17–21; 18:21–24; 19:17–21.
24. See Joel 2:30–31; Hag 2:6–7.
25. 2 Pet 3:8–9.
26. Nah 1:6; Mal 3:2.
27. Rev 6:16; see Gen 3:8.

There is no hint in the Revelation that supports universalism. Those who reason that sooner or later God's mercy prevails and everyone gets out of the hell they have chosen—that everyone meets Jesus, whether they are atheist or agnostic, Muslim or Hindu—cannot base their conclusion on the book of Revelation. Some popular Christians have said that there is no final judgment and that the wrath of God never needed to be propitiated by Christ's substitutionary atonement. One leading contender for this perspective is Rob Bell, who speculates, "What makes us think that after a lifetime, let alone hundreds or even thousands of years, somebody who has consciously chosen a particular path away from God suddenly wakes up one day and decides to head in the completely opposite direction?"[28] Bell believes that everybody is saved sooner or later, whether knowingly or anonymously, in this life or in the ages to come. Heaven and hell are within you, and eventually heaven wins. Bell resolves the dilemma of human destiny not through divine providence, but through the eventual good sense of the existential self to determine the right path in open-ended freedom.

In the Revelation there is a powerful sense of the utter finality of God's judgment and a vivid description of the unthinkable and persistent rejection of God's mercy. John appears to be drawing here on the Prophet Isaiah's description of the Day of the Lord:

> And the haughtiness of man shall be humbled, and the lofty pride of men shall be brought low, and the Lord alone will be exalted in that day. And the idols will utterly pass away. And the people shall enter the caves of the rocks and the holes of the ground, from before the terror of the Lord, and from the splendor of his majesty, when he rises to terrify the earth.[29]

It boggles the mind that people prefer self-annihilation to humbling themselves before God.[30] Divine mercy drags out the end again and again, but the conditions for salvation and damnation do not change: they are fixed. John's vision of the end warns us that people are angry enough to prefer death to the atoning sacrifice of the Lamb.[31] The sixth

---

28. Bell, *Love Wins*, 104–5.

29. Isa 2:17–19.

30. Luke 23:29–30.

31. Volf, *A Public Faith*, 50. "The book of Revelation rightly refuses to assume that all evil will either be overcome by good or self-destruct. It therefore cannot exclude the possibility of divine coercion against persistent and unrepentant evildoers. Those who refuse to be redeemed from violence to love by the means of love will be excluded from

seal affirms both hope and despair: the faithful are saved, while the "earth dwellers" are lost. Jacques Ellul is helpful when he writes, "Revelation is disconcertingly unsentimental in its portrayal of both God and evil. Indeed, much of the therapeutic force of the Apocalypse may well be to purge us of some of our fantasies concerning God."[32] All these abominable images of judgment "are under the cover, under the signification, under the embrace of the love of the Lamb."[33]

Christ has "disarmed the powers and authorities, he made a public spectacle of them, triumphing over them by the cross."[34] "Yet at the present we do not see everything subject to them. But we do see Jesus, who was made a little lower than the angels for a little while, now crowned with glory and honor because he suffered death, so that by the grace of God he might taste death for everyone."[35] The bad news is that the four horses of the apocalypse are still riding hard—evil runs wild. The good news is that Christ and his salvation are the supreme realities, not evil. And living by God's grace for the sake of Christ does not remove us from these harsh realities, but places us in the midst of them. "Do not be overcome by evil, but overcome evil with good."[36] "I have told you these things, so that in me you may have peace. In this world you will have trouble. But take heart! I have overcome the world."[37]

We live between two exclamations. The four living creatures say in a voice like thunder, "Come!" and the four wild stallions of conquest, war, scarcity, and disease ride hard across the human plane. But there is

the world of love. . . . In the context of the whole Christian faith, it is best described as a symbolic portrayal of the final exclusion of everything that refuses to be redeemed by God's suffering love. Will God in fact exclude some human beings in the end? Not necessarily. I called the divine coercion 'possible,' for it is predicated on human refusal to be made into the world of love. Will some people refuse? I hope not—and the Bible along with the best of the Christian tradition has never affirmed with certainty that some will refuse and therefore be excluded. The crucial question for our purposes is whether this possible divine coercion at the end of history sanctions actual human violence in the middle of it. The response that resounds throughout the New Testament, including the book of Revelation, is a loud and persistent no! Though imitating God is the height of holiness, there are things that only God may do. One of them is to deploy violence" (Volf, *A Public Faith,* 50). Volf's perspective here may be too sanguine. God's judgment of evil is not only possible, it is promised.

32. Mangina, *Revelation,* 97.

33. Ellul, *Apocalypse,* 123.

34. Col 2:15.

35. Heb 2:8–9.

36. Rom 12:21.

37. John 16:33.

another exclamation in the Revelation that focuses our attention. Jesus says, "Look, I am coming soon!"[38] He repeats the promise three times for emphasis. And the Spirit and the bride say, "Come!" And John encourages all who have ears to hear say "Come!" adding, "Let those who are thirsty come; and let all who wish take the free gift of the water of life."[39] To be faithful and fruitful the church must embrace both exclamations. We are not surprised by evil; we know it's coming, and hard. And we know the only redemptive resolution and restoration is the coming of Jesus, the Alpha and Omega, the Lamb of God, who takes away the sin of the world.

Chapter six ends with a rhetorical question: "For the great day of their wrath has come, and who can withstand it?"[40] Who, indeed? Who can stand when the sun goes black, the moon turns red, and the mountains give way? The answer is no one. The biblical understanding of human depravity and the secular philosophy of nihilism hold this truth in common. Nihilism admits humanity cannot stand, but a biblical understanding of depravity knows why. Secular culture vacillates between optimism and despair.

Jonathan Edwards is remembered for his famous "Sinners in the Hands of an Angry God" sermon, preached in the town of Enfield, Connecticut, on July 8, 1741. His text was from Deuteronomy: "Have I not kept this in reserve and sealed it in my vaults? It is mine to avenge; I will repay. In due time their foot will slip; their day of disaster is near and their doom rushes upon them."[41] Edwards began his sermon by asserting with conviction: "There is nothing that keeps wicked people at any one moment out of hell, but the mere pleasure of God . . . his sovereign pleasure."[42] "What are we," Edwards asked, "that we should think to stand before him, at whose rebuke the earth trembles, and before whom the rocks are thrown down?" Edwards pictured unconverted people walking over the pit of hell on a rickety bridge about to give way. Instead of turning to God they devised schemes to evade the judgment of God, but of course, "death outwitted them and God's wrath was too quick for them."[43] Edwards reasoned that people without God have no safety net. They are held in the hand of God over the pit of hell, "all that preserves them every

38. Rev 22:12.
39. Rev 22:17.
40. Rev 6:17.
41. Deut 32:34–35.
42. Edwards, "Sinners in the Hands of an Angry God," 50.
43. Ibid., 50–51.

moment is the mere arbitrary will, and uncovenanted, unobliged forbearance of an incensed God."[44]

Edwards warned, "However unconvinced you may be now of the truth of what you hear, by and by you will be fully convinced of it."[45] He challenged his listeners to consider the worst punishment they could possibly imagine on earth, and that is nothing compared to the fierceness of the wrath of God. Edwards quoted the words of Jesus: "I tell you, my friends, do not be afraid of those who kill the body and after that can do no more. But I will show you whom you should fear: Fear him who, after the killing of the body, has power to throw you into hell. Yes, I tell you, fear him."[46] Edwards warned, "How dreadful is the state of those that are daily and hourly in danger of this great wrath and infinite misery! But this is the dismal case of every soul in this congregation that has not been born again, however moral and strict, sober and religious, they may otherwise be."[47] According to the Revelation, Jonathan Edwards preached the gospel the way it should be preached. Edwards believed in eternal damnation and in the power of the gospel to save for all eternity. What Edwards preached is true: "But today, you have an extraordinary opportunity, a day wherein Christ has thrown the door of mercy wide open, and stands calling, and crying with a loud voice to poor sinners. . . . How awful it is to be left behind on that day!"[48]

44. Ibid., 55.
45. Ibid., 57.
46. Luke 12:4–5.
47. Edwards, "Sinners in the Hands of an Angry God," 62.
48. Ibid., 63.

16

Deliverance in Tribulation

⌁· Revelation 7:1–17 ·⌁

[7:1–8] *After this I saw four angels standing at the four corners of the earth, holding back four winds of the earth to prevent any wind from blowing on the land or on the sea or on any tree. Then I saw another angel coming up from the east, having the seal of the living God. He called out in a loud voice to the four angels who had been given power to harm the land and the sea: "Do not harm the land or the sea or the trees until we put a seal on the foreheads of the servants of our God." Then I heard the number of those who were sealed: 144,000 from all the tribes of Israel.*

From the tribe of Judah 12,000 were sealed, from the tribe of Reuben 12,000, from the tribe of Gad 12,000, from the tribe of Asher 12,000, from the tribe of Naphtali 12,000, from the tribe of Manasseh 12,000, from the tribe of Simeon 12,000, from the tribe of Levi 12,000, from the tribe of Issachar 12,000, from the tribe of Zebulun 12,000, from the tribe of Joseph 12,000, from the tribe of Benjamin 12,000.

IF THE REVELATION IS taken out of the twilight zone, some pretty amazing things happen. It is no longer complicated religious calculus, but the compelling call to patient endurance and faithfulness intended by God. The Apostle John invents no new truth; the truth is still the same: God in

Christ is reconciling the world to himself. Salvation is by grace through faith, and the atoning sacrifice of the cross of Christ is central to our faith. Evil charges forth, but it is not the supreme reality. Heaven and hell are real. Salvation and judgment are coming. Jesus is Lord. The interpretive key for understanding the Revelation is the Bible. The Apostle John is creatively sharing the gospel, revealing the risen Lord, calling for faithfulness, and comforting the saints.

He was an artist whose palate of symbols and metaphors included all the primary colors of biblical truth. He mixed and blended these symbols from the Old and New Testaments into vivid images and high-impact truth. In chapter seven his subject is eternal security. He affirms the words of Jesus, "I tell you the truth, whoever hears my word and believes him who sent me has eternal life and will not be condemned; he has crossed over from death to life."[1]

The 144,000

The last chapter ended with a question: "Who can withstand?" Revelation seven answers that question. The unsealings recorded in chapter six reveal the complexity and perversity of evil, but "the unsealings are more than matched by the sealings that protect persons of faith from the eternal consequences of historical evil."[2] Four angels are waiting at the four corners of the earth.[3] The stampede of evil is superseded by supersonic evil; the four horses of the apocalypse are transcended by four angels who cover the four points of the compass and everything in between. But the angels are prevented from causing harm until the servants of God are sealed.

The importance of sealing the servants of God has its roots in Ezekiel's vision. The righteous who grieve over the wickedness tolerated in Jerusalem are marked for preservation. The sealing was a figurative way of saying the Lord knew and protected each person who belonged to him. "Then the Lord called to the man clothed in linen who had the writing kit

---

1. John 5:24.

2. Peterson, *Reversed Thunder*, 82.

3. Mangina, *Revelation*, 109. Mangina: "Four is the number of the cosmos, of created totality, as we saw with the four living creatures in the heavenly worship. Charged with power over the elements of earth, air, water, and fire, these angels have been granted authority to restrain or set loose the fury of God's judgment upon the world" (*Revelation*, 109).

at his side and said to him, 'Go throughout the city of Jerusalem and put a mark on the foreheads of those who grieve and lament over all the detestable things that are done in it.'" In Ezekiel's vision the Lord gave specific directions: "Follow him through the city and kill, without showing pity or compassion. Slaughter the old men, the young men and women, the mothers and children, but do not touch anyone who has the mark."[4]

The metaphor of sealing goes back to circumcision and the Passover, when the people of God were identified by the shedding of blood. Circumcision was a sign of the covenant between Yahweh and Abraham and his descendants, and the blood on the doorposts on the night of the Passover in Egypt preserved the life of every firstborn male.[5] The Apostle Paul used the language of sealing to describe God's stamp of ownership on those in Christ: "God's solid foundation stands firm, sealed with this inscription: 'The Lord knows those who are his.'"[6] "Having believed, you were marked in him with a seal, the promised Holy Spirit, who is a deposit guaranteeing our inheritance until the redemption of those who are God's possession—to the praise of his glory."[7] "Now it is God who makes both us and you stand firm in Christ. He anointed us, set his seal of ownership on us, and put his Spirit in our hearts as a deposit, guaranteeing what is to come."[8] "As the imperial seal showed what belonged to the emperor, so the Christian 'seals' of baptism and the Holy Spirit showed what belonged to God."[9]

Who then are these servants of God, these 144,000 from all the tribes of Israel? This symbolic number, twelve squared then multiplied by a thousand, signifies the believing community. Jews and Gentiles are included together. The number represents all those who are preserved and protected at the end of the age. Not a single soul is lost. Some commentators believe that the 144,000 refer exclusively to ethnic Jews because of the reference to the twelve tribes of Israel.[10] But it is important to note

4. Ezek 9:3–6.

5. Gen 17; Exod 12.

6. 2 Tim 2:19.

7. Eph 1:13–14.

8. 2 Cor 1:21–22.

9. Mangina, *Revelation*, 110.

10. We conclude that the symbolic number represents the twelve tribes of Israel and the twelve apostles squared (Rev 14:1–5; 21:12–14). The tribe of Judah is listed first, emphasizing both the messianic (Gen 49:10) and the military nature (Num 2:3; 7:12; 10:14) of the arrangement. The tribe of Joseph represents Ephraim (Ezek 37:15–23) and there is no special significance to the omission of Dan. Some scholars have speculated

that John has already applied the Old Testament promises made to Israel to the church and he has defined the "true Jew" as a follower of Christ, whether Jew or Gentile.[11] The church is the community of the New Jerusalem and the destiny of the people of God is not divided between Jews and Gentiles.[12] As the apostle said so clearly: "There is neither Jew nor Gentile, slave nor free, male nor female, for you are all one in Christ Jesus. If you belong to Christ, then you are Abraham's seed, and heirs according to the promise."[13] Jesus has won the victory through his sacrificial death on the cross, not only for Jews, but for all God's people from all the nations. "St. John hears the number of the sealed as 144,000. When he looks, he sees a multitude that no one can number. Sound is 'rhymed' with sight."[14]

The Great Multitude

[7:9–17] *After this I looked, and there before me was a great multitude that no one could count, from every nation, tribe, people and language, standing before the throne and in the front of the Lamb. They were wearing white robes and were holding palm branches in their hands. And they cried out in a loud voice: "Salvation belongs to our God, who sits on the throne, and to the Lamb." All the angels were standing around the throne and around the elders and the four living creatures. They fell down on their faces before the throne and worshiped God, saying: "Amen! Praise and glory and wisdom and thanks and honor and power and strength be to our God for ever and ever. Amen!" Then one of the elders asked me, "These in white robes—who are they, and where did they come from?" I answered, "Sir, you know." And he said, "These are they who have come out of the great tribulation; they have washed their robes and made them white in the blood of the Lamb. Therefore they are before the throne of God and serve him day and night in his temple; and he who sits on the throne will spread his tent over them. Never again will they hunger; never again will they thirst. The sun will not beat down on them, nor any scorching heat. For the Lamb at the center*

---

that the tribe of Dan was suspected of apostasy.

11. Rev 2:9, 26–27; 3:9, 12.

12. Rev 21:9–13; Rom 11:25–32.

13. Gal 3:28–29; see Matt 19:28; Phil 3:3; Gal 6:16; 1 Cor 10:11; Eph 2:12, 19: 3:6; 1 Pet 2:9–10.

14. Peterson, *Reversed Thunder*, 84.

before the throne will be their shepherd; he will lead them to springs of living water. And God will wipe away every tear from their eyes.'"

The true Israel is "a great multitude that no one could count, from every nation, tribe, people and language, standing before the throne and in front of the Lamb."[15] Chapter seven is divided in two parts, like two stanzas of the same hymn. Both stanzas picture the people of God: the first stanza describes the last generation of believers, who experience the final collapse of civilization. They are sealed by the blood of the Lamb and delivered victoriously by the Lion of Judah; their salvation is assured. The second stanza illustrates the great multitude who have come out of the great tribulation. Together these two groups make up the body of Christ and stand as one before the throne. They embody the success of the great commission. Their white robes signify the purity of the righteousness of Christ. Their palm branches symbolize their celebration and adoration of God. Their loud voices proclaim the truth without hesitation or equivocation: "Salvation belongs to our God, who sits on the throne, and to the Lamb." And their affirmation harmonizes with the great choir in heaven, who declare boldly, "Amen! Praise and glory and wisdom and thanks and honor and power and strength be to our God for ever and ever. Amen!" Richard Bauckham explains,

> The vision of the 144,000 and the innumerable multitude in chapter 7 forms a parallel to that of the Lion and the Lamb in chapter 5. Just as in 5:5–6, John *heard* that the Lion of Judah and the Root of David had conquered, but *saw* the slaughtered Lamb, so in chapter 7 he *hears* the number of the sealed (7:4) but *sees* an innumerable multitude (7:9). It seems likely, therefore, that the relation between the 144,000 and the innumerable multitude is intended to be the same as that between the Lion and the Lamb.[16]

The Messianic Army and True Militancy

This 144,000 signifies the army of the conquering Messiah. "Jesus is not only our Friend, but our Commanding Officer. . . . We disciples are not only his family; we are his troops."[17] This army fights with the strategic

15. Rev 7:9.

16. Bauckham, *The Climax of Prophecy*, 215–16.

17. Bruner, *The Gospel of John*, 891.

initiatives and tactically shrewdness of the sacrificial Lamb of God. "The weapons we fight with are not the weapons of the world."[18] The vision of a messianic army under the leadership of the Lamb fits with the Apostle Paul's description of the full armor of God. "All the armor language is a way to talk about identification with God and his purposes."[19] To recognize "the devil's schemes" is to see the world from God's perspective. There is a demonic source and energy behind atrocities and catastrophes. Human culpability plus demonic activity magnifies and compounds evil beyond human calculation. These are the evils of genocide, the sex slave industry, the brainwashed child warriors of Uganda, witchcraft and animism, and the ideological captivity of the West.

In Hitler's Germany leading up to and during World War II, German Christendom was divided between the German Christian movement, which was pro-Nazi, and the Confessing Church, known for its courageous resistance to the Führer and the Third Reich. German Christians were known for being anti-Jew, anti-doctrine, and strong supporters of a "manly" church. They emptied the apostle's armor metaphor of all biblical meaning and filled it with Nazi propaganda. In an effort to appease the Nazi and neo-pagan critics who charged the church with weakness, humility, and defeatism, German Christians identified themselves as the "storm troopers of the church." As they said, they didn't want a church for old ladies—they wanted a soldier's church with manly qualities. German Christians claimed that their militant, nationalistic church inspired bravery, hardness, and heroism. They claimed that the German nature demanded a "fighting Christ," not a cowardly Christ who assumed the guilt of others. As one leading German Christian said, "We can naturally have nothing to do with a little lamb kind of Christianity."[20]

The Confessing Church saw through this blasphemy. They called out the German Christian anti-Jew, anti-doctrine, manly church for what it really was—heresy. They risked their lives to stand up to Hitler. German Christians and their "manly" church capitulated to the horrors of Nazism, while Confessing Church leaders Martin Niemoller, Dietrich Bonhoeffer, Karl Barth, and many others risked their lives to defend the faith. The "manly" church was the weak church, a tool in the hand of Hitler, used for his demonic advantage. But the Confessing Church was the strong church, faithful to the Lord Jesus Christ and marked by the

18. 2 Cor 10:4.

19. Snodgrass, *Ephesians,* 339.

20. Bergen, *Twisted Cross,* 74.

cross. They put on the full armor of God and "[took their] stand against the devil's schemes."[21]

The right kind of militancy is essential if we are going to be useful in the Lamb's army. The tendency to politicize the witness of the church, whether to the left or right, confuses its testimony. When the militancy of an ideology is substituted for the militancy of the Lamb, Christians end up being driven more by fear than the gospel. A sure sign that the spirit of the 144,000 is missing is when Christians panic and say, "This is the end! There's no hope!" Tim Keller observes, "This may be a reason why so many people now respond to U.S. political trends in such an extreme way. . . . They become agitated and fearful for the future. They have put the kind of hope in their political leaders and policies that once was reserved for God and the work of the gospel."[22]

The vulnerability of Christians to spiritual deception only increases as they deploy the weapons of the world against their political opponents. The vitriolic rhetoric and slander expressed by Christians against politicians is an indication not of strength and boldness, but of fear and hate. Three vital factors deserve serious consideration: (1) the depth and intensity of evil, (2) the sociology of cultural change, and (3) a theology of the end. Failure to grasp any one of these perspectives leads to fear, anger, and a worldly militancy. Zeal for social change without a true awareness of evil, insight into culture, and confidence in God's sovereign control of the end produces frustration and resentment. The Revelation is an antidote to this uninformed zeal because it provides an in-depth understanding of evil that is consistent with the sociology of cultural change and a biblical view of the end. The mission of the 144,000 is not to change as many "hearts and minds" as possible and mount a political campaign to overturn laws protecting abortion rights and gay marriage. Their true mission is to "go and make disciples of all nations, baptizing them in the name of the Father and of the Son and of the Holy Spirit, and teaching them to obey everything I have commanded you."[23] Christians need to better understand how to be pro-life and pro-marriage without being intimidated by the world and lashing out in anger and fear.

The agenda for the 144,000 is not to change the world but to follow the Lamb "wherever he goes."[24] The culture belongs to the world,

21. Eph 6:11.

22. Keller, *Counterfeit Gods*, 99.

23. Matt 28:19–20.

24. Rev 14:4.

and that is not going to change. For many the American Dream stands for the pursuit of happiness, individual rights, and democratic rule. This national ideology is materialistic and pluralistic, dedicated to a form of tolerance that is intolerant of absolute truth claims. In the midst of the spiritual war Christians find themselves in, it is best to refrain from "nation building." The Christian before the world is like Jesus before Pilate. Believers must hear these words to stay on mission: "My kingdom is not of this world. If it were, my servants would fight to prevent my arrest by the Jewish leaders. But now my kingdom is from another place."[25]

The Great Tribulation

One of the elders asked John, "These in white robes—who are they, and where did they come from?" John deferred, "Sir, you know," and the elder was eager to explain. "These are they who have come out of the great tribulation; they have washed their robes and made them white in the blood of the Lamb." In other words, "They have been where you are, John, and look at them now!" The great tribulation is not only in the future, but in the here and now as well. It began at the cross and will end when Christ comes again; in the meantime, it continues. "In the world you will have tribulation," Jesus said. "But take heart; I have overcome the world."[26] Along a similar line, Peter encouraged believers, "Do not be surprised at the painful trial you are suffering, as though something strange were happening to you."[27]

The tribulations' intensities may vary, yet fierce resistance to the gospel continues, and the Christian is called to remain faithful. The struggles will be intense.[28] To all believers John offered encouragement: on this side of eternity we belong to the 144,000, signed, sealed, and delivered, while on the other side we belong to the great multitude. This company of the committed has responded to the great commission and passed through the great tribulation. This tribulation "consists of pressures to

25. John 18:36.

26. John 16:33.

27. 1 Pet 4:12. Osborne remarks: "The question arises as to how saints are to be at one and the same time protected and killed.... The answer is to realize that the two apply to different aspects of these last days. The saints are protected from the wrath of God but are not protected from the wrath of the beast. They will ... suffer from the persecution of the earth-dwellers" (*Revelation*, 302).

28. See Dan 12:1–4; Matt 24:15–31; Mark 13:14–27; Luke 21:20–28.

compromise the faith, these pressures coming from within the church community through seductive teaching and from without through overt oppression. . . . The greatness of the tribulation is the intensity of the seduction and oppression through which believers pass."[29] Joseph Mangina writes, "No one escapes the great tribulation. The real question for contemporary Western Christians is whether we view martyrdom as an exotic relic from an age long past, or whether we stand in solidarity with the martyrs who are even now offering up their costly witness."[30]

John's congregations identified this description with the Abrahamic blessing, and the palm branches recalled the Festival of Tabernacles.[31] The scene draws us back to the earlier description of the worship of the Lamb and evokes joyful worship.[32] The saints sing and pray with emotional abandonment and physical energy. They are shouting in a loud voice, standing to sing, and then falling down on their faces before the throne to pray. Extraordinary worship and prayer shifts our attention from ourselves and focuses on the mission of God and his eternal salvation, the forgiveness of sins and Christ's atoning sacrifice for our redemption. To be washed in the blood of the Lamb is not an archaic metaphor, but the very best way to understand our true worth. When we are assured of our salvation by God's grace through faith in Christ, our self-assurance and self-confidence will reflect our true identity in Christ.

Chapters six and seven, recounting the unsealing of evil and the sealing up of everlasting life, belong together. Chapter six concludes with a picture of judgment; chapter seven concludes with a picture of salvation. The Bible presents two destinies: hell and heaven; awful reckoning and awesome rejoicing. Followers of the Lamb keep both destinies in view. The worshiping multitude is the picture of human flourishing. The redeemed are centered around throne of the Lamb and blessed with purpose, security, provision, protection, and guidance. The pastoral images of shepherding are drawn from the Old Testament.[33] The Lord will wipe away the tears of the suffering church and restore true meaning and purpose to all of life.

---

29. Beale, *Revelation*, 433–34.
30. Mangina, *Revelation*, 115.
31. See Gen 16:10; 32:12; Lev 23:40-43; Neh 8:15.
32. Rev 4:1—5:14.
33. Isa 49:9; Ps 23.

17

Evil Unleashed

⌁· Revelation 8:1—9:21 ·⌁

[8:1–13] When he opened the seventh seal, there was silence in heaven for about half an hour. And I saw the seven angels who stand before God, and seven trumpets were given to them. Another angel, who had a golden censer, came and stood at the altar. He was given much incense to offer, with the prayers of all God's people, on the golden altar before the throne. The smoke of the incense, together with the prayers of God's people, went up before God from the angel's hand. Then the angel took the censer, filled it with fire from the altar, and hurled it on the earth; and there came peals of thunder, rumblings, flashes of lightning and an earthquake.

Then the seven angels who had the seven trumpets prepared to sound them. The first angel sounded his trumpet, and there came hail and fire mixed with <u>blood</u>, and it was hurled down on the earth. A third of the earth was burned up, and all the green grass was burned up.

The second angel sounded his trumpet, and something like a huge mountain, all ablaze, was thrown into the sea. A third of the sea turned into <u>blood</u>, a third of the living creatures in the sea died, and a third of the ships were destroyed.

The third angel sounded his trumpet, and a great star, blazing like a torch, fell from the sky on a third of the rivers and on the springs of water— the name of the star is Wormwood. A third of the waters turned bitter, and many people died from the waters that had become bitter.

The fourth angel sounded his trumpet, and third of the sun was struck, a third of the moon, a third of the stars, so that a third of them turned dark. A third of the day was without light, and also a third of the night.

As I watched, I heard an eagle that was flying in midair call out in a loud voice: "Woe! Woe! Woe to the inhabitants of the earth, because of the trumpet blasts about to be sounded by the other three angels!"

THE OPENING OF THE seventh seal is anticipated with reverential silence, intense prayer, and an all-out uproar in nature: "peals of thunder, rumblings, flashes of lightning and an earthquake." The first four trumpet blasts announce devastating judgment over the earth, oceans, rivers, and sky. There are layers of judgment and backup systems of destruction. John's choice of images and metaphors are familiar to students of the Bible. He draws upon a long history of plagues and punishments designed by God to check evil. Humanity has been in mortal danger ever since the fall, "For the wages of sin is death."[1] Only the mercy of God preserves the human race. The Bible says a great deal about judgment and the wrath of God, much more than many Christians care to admit. Salvation history is replete with warning, admonition, correction, and condemnation. Humankind is often "put on notice"; warning gives way to verdict, and indictment leads to sentencing. Catastrophic judgment is described from beginning to end. God is deadly serious about finishing off evil once and for all. "The certainty of God's just judgment at the end of history is the presupposition for the renunciation of violence in the middle of it."[2]

Trumpet Blasts of Judgment

Before the trumpets blow there is a period of silence in heaven. The silence in heaven is in contrast to the cacophony of babble and bluster on earth. What follows on earth is in response to prayer: not rote, repetitive prayer, but passionate, intense prayer.[3] The scene in heaven portrays the sacrificial nature of genuine prayer.[4] Prayer is fire from the

1. Rom 6:23.
2. Volf, *Exclusion and Embrace*, 302.
3. Rev 8:3; see 6:10.
4. Mounce, *Revelation*, 182.

altar hitting the earth with thunder, rumblings, flashes of lightning, and an earthquake. There is nothing meek and mild about these prayers. This is not a brass ensemble playing a courtly trumpet fanfare. These are bugle blasts of judgment announcing war against evil. They are orchestrating judgment; their jarring sound invokes a soul-churning battle cry. The Prophet Joel knew what the sound of the trumpet meant: "Blow the trumpet in Zion; sound the alarm on my holy hill. Let all who live in the land tremble, for the day of the Lord is coming. It is close at hand."[5] Jeremiah dreaded the sound the trumpet: "Oh, my anguish, my anguish! I writhe in pain. Oh, the agony of my heart! My heart pounds within me, I cannot keep silent. For I have heard the sound of the trumpet; I have heard the battle cry."[6]

What are we to make of this storm of hail and fire mixed with blood and hurled to the earth? Is this John's description of an atomic bomb and nuclear fallout? Some interpreters have thought so. Did John mean to describe a literal hail and lightning storm, one so fierce and destructive it would burn up a third of the earth's trees and all of the earth's grass? Fertile imaginations gone wild picture meteors crashing into rivers and streams and poisoning the water supply, erupting volcanoes spewing out deadly ash, and a cosmic energy brownout causing the lights to go out in the universe. But the purpose of these trumpet blasts is not to give a literal description of coming natural disasters: the purpose of the trumpets is to announce God's judgment against evil.

The first four trumpet blasts evoke the biblical memory of the Egyptian plagues, with which God liberated his people from oppression and bondage. The trumpet blasts can be heard above the decimal-defying dissonance of human depravity. The blare of the trumpet is like a car alarm in the middle of the night or the piercing alert of a smoke alarm. To a hard-hearted, hard-of-hearing humanity God announces judgment. The trumpets broadcast the de-creation of nature, the desecration of the cosmos, and the deconstruction of the world. The whole created order is in peril and we are put on notice.

God's wrath is literal, but the description of how the judgment is to be executed is figurative. We can debate what John had in mind when he spoke of hail and fire and rivers of blood, but we can hardly debate the meaning of God's judgment. This is what the trumpets are blaring in a

5. Joel 2:1.
6. Jer 4:19; see Josh 6:4–5; Zeph 1:14–16.

global Jericho, and the seemingly impenetrable walls of a this-worldly worldview are about to come crashing down.[7] The trumpet blasts announce creation's frailty. There is no safe place to flee from the consequences of evil. The Egyptian plagues were designed "to systematically demolish every god-illusion or god-pretension that evil uses to exercise power over men and women."[8] The trumpet blasts in the Revelation fulfill that same purpose. They herald the sovereignty of God against biological determinism, philosophical materialism, and metaphysical naturalism. Nature does not rule—God rules. The Egyptian plagues were used "to discredit the Pharaoh's claim to sovereignty and to establish the sovereignty of Yahweh in its place."[9]

The Egyptian plagues served a double purpose: they challenged the sovereignty of the Egyptian worldview and vindicated the word of God through his prophet Moses. The plagues punished the Egyptians for their hardness of heart and purged the Hebrews "of all envious admiration of evil."[10] We cannot extract the purpose of judgment from the plagues, because the clash of sovereignties will always result in judgment. G. K. Beale inspects the nuances of the dual nature of the Egyptian plagues and Revelation's trumpets to declare God's sovereignty over his creation and to harden the hearts of those who refuse to accept God's omnipotence: "The trumpets must ultimately be understood as punishments that further harden the majority of people. The trumpets are not intended to coerce unbelieving idolaters into repentance but primarily to demonstrate to them God's uniqueness and incomparable omnipotence. The trumpets also serve to demonstrate human hardness, which is expressed in persistence in idolatry (Rev 9:20–21) and their persecution of the saints (Rev 6:9–11)."[11]

Judgment is strewn throughout the Scriptures. The Revelation finishes what God began in Genesis; first, the flood, then the Tower of Babel, followed by the fate of Sodom and Gomorrah. The ten plagues against

---

7. Beale, *Revelation,* 468. Beale: "The primary background here is the story of the fall of Jericho, where trumpets announced the impending victory in a holy war. That this is at work in Revelation is evident from the parallel of seven trumpets blown by seven priests (Joshua 6) or seven angels (Revelation 8–9), who are priestly figures (15:5–6)" (*Revelation,* 468).

8. Peterson, *Christ Plays in Ten Thousand Places,* 162.

9. Ibid., 165.

10. Ibid., 162.

11. Beale, *Revelation,* 467.

Egypt fit this picture.[12] We recoil in horror at Israel's mandate to destroy the Canaanites. We are shocked at God's liberal use of the destructive conquest of Assyria, Babylon, and Rome to check evil and accomplish God's will. Contrary to popular opinion the New Testament does not soften the hard-line messages of the Old Testament: it "actually engraves them more deeply."[13] Jesus drove the message of judgment home. "With great earnestness he called on everyone to repent and with great compassion he invited those weighed down with cares and sorrows to come to him for rest. Yet this very Jesus uttered the most terrible warnings, not once or twice, but again and again."[14]

John's vision alternates between powerful worship and devastating wrath. In this spiraling intensity of God's wrath the four plagues directed against nature (earth, oceans, rivers, and sky) correspond to the four horses of the apocalypse. The opening of the first four seals depict judgments against human sinfulness. The trumpets reveal the active involvement of God in bringing punishment upon a wicked world.[15] Just as Adam and Eve were forced to live in a hostile environment, so are we. The reality of the fall prevails, with no sign of easing. The severity of the ecological, pathological, political, and spiritual destruction is bad and getting worse. John revisits the Exodus plagues on a cosmic scale.

The correspondence between Pharaoh's rule and Caesar's dominion can be expanded to include the sovereign American self. We are a nation of little Pharaohs and Caesars, with each person intent on ordering his or her own private universe. But we are not the masters of the universe we think we are. As John's trumpet announcements prove, we are helpless before nature's upheavals. Floods, hurricanes, tornadoes, fires, earthquakes, global warming, and drought should impress upon us our vulnerability. We live on a fragile planet hurtling through space. Earth dwellers can either humble themselves before the living God or harden their hearts the way Pharaoh did.

---

12. Exod 7–11; 14:28.

13. Wenham, *The Goodness of God*, 21.

14. Ibid., 20. See Matt 5:29–30; 10:15, 28; 11:21–24; 12:31, 36, 41–42; 13:49; 16:26; 18:6–8; 25:30; Mark 8:36–37; Luke 10:12–15.

15. Beale, *Revelation*, 488. Beale: "The first four trumpet woes could also represent a wide range of sufferings brought on people because of their idolatrous trust in the temporary world system instead of in the eternal God. The sufferings are continual reminders of the impermanence of the idolatrous object of the earth-dwellers' trust. The sufferings are the deficiencies in the world's resources, which the ungodly depend on to meet their needs" (*Revelation*, 488).

The Apostle John's description of the complexity of evil spares the followers of the Lamb any illusion of world conquest. In a community marked by the cross, triumphalism is not an option. We "seek first his kingdom" and we "take captive every thought to make it obedient to Christ," not because we expect to heroically change the world, but because we have been called to be faithful.[16] Christians fight the impact of the fall and the consequences of evil, not with the weapons of the world, but in the full armor of God.[17] John's description of the trumpet blasts is a warning against underestimating the perversity of evil and the power of the rulers of this age.

To be faithful requires believers to distance themselves from the spirit of the age. In humility, the followers of the Lamb give up their ambition for worldly power and control. The Apostle Paul's description remains current: "Not many of you were wise by human standards; not many were influential; not many were of noble birth. But God chose the foolish things of the world to shame the wise; God chose the weak things of the world to shame the strong. God chose the lowly things of the world and the despised things—and the things that are not—to nullify the things that are, so that no one may boast before him."[18] It appears that the weaker believers are in the eyes of the world, the stronger they are spiritually. A person defined by the cross of Christ invariably appears foolish to the world. The Apostle John describes a culture in which Christians do not belong to the elite. They don't leverage institutional power and shape the social network. This is not because "they don't believe enough, or try hard enough, or care enough, or think Christianly enough, or have the right worldview."[19] Faithfulness to Christ runs contrary to the dominant culture, and the benefit of understanding this truth encourages humility, cultivates realism, reduces anxiety, removes false guilt, and builds resilience. Futility and cynicism are countered by a realistic appraisal of the power of evil. The inspiration for keeping the lampstand lit and the witness bright comes not from human charisma and confidence, but from the power and wisdom of the Holy Spirit.

16. Matt 6:33; 2 Cor 10:5.
17. 2 Cor 10:4; Eph 6:11.
18. 1 Cor 1:26–29.
19. Hunter, *To Change the World*, 89.

Apollyon's Army

[9:1–21] *The fifth angel sounded his trumpet, and I saw a star that had fallen from the sky to the earth. The star was given the key to the shaft of the Abyss. When he opened the Abyss, smoke rose from it like the smoke from a gigantic furnace. The sun and sky were darkened by the smoke from the Abyss. And out of the smoke locusts came down on the earth and were given power like that of scorpions of the earth. They were told not to harm the grass of the earth or any plant or tree, but only those people who did not have the seal of God on their foreheads. They were not allowed to kill them but only to torture them for five months. And the agony they suffered was like that of the sting of the scorpion when it strikes. During those days people will seek death but will not find it; they will long to die, but death will elude them.*

The locusts looked like horses prepared for battle. On their heads they wore something like crowns of gold, and their faces resembled human faces. Their hair was like women's hair, and their teeth were like lion's teeth. They had breastplates like breastplates of iron, and the sound of their wings was like the thundering of many horses and chariots rushing into battle. They had tails with stingers, like scorpions, and in their tails they had power to torment people for five months. They had as king over them the angel of the Abyss, whose name in Hebrew is Abaddon and in Greek is Apollyon (that is, Destroyer). The first woe is past; two other woes are yet to come.

The sixth angel sounded his trumpet, and I heard a voice coming from the four horns of the golden altar that is before God. It said to the sixth angel who had the trumpet, "Release the four angels who are bound at the great river Euphrates." And the four angels who had been kept ready for this very hour and day and month and year were released to kill a third of the world's people. The number of the mounted troops was two hundred million. I heard their number.

The horses and riders I saw in my vision looked like this: Their breastplates were fiery red, dark blue, and yellow as sulfur. The heads of the horses resembled the heads of lions, and out of their mouths came fire, smoke and sulfur. A third of the people were killed by the three plagues of fire, smoke and sulfur that come out of their mouths. The power of the horses was in their mouths and in their tails; for their tails were like snakes, having heads with which they inflict injury.

The rest of the people who were not killed by these plagues still did not repent of the work of their hands; they did not stop worshiping demons, and idols of gold, silver, bronze, stone and wood—idols that cannot see or hear or walk. Nor did they repent of their murders, their magic arts, their sexual immorality or their thefts."

THE FIFTH TRUMPET BLAST is introduced by an eagle flying in midair and calling out in a loud voice, "Woe! Woe! Woe to the inhabitants of the earth, because of the trumpet blasts about to be sounded by the other three angels!"[20] This ominous warning comes as the fifth trumpet sounds and a star falls from the sky to the earth. The star unlocks the abyss and releases an army of locusts from a bottomless pit. The extent and intensity of these evil "woes" is demonic. When the shaft of the abyss is opened, evil escalates exponentially; the lid on evil is blown off. The fallen star invokes the memory of satanic activity.[21] The fifth trumpet signifies the free reign of evil. The "god of this world" is busy blinding the minds of unbelievers, "so that they cannot see the light of the gospel that displays the glory of Christ, who is the image of God."[22]

The message is clear: God is sovereign over evil. Demonic agents are unable to make a move without God's permission. The fallen angel who unlocks the abyss uses a metaphoric key to release the evil powers. But why does the Lord allow this fallen star to open the abyss and escalate the power of evil? The fifth trumpet blast unveils a cosmic parable, revealing what believers know to be true about evil and judgment: "God gave them up in the lusts of their hearts to impurity . . . God gave them up to dishonorable passions . . . God gave them up to a debased mind to do what ought not to be done."[23]

The Apostle John's first woe recalls the Prophet Joel's graphic description of devastation wrought by an onslaught of locusts.[24] But these wild creatures are not ordinary locusts; they are more like war horses prepared for battle. Their gold-crowned heads have the look of victory, their appearance is hauntingly human, and their long flowing hair is a sign of beauty and vitality. Their teeth are fierce like a lion's and their

20. Rev 8:13.

21. Luke 10:18. This fallen star is not the same as the "angel coming down from heaven" in Revelation 20:1.

22. 2 Cor 4:4.

23. Rom 1:24, 26, 28.

24. Joel 2.

iron breastplates suggest invincibility. Their wings make them mobile and their tails sting mercilessly. This demonic evil is under the royal rule of Apollyon, the "Destroyer"—the name, title, and image point to Satan. John may have intended a hidden meaning behind this name. The Greeks derived the name Apollo from the same Greek verb that is the root of Apollyon. The Roman emperor Domitian assumed the name Apollo. The reigning Caesar may have struck John as the appropriate symbol for the evil underworld. "The locust was one of the symbols of the god Apollo."[25]

The sixth trumpet signals the release of four angels, "who are bound at the great river Euphrates."[26] These four angels have been waiting for this very moment. They release a two-hundred-million-man army mounted on fire-breathing monsters. These armored war horses bear the heads of lions and belch out fire, smoke, and sulfur. Three devastating plagues come out of their mouths, wiping out a third of the people. But no matter how devastating these judgments are, people refuse to repent and turn from their wicked ways.[27] But there is still more to come. "The first woe is past; two other woes are yet to come."[28] Each step spirals into more horrific episodes of evil and destruction. The first woe describes pain and torment. The second woe leads to death, as a third of mankind is wiped out by the two-hundred-million-man army mounted on fire-breathing monsters. This unimaginable calvary does not symbolize an actual military attack with napalm, cruise missiles, or fifteen-ton bunker busters; John never intended a literal description of weapons of mass destruction. The third woe is left dangling, ready to fall. It is pending and there is no end in sight.

John wrote in metaphor and symbol. "Wormwood" is shorthand notation for bitterness and death.[29] The release of the four angels who were bound at the great river Euphrates and the march of a two-hundred-million-man army does not point to Russia or China, but to the power of evil emanating from the cradle of human civilization.[30] Evil is systemic to the human condition. The five-month locust infestation (five months being the life cycle of locusts) describes a limited period of time in which nature attacks people who do not belong to God with such ferociousness

25. Mounce, Revelation, 198.

26. Rev 9:14.

27. Rev 9:20–21; see Rev 6:15–17.

28. Rev 9:12.

29. Rev 8:11; see Jer 9:12–15.

30. Rev 10:14–16.

that they would rather die than go on living. In the Spirit, John's images of war and destruction were given to impress believers with the wrath of God. The trumpet blasts do more than announce the pending judgment: they produce shock and awe. Each powerful blast projects graphic pictures of disaster and devastation. John keeps "piling up the monstrous metaphors" to show that the "demons are ferocious and dreadful beings that afflict people in a fierce, appalling, and devastating manner."[31] His metaphors point to Satan, the ancient serpent, whose ambition from the beginning has been to deceive and destroy. From the serpent's line in Genesis, "did God really say . . . ?" to the description in the Revelation, "the power of the horses was in their mouths and in their tails; for their tails were like snakes, having heads with which they inflict injury," Satan's purpose has always been to betray and torment. What is said here corresponds to what the Apostle Paul wrote to the Thessalonians.[32]

God's holy love will stop at nothing. The six trumpet blasts of warning and doom show the extent to which God will go to get the world's attention. In this cosmic confrontation, God will even destroy his own creation to bring humanity to its senses.[33] The Apostle John's prophecy describes an intensity of evil that is foreign to the imagination of most American Christians. We are in the habit of ignoring the truth of God's judgment. But if God goes to such lengths to warn humanity, should we not be more concerned to declare the gospel in the face of evil? "We may need to challenge more, and comfort less, in our evangelism and discipleship."[34] The trumpet judgments are "strictly limited." "They are warning judgments," insists Richard Bauckham, "designed to bring humanity to repentance." But they don't work. "Judgments alone, it is implied, do not lead to repentance and faith."[35] What is apparent is that God provides "sufficient opportunities for spiritual reform," proving not only his sovereignty but his justice.[36] The Apostle Peter said it well: "The Lord is not slow in keeping his promise, as some understand slowness. Instead he is patient with you, not wanting anyone to perish, but everyone to come to repentance."[37] "God will judge," writes Miroslav Volf, "not because God

31. Beale, *Revelation,* 510.

32. 2 Thess 2:7–10.

33. Wilcock, *Revelation,* 95.

34. Lovelace, "Evangelicalism," 25.

35. Bauckham, *The Theology of the Book of Revelation,* 82.

36. Beale, *Revelation,* 518.

37. 2 Pet 3:9.

gives people what they deserve, but because some people refuse to receive what no one deserves; if evildoers experience God's terror, it will not be because they have done evil, but because they have resisted to the end the powerful lure of the open arms of the crucified Messiah."[38] To put this another way, to resist the love of God is the greatest evil we will ever do.

If God's wrath and the consequences of evil are imaginary, if there is no final judgment day, if there is no hell, then Christians have no reason to shout "Fire!" But if the house is burning and danger is imminent, then Christ's love motivates believers to "rescue the perishing and care for the dying." John shouts "Doom!" and "Danger!" at the top of his lungs with his Spirit-inspired vision. But against all reason many, refuse to get out of the burning building.

38. Volf, *Exclusion and Embrace*, 298.

18

Witness

◦ Revelation 10:1–11 ◦

[10:1–11] *Then I saw another mighty angel coming down from heaven. He was robed in a cloud, with a rainbow above his head; his face was like the sun, and his legs were like fiery pillars. He was holding a little scroll, which lay open in his hand. He planted his right foot on the sea and his left foot on the land, and he gave a loud shout like the roar of a lion. When he shouted, the voices of the seven thunders spoke. And when the seven thunders spoke, I was about to write; but I heard a voice from heaven say, "Seal up what the seven thunders have said and do not write it down."*

Then the angel I had seen standing on the sea and on the land raised his right hand to heaven. And he swore by him who lives for ever and ever, who created the heavens and all that is in them, the earth and all that is in it, and the sea and all that is in it, and said, "There will be no more delay! But in the days when the seventh angel is about to sound his trumpet, the mystery of God will be accomplished, just as he announced to his servants the prophets."

Then the voice that I had heard from heaven spoke to me once more: "Go, take the scroll that lies open in the hand of the angel who is standing on the sea and on the land." So I went to the angel and asked him to give me the little scroll. He said to me, "Take it and eat it. It will turn your stomach sour, but in your mouth it will be as sweet as honey." I took the little scroll from the angel's hand and ate it. It tasted as sweet as honey in my mouth, but when I had eaten it, my stomach turned sour. Then I was told, "You must prophesy again about many peoples, nations, languages and kings."

JOHN'S VISION OF THE mighty angel "coming down from heaven" refocuses the followers of the Lamb on their crucial responsibility. Robed in a cloud, with a rainbow above his head and his face shining like the sun, the angel reminds believers of how they are to be *in* the world, but not *of* the world. Ever since we learned that only the Lamb was worthy to open the scroll we have been waiting expectantly for full disclosure—the message that lies behind the seals. The impact of the stampede of evil and the trumpet blasts of judgment have not changed mercy-resistant hearts. People still refuse to repent and turn to Christ for salvation, and the vile message of Satan continues to cause untold injury. The people "who were not killed by the plagues" would rather die than repent and worship the living God.[1] Trumpeted doom introduces the witnessing church in action. The lid has been lifted, evil is unleashed, and its devastating impact is global. No one can escape the trio of woes, except those who have been sealed by the living God. The earth is ravaged and the wrath of God is released against unrepentant, godless, self-worshiping idolaters.

Yet evil and judgment are never the last word, nor is evil ever the whole picture. Before heaven proclaims that "The kingdom of the world has become the kingdom of our Lord and of his Christ, and he shall reign forever and ever," earth receives Christ's final witness.[2] Between orchestrated judgments and the hallelujah chorus, the mission of the church is described. The followers of Christ do not run for cover when they hear the trumpet blasts; for them, the sound of the trumpet is a call to witness. They cannot change the world, but they can be transformed by Christ in the world. Only God can change the world. Salvation and judgment await. In the meantime, the church is called to love as Christ loves the world. They "regard no one from a worldly point of view," because they have been given "the message of reconciliation" and appointed "Christ's ambassadors."[3]

The followers of the Lamb live in anticipation of the fullness of life promised in Christ. Everlasting life has already begun. The abundant

1. Rev 9:20.
2. Rev 11:15.
3. 2 Cor 5:16–21.

life is now.[4] God intended believers "to grasp the organic connection between what we are called to do and become in the present and what we are promised as full, genuine human life in the future."[5] Our witness is not about our happiness or fulfillment. "It's about God and God's kingdom, and [our] discovery of genuine human existence by the paradoxical route—the route God himself took in Jesus Christ!—of giving [ourselves] away, of generous love which constantly refuses to take center stage."[6]

Jesus is described as "the faithful witness" and those who follow him bear witness to his gospel. The church finds in Antipas—the only named disciple in the book of Revelation—her true identity. Christ calls this martyr "my faithful witness," and that is what we are to become.[7] In chapters ten and eleven, the church is called to witness by the mighty angel, the old apostle, and the two witnesses. These two witnesses are martyred and resurrected before the watching world. They embody the life and witness of the church. Loud voices in heaven celebrate the church's commission and cheer her on. The twenty-four elders pray before the throne of God for the church, and announce that "the time has come" for judgment and reward.

The Mighty Angel

In John's one act drama the witness of the church reaches its high point. There is a positive tension between the heavenly authority of the mighty angel and the earthly vulnerability of the witnessing church. Out of love, God intended this glorious paradox. In the tradition of Jesus, the witnessing church offers no coercion or manipulation; the gospel is never imposed on the world. The mighty angel coming down from heaven, robed in a cloud, encircled by a rainbow, whose face is shining like the sun and whose legs are like fiery pillars, is the picture of divine authority. But the gospel is always delivered with lamb-like vulnerability. The mighty angel recalls the earlier mighty angel, who proclaimed in a loud voice, "Who is worthy to break the seals and open the scroll?"[8] John intended a parallel between the two angels and the two scrolls.

4. John 10:10.
5. Wright, *After You Believe*, 68.
6. Ibid., 70.
7. Rev 2:13.
8. Rev 5:2.

The mighty angel dominates the scene before us. "He planted his right foot on the sea, and his left foot on the land, and he gave a loud shout like the roar of a lion." The shout alone reminds us of the Lion of the tribe of Judah.[9] The Prophet Daniel described "one like a son of man, coming with the clouds of heaven."[10] Ezekiel envisioned a "figure like that of a man" surrounded by a brilliant rainbow in the clouds.[11] His face shining like the sun causes us to think of John's opening vision of "someone like a son of man."[12] His legs are like fiery pillars, recalling the Lord's guidance of the people of Israel in the wilderness.[13] All the descriptive features of this mighty angel remind us of God himself and Christ in particular, but John stops just short of drawing out this identification. The ambiguity may be a way of emphasizing the full spectrum of divine authority within the triune God, stretching from the angel of the Lord to one like a son of man. The presence of the mighty angel stands for the revelation of God in every form, from theophany to incarnation. The little scroll has the absolute backing of divine authority.

A voice from heaven silences the seven thunders to indicate that another series of plagues is unnecessary. We might have expected a fourth series of judgments impacting half of the earth; the seals covered a quarter of the earth, and the trumpets a third. But an additional stage leading up to the full judgment of the bowls is preempted.[14] The purpose of divine judgment—to lead sinners to repentance—has been met with resistance every step of the way. People would rather blame God than repent and turn from their idolatrous ways. In the face of judgment, earth dwellers insist on rebellion. Their commitment to idolatry, violence, and sexual immorality is unwavering.

The mighty angel takes an oath reminiscent of Daniel's prophecy. Daniel envisioned "The man clothed in linen, who was above the waters of the river" lifting his right hand and left hand toward heaven, swearing "by him who lives forever," and saying, "It will be for a time, times and half a time. When the power of the holy people has been finally broken, all these things will be completed."[15] Heavenly authority and human

9. Rev 5:5.

10. Dan 7:13.

11. Ezek 1:26–28.

12. Rev 1:12–16.

13. Exod 13:22.

14. Bauckham, *The Theology of the Book of Revelation*, 82.

15. Dan 12:7; Rev 6:11.

weakness are set in juxtaposition. The full number of martyred believers is about to be reached. The church is given no hint of success and every indication of suffering. The loud voice of the mighty angel with one foot planted on the sea and the other planted on land is in stark contrast to the exiled disciple who is about to have a stomachache.

The "little scroll" in the hands of the mighty angel is distinguished from the scroll opened by the Lamb in chapter five only by size. The believer's ability to bear witness is a little book or booklet compared to Christ's volume, but it is the same message—the gospel of Jesus Christ. The scrolls may not be identical but they share a similar meaning. Both scrolls are "symbolic of God's plan of judgment and redemption, which has been inaugurated by Christ's death and resurrection," and both scrolls "concern the destiny of peoples, nations, tongues, and tribes/kings."[16]

Take and Eat

John is told by the mighty angel to eat the book. Like Ezekiel the watchman, John is called to take in God's intelligible revelation as if it were food.[17] Christ's disciples follow the lead of the prophets. Faith in the Lord Jesus is far more radical than we ever dreamed it would be. Those who limit faith to positive sentiments and good ideas soon find that God and his Word are greater more than we bargained for. The Bible endangers our old way of living. No number of well-crafted sermons will ever replace the importance of hearing the whole counsel of God personally and prayerfully. We cannot live off the spiritual experience of others; we need to take in the word of God for ourselves. Nor does it work for us to experience God for ourselves alone. The goal of worship is not an enriched spiritual life, but a life useful for God's kingdom work. Devotion that leads only to positive personal feelings forsakes God's call to witness.

The vivid analogy of eating dates back to the prophets Ezekiel and Jeremiah, who were commanded to eat God's revelation.[18] The prophets took in the intelligible revelation of God as if it were food. They were to live, as we are to live, not on spiritual recipes for better living, but on the word of God itself. Feeding on God's revelation is the ultimate picture of

16. Beale, *Revelation,* 527. See Rev 5:9–10; 10:11.

17. Ezek 3:3.

18. Ezek 2:8—3:3; Jer 15:16.

personal participation. We cannot stand aloof or sit in judgment of the truth of God when we are eating it up! As long as we are talking about religion we can intellectualize the faith, but the moment we begin to take it in and absorb it into our bloodstream we are transformed by it. There is a huge difference between a motivational talk from Jesus and the gospel of Christ transforming every fiber of our being!

"Take and eat" evokes the Eucharist and recalls the promise of the Savior: "Here I am! I stand at the door and knock. If anyone hears my voice and opens the door, I will come in and eat with them, and they with me."[19] The mission of God depends on this eating. It is not the rote ritual of observing Lord's Supper that will satisfy this appetite and strengthen the church for witness—only a steady diet of the word of God will equip the saints for the works of service, "so that the body of Christ may be built up until we all reach unity in the faith and in the knowledge of the Son of God and become mature, attaining to the whole measure of the fullness of Christ."[20]

Malnourished Christians

Have we given up on a close, careful, life-shaping reading of the biblical text? Perhaps it has never been easy to ingest the word of God. But in this age awash with Christian resources at our fingertips, designed for easy accessibility and composed at a fourth grade reading level, we have nearly hit the wall when it comes to hearing God's word. The canon for most Christian young people is not the canon of Scripture but Hollywood's cinematic blockbusters. Pastors lament biblical illiteracy and Christian publishers justify their popular best sellers as what the market wants. In an age of information overload there is "a famine of hearing the words of the Lord."[21]

A trained incapacity to think and communicate on anything other than the shallow level of small talk, sound bites, and instant messaging has been acquired over time with remarkable ingenuity. The culprits messing up communication can be identified easily enough. We have known what is happening, but we have been seemingly powerless to do anything about it. We have retreated from the Word by choosing numbers

19. Rev 3:20.
20. Eph 4:12–13.
21. Amos 8:11.

over thought, scanning over reading, and images over words. Ironically, we have chosen this for ourselves. Our intentional dumbing down has required sophistication and intelligence. We have undergone a cultural shift from words to images that has shrunk our attention spans and decreased our capacity to weigh ideas, compare and contrast assertions, connect one generalization to another, and understand what moves us.[22] The impact of retreating from the word, scanning over reading, cobbling together a customized worldview, and preferring images over words has not only changed the way we communicate, but the way we think.

When we "eat this book," our lives cannot help but be transformed. Mongolian believer Gantumur Badrakh shows what it means to translate the word of God into a new life. In 2001, he taught English at the Defense University of Mongolia. He was abruptly removed from his teaching position without explanation. Sometime later his principal told him that he was ordered by the commander to fire Gantumur because of his Christian faith. The principal defended Gantumur. Besides being an excellent English instructor, Ganturmur had never spoken of Christ in the classroom. The commander replied, "I don't care. He is teaching who he is, even without saying it."[23]

A Sour Stomach

"I took the little scroll from the angel's hand and ate it. It tasted as sweet as honey in my mouth, but when I had eaten it, my stomach turned sour."[24]

John's vision relates to Ezekiel's prophecy in three ways. First, we have noted the connection to the vision of the mighty angel.[25] Second, there is a direct parallel to the invitation to eat the scroll.[26] Third, Ezekiel's description of the eschatological temple of God corresponds with John's calling to measure the temple.[27] John's description of the two witnesses and the temple picks up Ezekiel's temple theme.[28]

22. Postman, *Amusing Ourselves*, 51, 54.

23. Gantumur Badrakh is a graduate of Beeson Divinity School. His story is used with permission.

24. Rev 10:10.

25. Ezek 1:26–28.

26. Ezek 3:3.

27. Ezek 40–48.

28. Rev 11:1–4.

John saw the Prophet Ezekiel as the epitome of the God-hardened communicator. After Ezekiel ate the scroll that "tasted as sweet as honey," he was sent home to his own people. The Lord made it clear that Ezekiel's apparent lack of success in changing lives was not his fault. He did not lack the divine authority, human courage, or Spirit-led creativity necessary to drive God's message home. Yet he knew from the beginning that he was being sent to a people who were "obstinate and stubborn."[29] With divine authority the prophet delivered God's message relentlessly for some twenty years (593 BC–573 BC) without the benefit of acceptance. Ezekiel was conscious of undertaking his ministry of the word in the power of the Spirit of God. "The Spirit then lifted me up and took me away, and I went in bitterness and in the anger of my spirit, with the strong hand of the Lord on me."[30]

The Apostle John compares the witness of the church to the witness of Ezekiel. The message of God's sovereign will and redemptive love is "sweet." The church has good news to proclaim and practice in a lost and needy world, but this "sweet" gospel meets with "bitter" resistance. "The gospel, although it embodies God's 'yes' to humanity, is also the occasion of offense. It is vulnerable to rejection, and this rejection will be aimed not just at the message but at the messenger."[31] Ezekiel confronted what we experience today: the easy dismissal of God's revelation, the entitlement of personal opinion, and the bias in favor of existential-felt needs. Ezekiel knew the power of God's enduring truth. It may have been sweet to the taste, "as honey in my mouth," but it was difficult to swallow and he "went in bitterness and in the anger of [his] spirit, with the strong hand of the Lord upon [him]." The followers of the Lamb abide in the enduring tradition of Ezekiel and John. They are sensitive to the beauty and power of the gospel to meet the eternal needs of people for whom Christ died. They have heard the divine imperative, "You *must* prophesy again about many peoples, nations, languages and kings."[32]

Christ's witness is vulnerable to distortion and corruption. Egos and idols get in the way of the gospel. For believers, any form of elitism "is despicable and utterly anathema to the gospel they cherish."[33] "Once we are clear about our own role, as bit-players in God's great drama," writes

29. Ezek 2:4.

30. Ezek 3:14.

31. Mangina, *Revelation*, 132.

32. Rev 10:11.

33. Hunter, *To Change the World*, 94.

N. T. Wright, "we are free, in a way that we might not have been if we were still struggling to think of ourselves as moral heroes in the making, to see what an astonishing vocation we actually have, and hence to reflect on how that works out in the present time."[34] The divine imperative to witness "moves in the opposite direction of social theory."[35] What works in the world doesn't work in the church. The authority and source of the message lies outside of culture and cannot be judged as having any practical value by culture. The world cannot help the church deliver the gospel, because everything the world stands for counters and contradicts the gospel. If we deliver a generic gospel of the parenthood of God and the brotherhood of man, then the world can embrace it. If we are pushing a God and country gospel, or a prosperity gospel, or a felt-need gospel, then the world can endorse it. But if we preach Jesus Christ crucified, we are setting ourselves up for rejection. The Jesus-is-Lord gospel has no voice on Wall Street or in Hollywood. The gospel of the Lamb is not considered authoritative speech at Harvard or Stanford. It has no political clout or entertainment value. The gospel that says "the wages of sin is death, but the gift of God is eternal life in Christ Jesus our Lord" is not accepted in a court of law or in the public press.[36]

The gospel is neither drawn from the ideologies of the world nor driven by the powers of the world. Christ's gospel must be free from the will to power. Beatitude-based belief, with salt and light impact, seeks heart righteousness, not political power or social leverage. The gospel of free grace is free of coercion and manipulation. And those who bear faithful witness to the gospel should never expect the world's approval.

---

34. Wright, *After You Believe*, 71.
35. Hunter, *To Change the World*, 95.
36. Rom 6:23.

19

The Measure of the Mission

⤙· Revelation 11:1–19 ·⤚

[11:1–14] *I was given a reed like a measuring rod and was told, "Go and measure the temple of God and the altar, with its worshipers. But exclude the outer court; do not measure it, because it has been given to the Gentiles. They will trample on the holy city for 42 months. And I will appoint my two witnesses, and they will prophesy for 1,260 days, clothed in sackcloth." They are the two olive trees and the two lampstands, and they stand before the Lord of the earth. If anyone tries to harm them, fire comes from their mouths and devours their enemies. This is how anyone who wants to harm them must die. They have power to shut up the sky so that it will not rain during the time they are prophesying; and they have power to turn the waters into blood and to strike the earth with every kind of plague as often as they want.*

Now when they have finished their testimony, the beast that comes up from the Abyss will attack them, and overpower and kill them. Their bodies will lie in the public square of the great city, which is figuratively called Sodom and Egypt, where also their Lord was crucified. For three and a half days many from every people, tribe, language and nation will gaze on their bodies and refuse them burial. The inhabitants of the earth will gloat over them and will celebrate by sending each other gifts, because these two prophets had tormented those who live on the earth.

But after the three and a half days the breath of life from God entered them, and they stood on their feet, and terror struck those who saw them. Then they heard a loud voice from heaven saying to them, "Come up here." And they went up to heaven in a cloud, while their enemies looked on.

At that very hour there was a severe earthquake and a tenth of the city collapsed. Seven thousand people were killed in the earthquake, and the survivors were terrified and gave glory to the God of heaven. The second woe is passed; the third woe is coming soon.

JOHN'S COMMISSION TO "PROPHESY again about many peoples, nations, languages and kings" leads to the work of measuring the temple of God.[1] The commission and the command go hand in hand. The contrasting images of the mighty angel and the old apostle underscore the tension between authority and vulnerability. John is called to cordon off the temple of God, the altar, and the worshipers from the Gentiles. The word of God serves as the measuring tool. The preached word, the prayed word, the sung word, and the lived word function to secure and protect the people of God. This is what it means to "go and make disciples of all nations, baptizing them in the name of the Father and of the Son and of the Holy Spirit, and teaching them to obey everything I have commanded you."[2] The images identify the eschatological community of God made up of individuals from every people, nation, language, and nationality. The measuring of the temple corresponds to the sealing of the 144,000. "Believers throughout the entire Christian age are in view."[3]

Drawing Boundaries

The gospel is as exclusive as it is inclusive. The message is addressed to every people group, nation, language, and political order, but it identifies, defines, and separates. To measure is to draw a line, set a boundary, and seal the membership. To identify true worshipers is to determine who is in and who is out. The court of the Gentiles is the arena of the pagans, and its inhabitants are excluded from worship by their own choice. John sees two cities at war: the Holy City that is being trampled, on and the great

1. Rev 10:11.
2. Matt 28:19–20.
3. Beale, *Revelation*, 561.

city that has the appearance of power but is certainly doomed. The opposition to the witness is international and violent. To measure the temple of God is to protect the people of God, but the nature of this security system is very different from erecting another "dividing wall of hostility."[4] In an effort to preserve the purity and integrity of their heritage, the Jews built a moral and spiritual barrier between themselves and the rest of humanity. Nowhere was this moral and spiritual wall more evident than in the literal stone wall that surrounded the temple in Jerusalem. The outer court of the Gentiles surrounded the temple, and excluded Gentiles from entering it. The Jewish historian Josephus described signs in Greek and Latin posted on pillars warning foreigners not to enter. Archeologists have discovered two of these signs, one of which is on display in a museum in Istanbul and reads, "No foreigner may enter within the barrier and enclosure around the temple. Anyone who is caught doing so will have himself to blame for his ensuing death."[5]

The act of measuring circumscribes the identity of the people of God. John is like a watchman on duty. He is entrusted with a life-saving responsibility—people's lives depend on being within the boundary of God's will and word. To be good watchmen does not require ingenuity or eloquence, but it does require that we remain alert to the will of God and the welfare of the people of God. The task itself may be simple, but the responsibility is great: faithfulness is the key.

The role of the watchman was on the mind of the Apostle Paul; it is evident in his many warnings. He listed "the acts of the sinful nature" for the Galatian believers and concluded, "I warn you, as I did before, that those who live like this will not inherit the kingdom of God."[6] It is reflected in his warnings to the believers in Corinth: "I am not writing this to shame you, but to warn you, as my dear children."[7] And in his warning to the believers in Thessalonica, "Warn those who are idle, encourage the timid, help the weak, be patient with everyone."[8] Paul even advised believers to hand a professing believer over to Satan so "the sinful nature may be destroyed and his spirit saved on the day of the Lord."[9] He advised

---

4. Eph 2:14.
5. Stott, *God's New Society*, 92.
6. Gal 5:21.
7. 1 Cor 4:14.
8. 1 Thess 5:14.
9. 1 Cor 5:5.

Timothy, "Warn them before God against quarreling about words."[10] The metaphor of the watchman parallels the Apostle Paul's challenge to Timothy to guard what had been entrusted to his care.[11] It is consistent with Jude's warning to "contend for the faith that was once for all entrusted to the saints."[12] The Apostle Peter challenged believers, "be on your guard so that you may not be carried away by the error of the lawless people and fall from your secure position."[13]

Discernment is never easy. Knowing where and when to draw boundaries is challenging. The impulse may be strong to be "set free from the claustrophobic confinement of sectarianism, opening wide windows and doors to wherever the wind of the Spirit is blowing."[14] But we face the danger of compromising the gospel when we fail to recognize the "false teachers among [us]," who "secretly introduce destructive heresies" and "bring the way of truth into disrepute."[15] Are we free to commend a church leader who questions the virgin birth and bodily resurrection of Christ because they have a winsome personality and gracious manner? The boundaries called for by the word of God are not arbitrary, and they were not meant to be drawn selectively. We cannot guard the church against consumerism and then accept the culture's notions of sex. To be in the world but not of the world is not so easily done. We may take pride in our conservative theology and our staunch moral stand, but be downright worldly in our neglect of the poor and in our greedy ambition for wealth. Our doctrinal stance may be conservative, but our devotion to sports and material success may be idolatrous. We may never miss a Sunday worship service, but we may also spend the rest of the week living only for the self. Ironically, many conservative churches reflect their worldliness in how they go about evangelism and church growth. In the name of winning souls they think like Madison Avenue and act like Walmart.

The gospel doesn't write the culture off. We cannot wash our hands of the whole mess to go about being nice to our friends and living a nice Christian life. Nor does the gospel permit us to become one with the culture, enmeshed in a live-and-let-live ethos that is at its root antichrist. The challenge for the church is to "relate to the world within a dialectic of

10. 2 Tim 2:14.

11. 1 Tim 6:20; 2 Tim 1:14.

12. Jude 3.

13. 2 Pet 3:17.

14. Peterson, *The Pastor*, 68.

15. 2 Pet 2:1–2.

affirmation and antithesis."[16] We are called to engage the world in a way that is a true benefit to everyone. In the Spirit, we are empowered to have a prophetic, fruitful, and insightful witness.

The Temple of God

The imagery of the temple and the altar corresponds to the Prophet Ezekiel's description of the eschatological temple (Ezek 40–48). Ezekiel's prophecy gathers up all the Old Testament ideals for the temple, including the priesthood, the sacrificial system, and the land. Ezekiel pointed beyond a literal reconstruction of the temple. He envisioned the perfect fulfillment of God's promise. The indwelling presence of God, as envisioned by Ezekiel's prophecy, was fulfilled in the coming of Jesus, who completed all that the temple stood for, in ways that Ezekiel may never have imagined.

In the book of Hebrews, Jesus is presented as the completion of the priestly sacrificial system. Christ is the mediator of the new covenant, the great high priest, who offers himself, once and for all, as the perfect sacrifice for our sins.[17] Through Christ we enter into his rest and through the blood of Jesus we have confidence to enter the most holy place. Everything in the old priestly worldview—the Jewish race, the land, the temple, the sacrifices, the priesthood, and the rituals—have been fulfilled and transcended in Christ. "Christians have no territorial center, no physical land or place that is the focus of faith and worship, because Jesus Christ has taken on the full theological and spiritual significance of all that land, city and temple had held for Israel and opened that significance up to people of all nations."[18]

16. Hunter, *To Change the World*, 231.

17. New Testament references to the new covenant present a dilemma for Dispensationalists, who argue with J. N. Darby that the promise of the new covenant applies only to Israel and do not apply to the church (Luke 22:20; 1 Cor 11:25; 2 Cor 3:6; Heb 8:7–13; 9:15; 12:24). Darby insisted that the new covenant was made exclusively with Israel and was to be fulfilled on earth. He tried to resolve the problem by arguing that the church experienced spiritual blessing and the forgiveness of sins, but that did not mean the law was written on believers' hearts (see Henzel, *Darby, Dualism and the Decline of Dispenationalism*, 134–35). Later Dispensationalists have argued a dual new covenant theory. John F. Walvoord wrote, "Most premillenarians (Darby excepted) would agree that a new covenant has been provided for the church, but not the new covenant for Israel" (Walvoord, *The Millennial Kingdom*, 210, quoted in Henzel, *Darby, Dualism, and the Decline of Dispensationalism*, 171).

18. Wright, *The Mission of God*, 341.

The New Testament applies Ezekiel's temple imagery to the church. All those in Christ are "members of God's household, built on the foundation of the apostles and prophets, with Christ Jesus himself as the chief cornerstone. In him the whole building is joined together and rises to become a holy temple in the Lord."[19] Ezekiel's vision of a people who no longer defile God's holy name (Ezek 43:7) is fulfilled by a people who, in Christ, have crucified their sinful nature.[20] His vision of the new temple and of those who are "faithful to its design" have become the temple of the Holy Spirit.[21]

The destiny of the witnessing church is held secure through a defined period of opposition and persecution that lasts for a figurative forty-two months or 1,260 days. This three and a half years is a "broken seven," and recalls Daniel's prophecy: "The holy people will be delivered into his hands for a time, times, and half a time."[22] The number forty-two may stand for Elijah's ministry of judgment, when rain was withheld from Israel for three and a half years, a detail we would not know apart from Jesus telling us.[23] It may symbolize Israel's experience in the wilderness for forty-two encampments.[24] The trampling of the Holy City corresponds to the time when the woman, who is a figure for the people of God, is on the run and is protected in the wilderness for 1,260 days.[25] It also parallels the period when the beast of the sea is given forty-two months to exercise his power.[26]

Two Witnesses in Sackcloth

The two witnesses are dressed in sackcloth, a symbol of repentance and grief. "How we preach the gospel," writes Joseph Mangina, "is as important as when we preach it."[27] Once again absolute divine authority is contrasted with the vulnerability of the word of God. The church cannot

19. Eph 2:19–21.
20. Ezek 43:7; Gal 6:8.
21. Ezek 43:11; 1 Cor 6:19.
22. Mangina, *Revelation*, 135. See Dan 7:25; 9:27.
23. Luke 4:25; 1 Kgs 17–18.
24. Beale, *Revelation*, 565.
25. Rev 12:6.
26. Rev 13:3–5.
27. Mangina, *Revelation*, 136.

afford to throw its weight around and try to match the triumphalism of the "principalities and powers and the rulers of darkness." Sackcloth is the witnessing uniform of the church, because it goes with everything. The full armor of God fits with it perfectly, as do "compassion, kindness, humility, gentleness and patience."[28] "The proclamation of the gospel requires the telling of truth about human sin, including, although by no means limited to, that sin committed by the church itself. The church represents Jesus Christ to the world in the painful awareness that it will often misrepresent him. It is therefore clothed in sackcloth, modeling for the world that turning back to God is the appropriate response to the gospel."[29]

The imagery of the two olive trees and the two lampstands is drawn from the book of Zechariah to signify the witness-bearing power of the church in the last days. The witness of the church is validated in three ways: the two witnesses—brave and courageous; the two olive trees—productive and fruitful; and the two lampstands—discerning and illuminating. The three-fold, doubled-up confirmation of truth characterizes the witness of the church.[30] The spirit of God empowers the church's testimony by giving the body of Christ credibility, energy, and illumination. Nevertheless, the witness of the church meets with brutal persecution. The world treats the church the way the Jerusalem crowd treated Christ.[31]

When the Prophet Zechariah asked for an explanation of the lampstand and the two olive trees, the angel repeated the central thrust of all eight visions contained in Zechariah's prophetic ministry, saying, "This is the word of the Lord to Zerubbabel: 'Not by might nor by power, but by my Spirit,' says the Lord Almighty."[32] Once again, the humble, Spirit-dependent nature of the church's witness is emphasized. The angel goes on to explain that two figures stand at the center of God's revelation to Zechariah: Joshua, the high priest, and Zerubbabel, the political ruler. Together they symbolize the coming Messiah, the branch, who will build the temple of the Lord. "These are the two who are anointed to serve the Lord of all the earth."[33] The imagery in Zechariah's prophecy points forward to Christ—the living word, by the Spirit of Christ, the one and only essential authority needed to achieve God's kingdom purposes. In Christ,

28. Eph 6; Col 3:12.
29. Mangina, *Revelation*, 136.
30. Deut 19:15; John 8:17.
31. Rev 11:8.
32. Zech 4:6.
33. Zech 4:14.

we have what we need to pursue God's kingdom work. The Apostle John's praying imagination captured the essence of Zechariah's vision when he pictured Christ, the great high priest, shining like the sun in all its brilliance, walking amidst the lampstands. This juxtaposition of humble candle power and unlimited Son power remains in today's household of faith.[34]

The two witnesses are targets for persecution, but "If anyone tries to harm them, fire comes from their mouths and devours their enemies."[35] This may sound like a literal and violent defense of the gospel, but the truth of the matter is far from it. The paradox of divine authority and human vulnerability persists. The church is sent out into the world with an extraordinary power at its disposal. But it is the power of the word of God as "a consuming fire."[36] As the Lord said to Jeremiah, and declares to the church today, "I will make my words in your mouth a fire and these people the wood it consumes."[37] The two witnesses are like Elijah: they have "power to shut up the sky so that it will not rain."[38] They are like Moses, who was given power to strike the earth with plagues. John used militant images to capture the power of the word. Christ's mouth is like "a sharp, double-edged sword."[39]

Martyrs in the City

" . . . like those condemned to die in the arena. We have been made a spectacle to the whole universe, to angels as well as human beings."[40]

John has much more to say about the great city and the beast that comes up from the abyss, but he introduces the subject here to give the hearer perspective. The great city consistently refers to Rome in the Revelation.[41] Jerusalem is called Sodom by Isaiah and Ezekiel, but never designated as Egypt.[42] The reference to the crucifixion does not fix the location literally

34. Rev 1:12–16.
35. Rev 11:5.
36. Heb 12:29; Deut 4:24.
37. Jer 5:14.
38. 1 Kgs 17:1.
39. Rev 1:16; 2:12, 16; 19:15, 21; see Isa 11:4.
40. 1 Cor 4:9.
41. Rev 16:19; 17:18; 18:10, 16–21.
42. Isa 1:9–10; Ezek 16:46–49.

in Jerusalem. The great city stands for the depths of moral degradation and is a symbol of oppression and slavery.[43] "The great city in which the martyred church lies dead is the world under the wicked and oppressive sway of the Antichrist."[44] The beast of the abyss is not a single person anymore than the two witnesses are two literal people. The beast signifies all that is antichrist in the great city. The city, called Sodom and Egypt, represents the full extent of culture turned away from God. The great city signifies Rome or Jerusalem or San Diego or New York. John's description corresponds to Daniel's prophecy of the fourth beast: "He will speak against the Most High and oppress his holy people and try to change the set times and the laws. The holy people will be delivered into his hands for a time, times, and half a time."[45] Ever since Christ's sacrifice, the witness of the church has endured the cross. And the Sovereign Lord has determined that the witness of the gospel be given a set duration of forty-two months, or 1,260 days, or three and a half years. This is not "chronos" time, but "kairos" time; not literal time, but God's providential time. The numbers signify a period of grace. The world has been given a window of opportunity to respond to God's mercy.

The inhabitants of the great city despise God's grace, overpower the church, and kill the witnesses. These earth dwellers are those unbelieving idolaters who have been referred to throughout Revelation.[46] The "earth-dwellers" are outraged that the two witnesses, who stand for the witness of the entire church, preach a message not only of salvation but of judgment. Those who deny Christ and embrace idolatry will be subject to judgment.[47] For three and a half days it looks like defeat is the final outcome. The court of the Gentiles, the great city, the place called Sodom, the very place where the Lord was crucified, goes wild with excitement. The bodies are subject to public humiliation and desecration. They are left to rot in the street.[48]

The reason people from every tribe, language and nation can gaze upon the trampled remains of the church is not because of cable television coverage, but because of the global persecution of the church. The relationship of three and a half years of witness to three and a half days

43. Gen 19:4–11.
44. Mounce, *Revelation*, 227.
45. Dan 7:25.
46. Rev 3:10; 6:10; 8:13; 11:10; 12:12; 13:8, 12, 14; 14:6; 17:2, 8.
47. Beale, *Revelation*, 596. See Acts 17:30–31; 1 Thess 1:8–10.
48. Psalm 79 captures the horror of this scene.

of apparent defeat invites comparison to our Lord's earthly ministry and crucifixion. It is not surprising that the church should follow in the footsteps of her Savior and Lord. Nor is it surprising that the defeat is only apparent. The victory of the beast and the celebration of the great city is short-lived. Resurrection power rescues the faithful, those 144,000 who have been sealed. "After the three and a half days the breath of life from God entered them, and they stood on their feet, and terror struck those who saw them."[49] Once again the prophecy of Ezekiel shapes the meaning. The words come out of the prophet's vision of the valley of dry bones: "'Come, breath, from the four winds and breathe into these slain, that they may live.' So I prophesied as he commanded me, and breath entered them; they came to life and stood on their feet—a vast army."[50]

A loud voice from heaven says to them, "Come up here," inviting them to join the great multitude that "no one could count, from every nation, tribe, people and language, standing before the throne and in front of the Lamb."[51] John refers cryptically to a severe earthquake.[52] He uses two numbers to signify the just destruction of the great city; a tenth of the city collapses and seven thousand people are killed. The survivors are terrified and give "glory to the God of heaven."

How are we to interpret their response? Is this a grudging and dreaded recognition of the power of God, or a true act of faith and trust in the living God? Richard Bauckham interprets this as a "remarkably universal, positive result of the witnesses' testimony." Instead of the numbers indicating the totality of judgment (a tenth part of the city and the seven thousand people), Bauckham sees the numbers as an allusion to the faithful remnant.[53] Only this time, nine-tenths of the people escape judgment and one tenth are judged. Instead of the faithful remnant being saved, it is the faithful majority who are saved, because they have come to repentance and faith.[54] G. K. Beale sees the two numbers signi-

---

49. Rev 11:11.

50. Ezek 37:9–10.

51. Rev 7:9.

52. Rev 6:12; see 9:20–21.

53. 1 Kgs 19:18; Isa 6:13; Amos 5:3.

54. Bauckham, *The Theology of the Book of Revelation*, 87. He writes, "In this way, John indicates the novelty of the witness of the two witnesses over against the Old Testament prophets whom he has used as their precedents. This is especially the case in that the reference to the seven thousand alludes to the effect of Elijah's ministry. Elijah was to bring about the judgment of all except the faithful seven thousand, who were spared (1 Kgs 19:14–18). The two witnesses will bring about the conversion of all except

fying "the totality of unbelievers judged at the conclusion of history."[55] The response of the terrified survivors, who give glory to God, find their parallel throughout salvation history. The Apostle Peter admonished believers to "live such good lives among the pagans that, though they accuse you of doing wrong, they may see your good deeds and glorify God on the day he visits us."[56] Peter's admonition reflects the Sermon on the Mount, when Jesus said, "Let your light shine before others, that they may see your good deeds and glorify your Father in heaven."[57] The phrase "give glory to God" appears to have a range of meanings, from merely stating the truth about reality to whole-hearted worship of God. When confronted by Joshua for his theft and deception, Achan is told, "My son, give glory to the Lord, the God of Israel, and honor him."[58] King Nebuchadnezzar glorified Daniel's God enthusiastically, but there is no evidence that he gave up his Babylonian gods.[59] Beale writes, "Nebuchadnezzar was constrained to acknowledge God in much the same way as the world of unbelievers will at the end of the age."[60]

Worship and Witness

[11:15–19] *The seventh angel sounded his trumpet, and there were loud voices in heaven, which said: "The kingdom of the world has become the kingdom of our Lord and of his Messiah, and he will reign for ever and ever." And the twenty-four elders, who were seated on their thrones before God, fell on their faces and worshiped God, saying: "We give thanks to you, Lord God Almighty, the One who is and who was, because you have taken your great power and have begun to reign. The nations were angry, and your wrath has come. The time has come for judging the dead, and for rewarding your servants the prophets and your people who revere your name, both great and small—and for destroying those who destroy the earth."*

---

the seven thousand, who are judged" (*Theology*, 87).

55. Beale, *Revelation*, 603. See Rev 6:12–17.

56. 1 Pet 2:12.

57. Matt 5:16.

58. Josh 7:19.

59. Dan 2:47.

60. Beale, *Revelation*, 604. See Phil 2:10–11.

Then God's temple in heaven was opened, and within his temple was seen the ark of his covenant. And there came flashes of lightning, rumblings, peals of thunder, an earthquake and a great hailstorm.

The seventh trumpet announces a worship scene that is in contrast to the grudging acknowledgment of the glory of God made by terrified survivors of the previous earthquake. In the spiraling intensity of the end, John's images converge, his descriptions overlap, and his meaning sharpens. The second woe passes as the witnesses of the church are persecuted to death, even as the seventh trumpet announces a tremendous worship scene in heaven. Once again, witness and worship are in sync, and heaven and earth are in tandem with the sovereign will of God.[61]

The third woe, like the sword of Damocles, still hangs overhead, threatening imminent danger. But the final trumpet heralds worship, not wrath. The trumpet is heard in heaven, not on earth, and signals thanksgiving, not doom. The trumpet announces the reign of God in Christ, the vindication of the saints and the finality of God's judgment. This ultimate thanksgiving is in a new key. The anger of the nations is in the past and the promise of God has arrived. We will be able to say with the twenty-four elders, who represent the people of God in their totality, "We give thanks to you, Lord God Almighty, who is and who was," and we will not add "who is to come" because Christ will have already come and begun to reign.[62] John's vision of God's open temple in heaven and the ark of the covenant inside symbolizes the very presence of God. Open access to the living, reigning triune God is the experience of all believers.

Through the faithful preaching and practice of God's word and sacrament a protective hedge is set around the body of Christ. To the glory of God and to the benefit of human flourishing true freedom is experienced. Jesus said, "If you hold to my teaching, you are really my disciples. Then you will know the truth, and the truth will set you free."[63] Measuring the temple is John's Spirit-inspired metaphor for preserving the integrity and authenticity of the church. This effort is essentially positive and life-affirming. As David extolled, "The boundary lines have fallen for me in pleasant places; surely I have a delightful inheritance."[64] Setting these parameters of gospel truth and Christian living is neither sectarian

61. Rev 11:15–19.
62. Rev 11:17.
63. John 8:31–32.
64. Ps 16:6.

nor schismatic, but the task requires prayerful discernment and biblical courage. We are holy surveyors mapping out the spiritual footprint of the household of faith.

To outsiders these distinctions and definitions may seem limiting and restrictive, even prejudicial and discriminatory. They are like the tourist who looks out over the ocean on a beautiful day and pays no heed to the lifeguard's warning of dangerous riptides, but swims out anyways and in no time needs to be rescued. Setting the standard is life affirming. As the Apostle Paul made clear, New Testament parameters are not meant to stifle, but to protect.

> Do not be deceived: Neither the sexually immoral nor idolaters nor adulterers nor male prostitutes nor practicing homosexuals nor thieves nor the greedy nor drunkards nor slanderers nor swindlers will inherit the kingdom of God. And that is what some of you were. But you were washed, you were sanctified, you were justified in the name of the Lord Jesus Christ and by the Spirit of our God.[65]

Some insiders "have become persuaded that the world beyond the church tells a bigger and better story than the gospel of the sovereignty and powerful coming of Jesus Christ."[66] They renegotiate the meaning of the gospel surreptitiously, emptying the good news of biblical meaning and filling it with worldly perspectives. They conform the church to "the constitution, definition, parameters, and conditions" of the world and its prevailing stories.[67] "Heresy in the church is the failure to tell that one story truthfully; it is a question of the truthfulness of Christian *teaching*." Doug Harink warns that false teachers often "live apparently saintly lives," but "shifts away from truthful Christian teaching often occur along with, and perhaps as justifications for, unfaithfulness in Christian living."[68]

The exclusivity of the gospel is best measured against the inclusivity of its invitation. As the Apostle Paul said so beautifully, "I am not ashamed of the gospel, because it is the power of God that brings salvation to everyone who believes."[69]

---

65. 1 Cor 6:9–11.
66. Harink, *1 & 2 Peter*, 164.
67. Ibid., 164.
68. Ibid., 166.
69. Romans 1:16.

20

The Christmas Story

ᯈ· Revelation 12:1–6 ·ᯈ

[12:1–6] *A great and wondrous sign appeared in heaven: a woman clothed with the sun, with the moon under her feet and a crown of twelve stars on her head. She was pregnant and cried out in pain as she was about to give birth. Then another sign appeared in heaven: an enormous red dragon with seven heads and ten horns and seven crowns on its heads. Its tail swept a third of the stars out of the sky and flung them to earth. The dragon stood in front of the woman who was about to give birth, so that it might devour her child the moment he was born. She gave birth to a son, a male child, who "will rule all the nations with an iron scepter." And her child was snatched up to God and to his throne. The woman fled into the wilderness to a place prepared for her by God, where she might be taken care of for 1,260 days.*

C. S. Lewis wrote, "History is a story with a well-defined plot pivoted on Creation, Fall, Redemption, and Judgment. It is indeed the divine revelation *par excellence,* the revelation which includes all other revelations."[1] John's Christmas story is the most dramatic story of all. The old apostle offers a cosmic perspective on the birth of Christ. His extraordinary nativity scene hits the canvas of our soul with impact. John pulls in "the word of God and the testimony of Jesus" against a backdrop of popular first-century myths. Thoroughly steeped in Old Testament

1. Lewis, *Mere Christianity,* 103.

images and New Testament truth, John drew on the pagan tradition for dramatic effect. We do something similar when we use plays, novels, and movies to present biblical theology in a fresh light.

John used mythology to declare the power of the incarnate Son of God to defeat the evil one.[2] His congregations knew the story of the great dragon Python. When Python sought to kill Leto, who was pregnant with Zeus' child, Poseidon hid Leto on an island until she gave birth to Apollo. After only four days Apollo was strong enough to slay the dragon. John used the images and metaphors of his time to communicate the good news of Jesus Christ, but even then, the Old Testament and the ministry of Jesus takes precedence in shaping the story.[3] Pastor Darrell Johnson writes,

> Every culture in every corner of the globe has myths about humanity's struggle for peace. Every culture in every place has its "Star Wars." Pluralism is nothing new. The gospel has always had to compete for peoples' hearts and minds. Every culture had its "metanarrative," its "deep story," which seeks to make sense of life. The story, or worldview, is the set of glasses through which a culture looks at the world.[4]

Two Signs and the Child

In the tradition of the fourth Gospel, the apostle used a series of signs to tell the story.[5] The term "sign" is one of John's "signature words," which he used "to provide us with a comprehensive basis for belief that 'Jesus is the

---

2. Bauckham, *The Climax of Prophecy*, 197. Bauckham writes, "Apollo was well known throughout the cities of Asia, and the popularity of the story of Apollo's birth and his defeat of the Python is well attested by coins of the area. In a form of this story which was current by John's time, the dragon threatens and pursues Apollo's mother Leto at the time of the birth and is later slain by the god. Because of the dragon's connection with Apollo's birth, the case for supposing that Revelation 12:1–4 was deliberately intended to recall this story seems a good one, the best of many suggestions of specific myths supposed to underlie this chapter. The allusion is then partly an artistic device, identifying the Dragon as the enemy whom the divine Child will eventually slay" (*Climax*, 197).

3. Beale, *Revelation*, 625. Beale: "Indeed, the whole pagan mythological system including the Roman emperor's claims to deity (some emperors identified themselves with Apollo), is none other than the devil's lie. John was certainly as capable as English poets of almost two millennia later who intentionally utilized mythical material in order to give it a Christian interpretation" (*Revelation*, 625).

4. Johnson, *Discipleship on the Edge*, 219.

5. Rev 12:1; 15:1.

Messiah, the Son of God, and that through believing you may have life in his name."[6] The first sign is "great and wondrous": a pregnant woman clothed with the sun, with the moon under her feet and a crown of twelve stars on her head, cries out in pain, because she is in labor and is about to give birth. The identity of this dazzling woman is rooted in the word of God and the testimony of Jesus. John's vision draws on the historical narrative, from Eve to Mary. The image encompasses Israel and the daughter of Zion, extending all the way to the bride of Christ. The woman represents all the people of God. She embraces salvation history from start to finish. She is the faithful community, symbolized by the sun and moon and twelve stars in Joseph's dream.[7] God has clothed her with the garments of salvation, arrayed her in a robe of righteousness, and adorned her with jewels.[8] She is gloriously beautiful. In spite of her vulnerable state, her heavenly brightness reflects her heavenly identity.

With a swift brushstroke John represents the entire biblical community. No single individual is identified here, but we cannot help but think of Mary, the first Christian disciple. The meaning of her identity precedes her. She is the one spoken of by the Prophet Isaiah: "The Lord himself will give you a sign: The virgin will conceive and give birth to a son, and will call him Immanuel."[9] The image of the vulnerable but victorious woman goes back to Eve, whose seed will crush the head of the serpent.[10] This woman stands for the people of God, the messianic community, and the bride of Christ. John used a multilayered metaphor to represent all those who confront the great dragon.

The second sign is an enormous red dragon with seven heads and ten horns and seven crowns on its heads. Like the first sign, this second sign invokes a range of biblical references. John has in view the crafty serpent in the garden who deceived Eve into thinking that God lied to elevate himself.[11] The great red dragon is described in the Psalms as a multiheaded Leviathan.[12] Isaiah promised that the Lord will slay the great sea monster Leviathan, the gliding serpent, with his sword.[13] Based on

6. Peterson, *Christ Plays in Ten Thousand Places*, 92, 97. See John 20:31.

7. Gen 37:9; Joseph is the twelfth star.

8. Isa 61:10.

9. Isa 7:14; Matt 1:22–23.

10. Gen 3:15.

11. Gen 3:1–5.

12. Ps 74:13–14.

13. Isa 27:1.

Scripture, the metaphor of the dragon paints a graphic picture of evil, but John was also using the popular image of the dragon in first-century culture. The serpent was associated with three major cults in the cities of Asia Minor (Asklepios, Dionysos, and Zeus). The image of the snake was "the most pervasive image of pagan divinity" confronting the seven churches in Asia Minor.[14] John artistically selected this symbol as a kind of logo for all the evil God intended to defeat through the birth of this child. This all-encompassing characterization of evil includes the devil individually, as the chief architect of evil and the primary foe of the woman. The enormous red dragon is described in six ways. Red represented blood and death.[15] His seven heads, ten horns, and seven crowns symbolize the completeness of his worldwide oppressive power. He has the power to disrupt the cosmos and fling the stars out of the sky. Creation is subject to the dragon's whimsical destructive impulses, which can result in global chaos. The final descriptive note pictures the dragon standing in front of the woman, poised to devour the woman's child the moment he s born. As with the first sign, the second sign has layers of meaning. The great dragon represents evil in its totality, including the pagan deities in the regional culture, the devil as evil's individual representative, and the oppressive power of the imperial cult.[16]

The third focus in John's praying imagination is not a sign, like the woman or the dragon, but a person. "The child does not point beyond himself to another reality—he *is* the reality. We are not going to find a literal woman clothed in the sun. We are not going to find a literal dragon with seven heads and ten horns. But we are going to find a male child, a son."[17] A single line from Psalm 2 identifies this child: he will rule all the nations "with an iron scepter."[18] The line is repeated twice, once here and then again toward the end of this section.[19] This child is none other than the Lion of the tribe of Judah, the Root of David, the triumphant Lamb who was slain, the King of kings and Lord of lords.[20]

14. Bauckham, *Climax of Prophecy*, 196.

15. See Rev 17:3–6.

16. Bauckham: "The Dragon is a fine example of John's capacity to envision figures of Old Testament texts and to raise them to a new imaginative life by exploiting the vital symbolism of his readers' environment" (*Climax of Prophecy*, 198).

17. Johnson, *Discipleship on the* Edge, 221.

18. Ps 2:9.

19. Rev 19:15.

21. Rev 5:5–12; 19:15–16.

John's unique vision of the nativity intersects with real history in the birth of a child in Bethlehem.[21] John's story agrees with Mary's song. The two accounts deliver a similar message. Her sung prayer resonates with John's praying imagination: "My soul glorifies the Lord . . . the Mighty One has done great things for me—holy is his name. . . . He has brought down rulers from their thrones but has lifted up the humble. He has filled the hungry with good things but has sent the rich away empty."[22] John's Christmas story rings true with Matthew's account. Bethlehem became ground zero in the drama of salvation history. The Apostle John did not hesitate to paint a picture of Bethlehem with his Spirit-inspired words, making Bethlehem the center of the cosmic struggle between God's grace and Satan's power. That precious moment in Bethlehem, quiet and serene, filled with wonder and worship, was nothing less than God's D-Day invasion; the beaches have been stormed. At long last heaven threatens hell. The devil confronts the Incarnate One, not with gifts of adoration (gold, frankincense, and myrrh), but with strategies of annihilation (deception, treachery, and malice). Jesus' birth excites more than wonder—it excites evil. John impresses upon us the real meaning of Christmas. God defeats the enormous red dragon with a baby, who is Christ the Lord. John's nativity scene gives us the meaning of the manger!

From the moment he is born the devil is out to get this child. We see the devil's strategy at work in Herod's Gestapo-like raid on Bethlehem, slaughtering the innocents.[23] Herod's jealous and paranoid protection of his power reflected the devil's quest for power. We see the devil's work in the wilderness when he led Jesus "to a very high mountain and showed him all the kingdoms of the world and their splendor. 'All this I will give you,' he said, 'if you will bow down and worship me.' Jesus said to him, 'Away from me, Satan! For it is written: "Worship the Lord your God, and serve him only.""[24] The devil is there when the people threaten to stone Jesus because he said "I and the Father are one."[25] He is there in Judas's betrayal and Peter's denial. He is present in the Sanhedrin's deliberations. He has a front-row seat when Pilate washes his hands of justice and righteousness. He is there at the cross. From the birth of the Christ child on, the devil stands ready to devour the One who has come to bring salva-

22. Luke 1:30–33.
23. Luke 1:46–53.
24. Matt 2:16–18.
1. Matt 4:8–10.
25. John 10:30.

tion. The Apostle John places the incarnation and the ascension of Christ side by side: one moment the woman gives birth, and the next moment "her child [is] snatched up to God and to his throne."

In this one act drama, John insists on the immediacy of the totality of God's will. It is as if everything is happening in a single moment. The incarnation and the ascension stand side by side. But since the iron scepter rule of Christ remains in the future, the devil continues to be the archenemy of the woman and her offspring. "Your enemy the devil prowls around like a roaring lion looking for someone to devour."[26] The dragon fights with everything he has, because he has nothing left to lose. He is already a convicted murderer, rapist, and fraud. He only knows how to deceive, accuse, and lie. "What identity does the devil have, other than the sheer untrammeled exercise of power?"[27] The woman, who represents the people of God, is on the run. She has to flee "into the wilderness to a place prepared for her by God, where she might be taken care of for 1,260 days." During this period of tribulation that lasts from Christ's ascension to his return, the followers of the Lamb are referred to as "the holy city," "the two witnesses," "the woman," and "God's people."[28] Each reference is to the same persecuted community of believers who are protected and nurtured by God in the wilderness for a relatively brief and sovereignly appointed time. This time is represented symbolically in several ways: forty-two months, 1,260 days, "a time, times and half a time."[29] Each reference is to three and a half years of persecution, a symbolic duration that cuts perfection (seven years) in half. John did not pull the number out of thin air. Moses recorded forty-two stages of breaking camp as the Israelites moved across the wilderness to the promised land.[30] During the days of Elijah it did not rain for three and a half years.[31] Matthew framed his genealogy in forty-two generations, from Abraham to Jesus, in three sets of fourteen.[32] But the chief source for John's symbolic number is the prophecy of Daniel, who described a three-and-a-half-year period of persecution. A fourth and final beast "will speak against the Most High and oppress his holy people and try to change the set times and the laws.

3. 1 Pet 5:8.

27. Mangina, *Revelation*, 151.

28. Rev 11:2; 11:3; 12:6, 14; 13:6.

29. Rev 11:2, 3; 12:6, 14; 13:5.

30. Num 33.

31. Luke 4:25.

9. Matt 1:17.

The holy people will be delivered into his hands for a time, times and half a time."[33] "The symbol refers to the whole time the church is in the world, caught in the crunch of clashing kingdoms."[34]

Metanarrative

For some time the whole idea of the big story, the grand narrative, has come under fire. "The notion of an overarching canopy of objective truth has collapsed, leaving only tiny islands of subjective experience."[35] Our vision of the world is shrinking and the personal memoir outranks the metanarrative. One of the leading proponents of the collapse of the grand narrative was Jean-François Lyotard, a French philosopher and literary theorist. Lyotard argued that the all-encompassing philosophical explanations for reality were misguided and wrong. He assessed the Enlightenment quest for social progress and freedom through rationalism and science as a failure. He concluded that Marxism's theory of class conflict only resulted in more oppression and social injustice. He analyzed Freud's therapeutic worldview, which sought to reduce life to biology and sex, as woefully inadequate. Lyotard condemned all of these big-picture accounts of humanity for being too *theological*. He reasoned that they are fundamentally secular versions of a theistic worldview. He challenged any vision of life that relied on "transcendent and universal truth" and defined postmodern "as incredulity toward meta-narratives."

> This incredulity is undoubtedly a product of progress in the sciences: but that progress in turn presupposes it. To the obsolescence of the metanarrative apparatus of legitimation corresponds, most notably, the crisis of metaphysical philosophy and of the university institution which in the past relied on it. The narrative function is losing its functions, its great hero, its great dangers, its great voyages, its great goal. It is being dispersed in clouds of narrative elements.[36]

Lyotard advocated one's local narrative over a grand narrative. People's own stories are naturally truer to the chaos and disorder of the universe. They do a better job of capturing human diversity and individuality, and

33. Dan 7:25.
34. Johnson, *Discipleship on the Edge*, 205.
35. Tennent, *Invitation To World Missions*, 78.
13. Lyotard, *The Postmodern Condition*, xxiv.

they humbly refuse to project their story onto others. Some have argued that Lyotard's ironic self-professed claim to write "the great narrative of the end of great narratives" is itself a contemporary metanarrative and is thus self-refuting.[37] Christians agree with Lyotard's conclusion that many metanarratives are oppressive. What Lyotard said about the Enlightenment or Marx or Freud or capitalism fits with a Christian critique. "Incredulity toward metanarratives" makes sense when a grand narrative is used as a tool of oppression or a power play for the imagination of the weak and powerless.[38] The trouble comes when postmodernism paints all grand narratives with a simple brushstroke and then tosses the canvas into the garbage. Lyotard may offer a valid critique of religious and political ideologies, but to conclude that there is no overarching true metanarrative is its own ideology.

The Deep Story

Over and against all other grand narratives and local narratives, the Apostle John proclaimed Christ story as the very revelation of God. "That which was from the beginning, which we have heard, which we have seen with our eyes, which we have looked at and our hands have touched—this we proclaim concerning the Word of life."[39] The Apostle Peter expressed it this way: "For we did not follow cleverly devised stories when we told you about the coming of our Lord Jesus Christ in power, but we were eyewitnesses of his majesty."[40] Before the coming of Christ, the Apostle Paul said that humanity was "underage," enslaved by "the elemental spiritual forces of the world."[41] But "when the fullness of time had come, God sent forth his Son, born of a woman, born under the law, to redeem those under the law."[42]

---

37. Lyotard, *The Differend*, 135.

38. Lyotard, *The Postmodern Condition*, xxiv. Lyotard: "They allocate our lives for the growth of power. In matters of social justice and scientific truth alike, the legitimation of that power is based on its optimizing the system's performance—efficiency. The application of this criterion to all our games necessarily entails a certain level of terror, whether soft or hard: be operational (that is, commensurable) or disappear" (*Postmodern Condition*, xxiv).

39. 1 John 1:1.

40. 2 Pet 1:16.

41. Col 2:20.

42. Gal 4:3–5.

This "fullness of time" arrived nearly 1,800 years before Immanuel Kant declared *man had come of age* and Thomas Paine celebrated the *age of reason*. It came long before the age of the discoverers, the Enlightenment, the Industrial Revolution, the scientific age, and the computer age. Secularism ignores the fact that a biblical view of the world inspired the exploration of the world and the investigation of a rational universe. Christianity played a key role in the transition from astrology to astronomy, from magic to medicine, from superstition to science, from aristocracy to democracy, and from poverty to industry. Christians founded universities and hospitals, fought for emancipation, and carried the gospel to the ends of the earth. Christians believe that everyone has a story, but only one story redeems our story. God's salvation history is vital to the meaning and fulfillment of our own personal story. We arrive at the truth not by human ingenuity and scientific proof, but by the revelation of God. The gospel is neither manipulative nor coercive. A worldly ideology of power has no place in this truest of true stories. The essence of the story is the unfathomable humility of the incarnation of God.[43]

Lamb's Players

The followers of the Lamb need "a new determination to proclaim and herald the 'grand narrative' framed by creation, fall, incarnation, redemption, and a final eschatological climax of the divine/human drama to an increasingly postmodern world."[44] The motivation for this new determination cannot be fear or power; any sense of ulterior motive, intimidation, manipulation, or marketing will only confirm the world's cynicism and reinforce its prejudice against the gospel. Christians believe that "all people, in all times and places, need to discover the life-transforming narrative that is rooted in the person and work of Christ."[45] In other words, what we believe the world needs and longs for is not what the world thinks it needs and longs for. This is what makes the Revelation timely for believers. The only redemptive approach available to the church finds its sole source and strategy in the Lamb.[46]

43. Phil 2:6–8.

44. Tennent, *Invitation to World Missions*, 47.

45. Ibid., 47.

46. Ibid., 83. Tennent: "From the perspective of the Trinity, Jesus is the archetypal missionary. The first Western missionaries to arrive in Papua New Guinea may have believed that no one had ever traversed such a vast cultural divide as they. However,

21

The Easter Story

[12:7–17] *And there was war in heaven. Michael and this angels fought against the dragon, and the dragon and his angels fought back. But he was not strong enough, and they lost their place in heaven. The great dragon was hurled down—that ancient serpent called the devil, or Satan, who leads the whole world astray. He was hurled to the earth, and his angels with him. Then I heard a loud voice in heaven say: "Now have come the salvation and the power and the kingdom of our God, and the authority of his Messiah. For the accuser of our brothers and sisters, who accuses them before our God day and night, has been hurled down. They triumphed over him by the blood of the Lamb and by the word of their testimony; they did not love their lives so much as to shrink from death. Therefore rejoice, you heavens and you who dwell in them! But woe to the earth and the sea, because the devil has gone down to you! He is filled with fury, because he knows his time is short." When the dragon saw that he had been hurled to the earth, he pursued the woman who had given birth to the male child. The woman was given the two wings of a great eagle, so that she might fly to the place prepared for her in the wilderness, where she would be taken care of for a time, times and half a time, out of the serpent's reach. Then from his mouth the serpent spewed water like a river, to overtake the woman and sweep*

---

their experience pales in comparison to the great gulf that the Son of God crossed in the Incarnation" (*Invitation*, 83).

her away with the torrent. But the earth helped the woman by opening its mouth and swallowing the river that the dragon had spewed out of his mouth. Then the dragon was enraged at the woman and went off to make war against the rest of her offspring—those who keep God's commands and hold fast their testimony about Jesus.

THE BABE IN THE manger is none other than the Lord of history. Advent is not a season: it's a crisis, where adoration and annihilation converge. If Bethlehem was ground zero in the cosmic war between God and Satan, Golgotha was the epicenter. The Apostle John transports us from the cradle to the cross to the crown. He converges Advent and ascension in one glorious moment. To use words from Matthew's Gospel, John assures the church that "the gates of hell shall not prevail against it."[1] He confirms Isaiah's vision: "How you have fallen from heaven, morning star, son of the dawn! You have been cast down to the earth, you who once laid low the nations!"[2] What began at the incarnation was completed at the ascension. Satan's deceptive hold on the nations has been broken.[3] John's Christmas story becomes the Easter story. John's multilayered drama ends with the woman on the run. She symbolizes the people of God (the bride of Christ), and she is protected for a prescribed length of time. Her protection is described with images drawn from Israel's exodus and sojourn in the wilderness. The nature of the serpent's threat is also elaborated with imagery drawn from the Old Testament. In the midst of this unfolding drama, John reveals the cosmic impact of Christ's resurrection on the great dragon and heaven's bold up-tempo response.

The resurrection and ascension of Christ trigger a cosmic conflict. The devil is defeated by Michael and his angels in a battle reminiscent of the devil's earlier defeat at creation. Isaiah's description of the fall of the king of Babylon, which we have just cited, expands to include the fall of the devil: "How you have fallen from heaven, morning star, son of the dawn! You have been cast down to earth, you who once laid low the nations! You said in your heart, 'I will ascend to heaven; I will raise my throne above the stars of God.'"[4]

1. Matt 16:18.
2. Isa 14:12.
3. Acts 14:16.
4. Isa 14:12–13; see Ezek 28:12–17.

The prophets associated human tyrants with the demonic. This has the effect of both distancing and actualizing the figure of the devil. The devil never writes his own biography, but his diabolical nature is on graphic display in the devastating evil that is embodied in human form. I was studying this text the day a heavily armed young man entered an elementary school in Newtown, Connecticut, and killed twenty-six innocent and defenseless children and adults. Such an unspeakable horror ultimately has no other explanation than the power of evil described in the Bible. Lurking behind the facade of civilization is an evil that defies imagining. This is, as C. S. Lewis says, the devil's terrain. "Enemy-occupied territory—that is what the world is. Christianity is the story of how the rightful king has landed, you might say in disguise, and is calling us all to take part in a great campaign of sabotage."[5]

The war in heaven between Michael and Satan has its roots in Daniel's prophecy. The atoning death, bodily resurrection, and ascension of Jesus Christ ignite a climactic conflict in heaven. Michael is victorious over Satan, and the devil is hurled to the earth. His privileged place of accusation is gone, and his demonic power to slander and deceive is curtailed. John writes, "The great dragon was hurled down—that ancient serpent called the devil, or Satan, who leads the whole world astray. He was hurled to the earth, and his angels with him."[6] John's description of the great dragon recalls the words of Jesus, when he said, "I saw Satan fall like lightning from heaven."[7]

The Blood of the Lamb

The blood of the Lamb is a metaphor for the atoning sacrifice given by God to accomplish our salvation. The survivors of the great tribulation "have washed their robes and made them white in the blood of the Lamb."[8] The theme of the power of blood to remove sin's stain is found throughout the Bible.[9] And the ancient symbol conforms to the cleansing power of blood in the human body. Blood cleanses the body of toxins: carbon dioxide from the lungs, other toxins from kidneys, worn-out cells from the liver and spleen. Blood is a redemptive analogy signifying the

5. Lewis, *Mere Christianity*, 46.
6. Rev 12:9.
7. Luke 10:18.
8. Rev 7:14.
9. Lev 14; 1 John 1:7.

power of the blood of the Lamb to overcome the devil, "the accuser of our brothers and sisters, who accuses them before our God day and night."[10] The image of the altar merges with the image of the battlefield. God fights against Satan and sheds his blood on our behalf. The perfect sacrifice is also the perfect soldier, fighting for our freedom from sin's oppression and Satan's dominion. The writer of Hebrews expresses it well: "Since the children have flesh and blood, he too shared in their humanity so that by his death he might destroy him who holds the power of death—that is, the devil—and free those who all their lives were held in slavery by their fear of death."[11] The power of the blood of the Lamb is found not only in cleansing us from sin, but inspiring us to do battle against sin as well. "They triumphed over him by the blood of the Lamb and by the word of their testimony; they did not love their lives so much as to shrink from death."[12] The blood of the Lamb symbolizes Christ's sacrifice and inspires our sacrifice. "Without the shedding of blood there is no forgiveness," but because of Christ's sacrifice we are ready to struggle against sin, to the point of shedding our blood.[13]

The Essential Wilderness

Believers are in for a struggle. The devil is mad; "He is filled with fury." He has been defeated by the Lamb and he's fighting back like a wounded animal. "He knows that his time is short." John now explores the wilderness experience more thoroughly. The woman who gave birth to the child flees the dragon on the wings of an eagle and finds protection and provision in the wilderness for a specified length of time. The imagery of the eagle recalls God's protection of the Israelites.[14]

The people of God are sustained by the presence of God in the wilderness as they journey to the promised land. They admit that they are "foreigners and strangers on earth." They are "longing for a better country—a heavenly one." Like Abraham, they are "looking forward to the city with foundations, whose architect and builder is God."[15]

10. Rev 12:10.
11. Heb 2:14–15.
12. Rev 12:11.
13. Heb 9:22; 12:4.
14. Exod 19:4–6; see Deut 1:31–33; 32:10–12; Isa 40:3, 29–31.
15. Heb 11:10, 13, 16.

Wandering in a wilderness of trouble and trial is not what many modern believers have been told to expect. They were led to believe that life would be a lot easier with Jesus. All that talk of having your best life now, along with your dream marriage, your dream family, and your dream job, flies in the face of what John tells the church. Timothy Tennent writes,

> We must resist the pressure to treat people as "religious consumers" to whom we "market" the gospel and create some kind of "market share." This inevitably compromises the church, tempting her to proclaim a kind of minimalistic gospel that focuses on the least one has to do to be a Christian. This approach must be decisively abandoned and replaced with intensive discipleship objectives that produce a leaner, far more robust, culturally savvy, and theologically literate church.[16]

The Devil's Torrent

John paints a graphic picture of a rushing torrent from the serpent's mouth, threatening to wipe out everything in its path. "Then from his mouth the serpent spewed water like a river, to overtake the woman and sweep her away with the torrent."[17] The image of a raging torrent captures the nature of the devil's oppression. The world is drowning in the devil's deception. The serpent is spewing out lies and accusations. The sheer volume of deceptive words is overwhelming. The metaphor of a flood captures what faithful Christians are up against, both in John's day and our own. How do the followers of the Lamb keep from drowning? They are inundated by a constant flood of words and ideas inimical to Christ and his kingdom. No place is safe from the barrage of false ideologies and powerful cultural messages that belittle and strive to override the testimony of Jesus.

Consider the flood of falsehood that threatens to overwhelm believers. A believer's daily experience on a university campus is sobering. She begins her day in English class where her professor opens class with a quote from Salman Rushdie: "Literature is where I go to explore the highest and lowest places in human society and in the human spirit, where I hope to find not absolute truth but the truth of the tale, of the imagination

---

16. Tennent, *Invitation to World Missions*, 47.

17. Rev 12:15.

and of the heart."[18] He lectures the class on the myth of absolute truth and mocks the notion of divine revelation in the Bible. He equates the Bible with the Book of Mormon and the Qur'an, and argues that the educated mind cannot tolerate dependence on obsolete creeds and truth claims built on thin air.

Her next class is Introduction to Psychology, taught by the faculty advisor for the LGBTQ club on campus. Class begins with a discussion on repressive sexual patterns in society and family. The professor has made it clear that she will not even entertain the notion that marriage between man and a woman is normative for society. After class our student heads to her dorm, but to her surprise she finds her roommate in bed with a boyfriend, so she heads for Starbucks. Over a latte she reads Tom Wolfe's latest, *Back to Blood,* for class. If Wolfe is right, she thinks, we are a far more decadent culture than she had ever imagined. He describes a world devoid of friendship and even common decency. His characters are over-sexed adult adolescents. Later in the day she meets up with friends and heads to an evening meeting of an on-campus ministry, where the title of the night's presentation is "Breathing Room." It was a nice talk with some good jokes and stories about messy roommates and busy schedules, and the need to clean up the clutter in our lives, but it all left her feeling empty.

How easy it is for a Christian student on any typical day to be swept away by the devil's torrent. The devil uses it all, from an aggressive secular assault on the Christian faith to a superficial "Christian" talk. Believers are subject to a constant flood of perspectives that threaten to overwhelm the truth. Outright deception, accusation, and slander flow in the same raging current as innocuous speech about sports, fashion, business, and pop culture. The devil's propaganda campaign against God's word and the testimony of Jesus is as intense as it is pervasive.

The Lord's Protection

Believers cannot stop the demonic torrent, but they can be preserved in the midst of the flood. The Apostle John's image of the earth helping the woman "by opening its mouth and swallowing the river that the dragon had spewed out of his mouth" recalls God's preservation of the Israelites at the Red Sea. Pharaoh's army "sank like lead in the mighty waters," and

18. Rushdie, *The Hindu*, February 26, 1995.

Moses sang, "You stretch out your right hand, and the earth swallows your enemies."[19] When the families of Korah, Dathan, and Abiram spoke against Moses, he refused to defend himself. He relied solely on the Lord's supernatural defense of the truth. He did not wage war against their propaganda machine. Instead, Moses relied on the Lord, saying, "This is how you will know that the Lord has sent me to do all these things and that it was not my idea: If these men die a natural death and suffer the common fate of all human beings, then the Lord has not sent me. But if the Lord brings about something totally new, and the earth opens its mouth and swallows them, with everything that belongs to them, and they go down alive into the realm of the dead, then you will know that these men have treated the Lord with contempt."[20]

When the Lord dramatically intervened and the earth literally "opened its mouth and swallowed them and their households," the authority of Moses was validated and vindicated.[21] The message that John delivers to the church is that God will protect and preserve his witnesses. His word will not return to him void. Our responsibility is simple, yet demanding: keep God's commands and hold fast to the testimony of Jesus.

19. Exod 15:10, 12.
20. Num 16:28–30.
21. Num 16:32.

22

Filled with Wonder

⌒· Revelation 13:1–18 ·⌒

[13:1–18] *The dragon stood on the shore of the sea. And I saw a beast coming out of the sea. It had ten horns and seven heads, with ten crowns on its horns, and on each head a blasphemous name. The beast I saw resembled a leopard, but had feet like those of a bear and a mouth like that of a lion. The dragon gave the beast his power and his throne and great authority. One of the heads of the beast seemed to have had a fatal wound, but the fatal wound had been healed. The whole world was filled with wonder and followed the beast. People worshiped the dragon because he had given authority to the beast, and they also worshiped the beast and asked, "Who is like the beast? Who can make war against it?"*

The beast was given a mouth to utter proud words and blasphemies and to exercise its authority for forty-two months. It opened its mouth to blaspheme God, and to slander his name and his dwelling place and those who live in heaven. It was given power to make war against God's people and to conquer them. And it was given authority over every tribe, people, language and nation. All inhabitants of the earth will worship the beast— all whose names have not been written in the Lamb's book of life, the Lamb who was slain from the creation of the world. Whoever has ears, let them hear. "If anyone is to go into captivity, into captivity they will go. If anyone is to be killed with the sword, with the sword they will be killed." This calls for patient endurance and faithfulness on the part of God's people.

Then I saw another beast, coming out of the earth. It had two horns like a lamb, but it spoke like a dragon. It exercised all the authority of the first beast on its behalf, and made the earth and its inhabitants worship the first beast, whose fatal wound had been healed. And it performed great signs, even causing fire to come down from heaven to the earth in full view of everyone. Because of the signs it was given power to perform on behalf of the first beast, it deceived the inhabitants of the earth. It ordered them to set up an image in honor of the beast who was wounded by the sword and yet lived. It was given power to give breath to the image of the first beast, so that it could speak and cause all who refused to worship the image to be killed. It also forced all people, great and small, rich and poor, free and slave, to receive a mark on their right hands or on their foreheads, so that they could not buy or sell unless they had the mark, which is the name of the beast or the number of its name. This calls for wisdom. Let those who have insight calculate the number of the beast, for it is the number of a man. That number is 666.

JESUS' COMFORT, "DO NOT let your hearts be troubled. Trust in God; trust also in me," corresponds with his warning.[1] "If the world hates you, keep in mind that it hated me first. . . . If they persecuted me, they will persecute you also."[2] Jesus prepared the disciples for persecution. He explicitly warned his disciples so they would not go astray. He said, "The time is coming when anyone who kills you will think he is offering a service of God."[3] "In this world you will have trouble. But take heart! I have overcome the world."[4] Warning and comfort are commingled in Jesus' spiritual direction. To follow the Lamb was never billed as easy.[5]

An Unholy Trinity

We instinctively turn away from truth that discourages, but John insisted on describing evil. He revealed its complexity, exposed its malice, and

1 John 14:1.
2. John 15:18, 20.
3. John 16:2.
4. John 16:33.
5. John 17:14–18,

called it by name. Evil is more deeply rooted and more all encompassing than we ever imagined. The forces of evil work in tandem. The enormous red dragon makes war against God's people and empowers the seven-headed monster that rises up from the sea. The beast of the earth has the power and skill to deceive, intimidate, and manipulate humankind into submission. All those who receive the mark of the beast and pay homage to the image of the beast are set apart from the last generation of believers, who are signed, sealed, and delivered by the blood of the Lamb. With these three figures—the dragon, the beast of the sea, and the beast of the earth—John portrayed the power of evil.

Christ	//	Beast
1:16; 19:15	sword	13:10
5:6; 13:8	slain	13:3, 8
14:1	names on the forehead	13:16
5:9; 7:9	authority over every tribe, tongue	13:7; 17:15
5:8–14	universal worship	13:4, 8
2:27; 3:21	empowering authority	13:12–15
777	trinity	666
Spirit, John 16:14	empowering	13:12–15, Second beast

John's description of the beast of the sea draws on Old Testament imagery of sea monsters. This monster is empowered by the dragon, who gives the beast autonomy and authority. The seven heads and ten crowns signify the global impact of his oppressive power. The beast represents the Roman Empire. "Yet the beast is more than the Roman Empire. John's vision grew out of the details of his own historical situation, but its complete fulfillment awaits the final denouement of human history. The beast has always been, and will be in a final intensified manifestation, the deification of secular [and spiritual] authority."[6] John's depiction of the Roman

---

6. Mounce, *Revelation*, 252. Mounce writes, "It should be noted that the attitude toward the state in Revelation differs decidedly from Rom 13:1–6; 1 Tim 2:1–2; and 1 Pet 2:13–17. This is not because John differed from the other apostles regarding church and state. It is because of the developing historical situation of the first century. . . . an aggressive program of emperor worship was being forced upon the populace, supported by active persecution. In the clash of loyalties between God and emperor, the Christian had no choice but to obey the One who is the source of all authority. Only when the state continues to act within the limitations of its delegated authority can the believer freely submit to its regulations" (*Revelation*, 252).

Empire and its persecution of the church is a metaphor for successive political and spiritual forces of opposition against Christ and his church. The sea beast suffered a near-fatal head wound, but has recovered to the amazement of the whole world.[7] The devil is gaining momentum.

A Demonic Strategy

"The beast was given a mouth to utter proud words and blasphemies and to exercise his authority for forty-two months."[8] "The trampling lasts for forty-two months, that is, for a limited time. Once again we are informed that the forces of evil are on a leash and under God's control. As Christ indicated, the hour will strike when 'the times of the nations' will be fulfilled."[9] The beast is the devil's propaganda chief. "It opened its mouth to blaspheme God, and to slander his name and his dwelling place and those who live in heaven."[10]

The seduction of the soul can be beguiling. In *All Things Shining*, Berkeley professor Hubert Dreyfus and Harvard philosopher Sean Kelly challenge Americans to rediscover Homer and the Greek gods as a solution to their feelings of emptiness and aimlessness. Their thesis is that the best defense against nihilism and culture's pervasive sadness is a return to Homer's gods. Life is not about inner convictions and beliefs. Meaning does not exist outside of ourselves. Truth is beside the point. What matters most is being in sync with the gods. Dreyfus and Kelly want to restore the Greek pantheon. "To lure back these Homeric gods is a saving possibility after the death of God: it would allow us to survive the breakdown of monotheism while resisting the descent into a nihilistic existence."[11] The key to a hopeful life has more to do with riding a wave than abiding in the truth. Homer's gods are moods that attune us "to what matters most in a situation, allowing us to respond appropriately

---

7. Gen 3:15.

8. Rev 13:5; see 11:2, 3; 12:6, 14; 13:5.

9. Hughes, *Revelation*, 122. Hughes writes, "These 'times' are represented here by the 42 months, the same period over which the worship of the 'beast' extends (13:5), and also during which 'the woman' who is Christ's church is nourished and preserved by God (12:6, 14), where 1260 days and 'a time, and times, and half a time', respectively, are other ways of stating the same period" (*Revelation*, 122).

10. Rev 13:6.

11. Dreyfus and Kelly, *All Thing Shining*, 61.

without thinking."[12] Like a wave whooshing up, special experiences offer a moment of exhilaration. In the whooshing up we catch a glimpse of focused meaning—a meaning that lies both outside of us and within us. Not surprisingly, the authors claim that this new sense of transcendence, the whooshing up, can be found most readily in sports. "Sports may be the place in contemporary life where Americans find sacred community most easily."[13] Dreyfus and Kelly believe that the spirit of Homeric polytheism—"the whooshing up that focuses one for a while and then lets one go—is still available in American culture today."[14]

The devil's strategy is to convince sophisticated and intelligent people that religion is a matter of mystery and wonder minus the truth of salvation history. The hard truths about sin and guilt can be quietly set aside. Christ's cross is only a myth pointing to human significance. The incarnation is a special metaphor for the meaning of the person. The resurrection is a piece of poetic fiction reminding us that life persists and the memories of our loved ones live on. Over time this method of seduction proves almost irresistible. This popular form of spirituality pervades the arts and the human sciences, and captures the ethos of the university.

The seduction of the soul can be accomplished through something as simple as a humorous TED Talk.[15] Behavioral scientist Brené Brown says that she has discovered that vulnerability is the key to human relationships. The path to self-fulfillment is to embrace our vulnerability. Her work has shown that the secret behind our broken relationships is our failure to confront shame head on. We are paralyzed by our feelings of insecurity and unworthiness. On the computer screen we see a picture of an ugly swamp and she says, "Shame is the swampland of the soul." We need to rise up out of the muck of our feelings of inadequacy and courageously embrace our vulnerability. Brené Brown cuts out all the tough stuff to believe in and boils it all down to vulnerability. She sweeps away the problem of guilt, the depth of depravity, and the need for repentance. Life's solution is found apart from redemption—apart from the atoning sacrifice of Christ. The lie is convenient, practical, and can be told with lots of humor and fun stories about vulnerability.

There is a beautiful side to blasphemy that ruins the soul just as effectively as outright slander. If we even pretend that real redemption is

12. Ibid., 84.
13. Ibid., 192.
14. Ibid., 205.
15. Brown, "The Power of Vulnerability."

found in embracing our vulnerability, we have fallen into the language game of the beast. Brené Brown says, "If we are going to find our way back to each other, vulnerability is going to be that path." She concludes, "You are worthy of love and belonging. . . . We need to let ourselves be seen, deeply seen for who we are. We need to love with our whole heart and practice gratitude and joy. Believe that you are enough." On the screen is projected a woman's chest upon which it is written in black marker, "I am enough."

The Language Game of the Beast

Shockingly, it seems that the whole world prefers the beast over the Lamb. Everything about the antichrist beast communicates power and triumph, over and against the weakness of the Lamb. John doesn't use the word "antichrist" in the Revelation, but he used it in his letters: "You have heard that the antichrist is coming, even now many antichrists have come."[16] His definition of the antichrist is this: "Whoever denies that Jesus is the Messiah. Such a person is the antichrist—denying the Father and the Son."[17] This spirit of the antichrist can be found wherever the incarnation of Jesus is denied. John warns the believers that this spirit of denial and deception is "already in the world."[18]

The demonic attack is multifaceted, and mediated through the beast of the sea and the beast of the earth. "[The beast coming out of the earth] had two horns like a lamb, but it spoke like a dragon."[19] The second beast appears to be a parody of the Lamb who was slain, as its two-horned appearance "mimics the two witnesses, two lampstands, and two olive trees."[20] The beast is called a dragon and a false prophet because its primary duty is to convince the world to worship the beast of the sea.[21] The beast is an excellent communicator, with a rare combination of dragon-like authority and lamb-like gentleness. The beast knows how to be dramatically bold and manipulatively gentle. Like Adam and Eve in the garden, the church is vulnerable to the false prophet's deception.

16. 1 John 2:18.
17. 1 John 2:22.
18. 1 John 4:3; 2 John 7.
19. Rev 13:11; Dan 7:17; Deut 13:1; Mark 13:22; 2 Thess 2:9.
20. Beale, *Revelation*, 707.
21. Rev 16:13; 19:20; 20:10.

In a variety of compelling ways, the beast of the earth sows the seeds of doubt: "Did God say?" We are warned by John that the beast can match the witness of the church with whatever is needed: authority, humor, wit, power, even signs and wonder. The beast appeals to people on the basis of loyalty, patriotism, and self-interest. The beast that looks like a lamb and talks like a dragon is the antichrist's minister of propaganda. The success of the beast is unnerving. Its power of persuasion is coupled with sheer force, securing total domination. The beast of the earth forced everyone who wanted to participate in commerce to wear the mark of the beast, which was man's number, 666.

John's vision of the beast of the earth parodies Christ and the church. The satanic knock-off tries in every way imaginable to copy the true way. Christ gives the church resurrection authority; the devil gives the beast political authority. The church offers the gospel; the beast offers charisma. Christ seals and delivers his followers; the devil seals and delivers his followers. The devil boasts, "You have a Lamb, I have a lamb."

The unholy trinity is made up of the murderous red dragon, the seven-headed monster, and the beast of the earth, "a clumsy counterfeit of the magnificent true Lamb."[22] Every form of propaganda, blasphemy, manipulation, deception, and idolatry is encompassed by this comprehensive description of evil. Evil is embodied, empowered, and enshrined in the hideous strength of this unholy trinity. Evil is personified in the form of diabolical monsters. Evil reigns: "The whole world was filled with wonder and followed the beast."[23]

If the beast's chief weapon is deception, then the believer's necessary response is discernment. Intimidation is circumvented by insight. John is right. "This calls for wisdom. Let those who have insight calculate the number of the beast, for it the number of a man. That number is 666."[24] There are many theories as to who or what John meant by this number, but given the symbolic nature of all the numbers in the book, it seems best not to make a literal calculation.[25] The triple sixes are the antithesis to divine perfection. The number signifies "the completeness of sinful incompleteness found in the beast."[26] John's digital discernment fits with his description of the deification of the secular authority. If he had Nero

---

22. Peterson, *Reversed Thunder*, 123.
23. Rev 13:3.
24. Rev 13:18.
25. Beale, *Revelation*, 718–27.
26. Ibid., 722.

or Rome in mind, the number serves "as the parable nearest at hand for the unimaginable forms that historical evil will assume, the nearer we approach the end."[27]

The Strategy of the Lamb

The unholy trinity appears to have both strategic and tactical superiority. Believers were either persuaded or persecuted by the beast.[28] In the eyes of the world, failure is certain. Joseph Mangina writes, "The saints lose. This outcome will seem disappointing only to the extent that we embrace the beast's criteria for what constitutes success. The church that imagines it has a successful strategy for confronting the principalities and powers on their own terms had better think again."[29] Christ offers precious little by way of so-called strategies for success; there is no top ten list for popular church growth. All we have is a quote from the Prophet Jeremiah, when the Lord impatiently rebuked the people for their resistence to his will, as if to say, "Stop complaining and get with the program." The message is clear: what was necessary for Israel to accept in the days of Jeremiah is necessary now for the church to accept during the last days.

> If you're assigned to die, go and die; if assigned to war, go and get killed; if assigned to starve, go starve; if assigned to exile, off to exile you go![30]

John challenged believers to suffer according to the will of God. Instead of trying to escape the consequences of faithfulness in a fallen world, they were encouraged to accept the cost of discipleship. Instead of trying to outsmart the suffering or fight it or deny it, they were challenged to face it. This was not a passive acceptance of fate, but rather a passionate embrace of faithfulness. John shares the Apostle Paul's perspective: "I have been crucified with Christ and I no longer live, but Christ lives in me. The life I now live in the body, I live by faith in the Son of God, who loved me and gave himself for me."[31]

---

27. Mangina, *Revelation*, 167.
28. Rev 13:15.
29. Mangina, *Revelation*, 162.
30. Jer 15:2.
31. Gal 2:20.

The church is to be like Job, who was blindsided by the devil but faithful through it all. No-fear discipleship is the order of the day. We have not been given "a spirit of timidity but one of power, love, and self-discipline."[32] God is in control. The victory of Christ is assured. "In this world you will have trouble. But take heart! I have overcome the world."[33] We entrust ourselves to the providence of God. Patient endurance and faithfulness rule out revenge and retaliation. The world should never have to fear a Christian. Those who persecute, insult, threaten, slander, swindle, and murder Christians are never in danger of receiving the same treatment they perpetrate and perpetuate. Christians defend others and themselves from violence, slander, deception, and terrorism, but the disciple of the Lord Jesus Christ does not fight the way the world does. "For though we live in the world, we do not wage war as the world does. The weapons we fight with are not the weapons of the world."[34] The reason the followers of the Lamb don't fight fire with fire and render evil for evil is because of the victory of the cross.

32. 2 Tim 1:7.
33. John 16:33.
34. 2 Cor 10:3–4.

23

Keeping Perspective

◡· Revelation 14:1–13 ·◡

[**14:1–5**] *Then I looked, and there before me was the Lamb, standing on Mount Zion, and with him 144,000 who had his name and his Father's name written on their foreheads. And I heard a sound from heaven like the roar of rushing waters and like a loud peal of thunder. The sound I heard was like that of harpists playing their harps. And they sang a new song before the throne and before the four living creatures and the elders. No one could learn the song except the 144,000 who had been redeemed from the earth. These are those who did not defile themselves with women, for they remained virgins. They follow the Lamb wherever he goes. They were purchased from among the human race and offered as firstfruits to God and the Lamb. No lie was found in their mouths; they are blameless.*

BLASPHEMY AND BLUSTER GUSH from the unholy trinity. Deception and falsehood flow from these miracle-working monsters, but the followers of the Lamb know the Father's name, sing the new song, and keep themselves pure. The 144,000 stand on Mount Zion and sing a new song.[1] They represent "the totality of God's people throughout the ages," as well as the militant last generation of believers fighting to the end.[2] They are sealed against the woes of judgment. They join the innumerable multi-

1. Rev 14:1; Joel 2:32; Heb 12:22; Gal 4:26.
2. Beale, *Revelation*, 733; see Bauckham, *The Climax of Prophecy*, 229–32.

tude in praise and worship.[3] "Once again when John gestures toward the eschatological future, he falls naturally into language suggestive of music and hymnody."[4] In juxtaposition with the nightmare happening on earth, heaven is pulsating with a thunderous celebration. John projects his struggling congregations into the future experience of the victory of the Lamb. His reference to Mount Zion echoes the Lord's promise, "I have installed my king on Zion, my holy mountain."[5] Joyous worship erupts, like "the roar of rushing waters and like a loud peal of thunder."

The Apostle John's heavenly vision redescribes power in three ways: the power of worship, the power of obedience, and the power of proclamation. Instead of opting for the strategies of worldly power, which involve coercion, exploitation, and propaganda, John calls believers to make "other types of power imaginable."[6] Following the example of her Lord, the church operates with a "fundamentally different kind of social power."[7] Ordinary believers in their ordinary lives are called to take after Jesus in the world. They seek to practice Christlike intimacy with the Father, compassionate concern for others, and resilient witness in the world.

The Anthem

Praise songs drown out the deceiver's propaganda and remind us that the church is "first and foremost, a worshiping community whose life centers on the word of God."[8] Music is inspired by the God who sings. Melody, harmony, rhythm, and tone are not human inventions. King David credited God for his musical ability. "He put a new song in my mouth, a hymn of praise to our God."[9] Israel's priests gave God the credit for the song they sang. "By day the Lord directs his love, at night his song is with me—a prayer to the God of my life."[10] Music belongs to the chief musician. His acoustical world resonates with song. God designed not only

3. Rev 7:4–9.
4. Mangina, *Revelation*, 172.
5. Ps 2:6.
6. Hunter, *To Change the World*, 186.
7. Ibid., 188.
8. Ibid., 184.
9. Ps 40:3.
10. Ps 42:8.

the voice and ear, but the heart and spirit. Whatever creativity we express comes from God the Creator, who not only inspires praise, but also gives us the gifts with which to express it.

Music tells God's story in song. The dramatic turning points and breakthroughs in God's revelation are marked by hymns of praise. Prose gives way to poetry and dialogue to doxology. Narrative becomes declarative in anthems of praise. The Exodus is marked by the Song of Moses.[11] The birth of Christ is celebrated in Mary's Magnificat, Zechariah's Benedictus, and in the song of Simeon. Angels offer up an exclamation of praise in the gloria.[12] The early church confessed Christ in song. His humility and exaltation is celebrated in Paul's letter to the believers at Philippi in what is thought to be an early worship hymn.[13] They set their creeds to music: "He appeared in a body, was vindicated by the Spirit, was seen by angels, was preached among the nations, was believed on in the world, was taken up in glory."[14]

The Revelation anticipates powerful singing in the presence of God: Hymns of adoration, "Holy, holy, holy is the Lord God Almighty, who was, and is, and is to come"; Songs of redemption, "You are worthy to take the scroll and to open its seals, because you were slain, and with your blood you purchased people for God from every tribe and language and people and nation"; anthems of glory, sung with energy and enthusiasm, "Worthy is the Lamb, who was slain, to receive power and wealth and wisdom and strength and honor and glory and praise!"[15] The reason the Apostle John interchanged "saying" and "singing" in his description of heaven's worship was because he stressed the content of the message that was sung.[16] No matter how awesome a heavenly choir of "ten thousand times ten thousand" sounds, the message is never lost in the power of the music.[17] God's redemptive story is set to music from "the song of Moses the servant of God" to "the song of the Lamb" and all people will worship before the "King of the ages."[18]

---

11. Exod 15.
12. Luke 1:46–55, 67–79; 2:14, 29–32.
13. Phil 2:6–11.
14. 1 Tim 3:16.
15. Rev 4:8; 5:9, 12.
16. Rev 4:8, 10; 5:9, 12; 7:10, 12.
17. Rev 5:11.
18. Rev 15:3.

The Offering

In many churches the offering is taken after the choir sings the anthem. In this case, the offering is people, the 144,000, the firstfruits who belong to the Lamb. Those who sing the anthem of redemption are characterized in four ways: (1) They do not defile themselves with women, for they remain virgins; (2) They follow the Lamb wherever he goes; (3) They were purchased from among the human race and offered as firstfruits to God and the Lamb; and (4) They do not lie; they are blameless.

These four descriptive attributes define the true militancy of the 144,000 and the costly character of the followers of the Lamb. They manifest "the power to bless, unburden, serve, heal, mend, restore, and liberate."[19] Those who belong to God refuse to go to bed with the great prostitute of Babylon.[20] The image of sexual purity and virginity is used figuratively for spiritual purity and devotion to God. They have not drunk "the maddening wine of her adulteries." They have kept themselves pure for the "wedding of the Lamb."[21] They have not compromised with the great prostitute, nor have they been assimilated into the great city.

The second defining characteristic is discipleship. Wherever Jesus goes they go. The Lamb of God is their true center.[22] They not only believe *in* Jesus, they have the faith *of* Jesus. They are Beatitude-based believers with salt and light impact because they have taken his word to heart. They practice visible social righteousness and their hidden spirituality works itself out in true prayer, real giving, and genuine fasting. No middle-of-the road Christianity for this group. Every day is a choice between ambitions, visions, priorities, and masters—and every day Jesus wins. "The secret of the easy yoke," writes Dallas Willard, "is simple, actually. It is the intelligent, informed, unyielding resolve to live as Jesus lived in all aspects of life."[23]

The third validation is that they are a gift laid on the altar of God. Their value lies not in themselves, but in their grace-filled redemption. They are purchased by Christ "from among the human race" and they are "offered as firstfruits to God and the Lamb." "You are not your own," wrote the Apostle Paul. "You were bought at a price. Therefore honor God

19. Hunter, *To Change the World*, 193.
20. Ezek 23; Jer 3:1–10.
21. Rev 19:7; 2 Cor 11:2.
22. Rev 14:13; 19:14.
23. Willard, *The Spirit of the Disciplines*, 10.

with your bodies."[24] The very ones ostracized from the world economy are valued in God's economy.[25] They are "holy to the Lord, the firstfruits of his harvest."[26]

The fourth quality of the 144,000 is their integrity. "No lie was found in their mouths; they are blameless." Simple honesty will do more for the cause of Christ than complex arguments for the nature of truth. For those who have given up on truth in principle, truthful people are the only way they may see the truth. Being truthful liberates the believer from manipulation and posturing. We refuse to mimic "the cunning and craftiness of people in their deceitful scheming. Instead, speaking the truth in love, we will in all things grow up into him who is the head, that is, Christ." In the armor of God, the belt of truth refers to "speaking the truth in love" and speaking "truthfully to your neighbor." Truth is the "the truth that is in Jesus," and living truthfully.[27] Truth in doctrine; truth in praxis. This is the liberating truth found in Jesus' teaching and the truthfulness found in the imitation of Christ.[28]

These four qualities—sexual purity, obedient discipleship, a sacrificial life, and undaunted integrity—help to "disentangle the life and identity of the church from the life and identity of American society."[29] The Apostle John envisions a life that is fit for the priesthood of all believers. This is the offering that counts: not the checks tossed in the offering plate, but the offering of ourselves to Christ. John envisions a worship service where we leave our money in the pew and we give ourselves at the altar. We are "living sacrifice[s], holy and pleasing to God—this is true worship."[30] The Revelation weans us away from our preoccupation with the start of the Christian life and focuses our attention on the perseverance of faith. Life is not a sprint but a marathon; it's not over until it's over. Faithfulness to the end affirms our faith from the beginning. And the end in faithfulness to the end may be a long way off, but it is the only end worth pursuing. "Today we emphasize the New Birth," writes Peter Gilquist. "The ancients emphasized being faithful to the end. We moderns

24. 1 Cor 6:19.

25. Rev 13:17.

26. Jer 2:3.

27. Eph 4:14–15, 21, 25: 5:9.

28. John 8:31–32.

29. Hunter, *To Change the World*, 184. (In the place of "American" read Canadian, Chinese, Mongolian, etc.)

30. Rom 12:1; see 1 Pet 1:13–23.

talk of wholeness and purposeful living; they spoke of the glories of the eternal kingdom . . . the emphasis in our attention has shifted from the completing of the Christian life to the beginning of it."[31]

The Sermon

[14:6–13] *The I saw another angel flying in midair, and he had the eternal gospel to proclaim to those who live on the earth—to every nation, tribe, language and people. He said in a loud voice, "Fear God and give him glory, because the hour of his judgment has come. Worship him who made the heavens, the earth, the sea and the springs of water."*

A second angel followed and said, "Fallen! Fallen is Babylon the Great," which made all the nations drink the maddening wine of her adulteries.

A third angel followed them and said in a loud voice: "If anyone worships the beast and its image and receives its mark on their forehead or on their hand, they, too, will drink the wine of God's fury, which has been poured full strength into the cup of his wrath. They will be tormented with burning sulfur in the presence of the holy angels and of the Lamb. And the smoke of their torment will rise for ever and ever. There will be no rest day or night for those who worship the beast and its image, or for anyone who receives the mark of its name."

This calls for patient endurance on the part of the people of God who keep his commands and remain faithful to Jesus. Then I heard a voice from heaven say, "Write: Blessed are the dead who die in the Lord from now on." "Yes," says the Spirit, "they will rest from their labor, for their deeds will follow them."

Three angels deliver a three-point sermon, but it is not the kind of sermon we hear on Sunday morning. The midair mobility of the angels signifies their freedom to deliver "the eternal gospel" unhindered "to those who live on earth—to every nation, tribe, language and people."[32] The first message is succinct: "Fear God and give him glory, because the hour of his judgment has come. Worship him who made the heavens, the earth, the sea and the springs of water." This is the gospel Jesus preached on the shore of the Sea of Galilee, but the angel delivers the message with an increased sense of urgency. This is what God's messengers have been

31. Gillquist, "A Marathon We Are Meant to Win," 22.
32. Rev 14:6; see 8:13.

saying for millennia: "Today, if you hear his voice, do not harden your hearts."[33] Jesus' proclamation of the good news consistently warned of judgment.[34] The apostles sound a similar note of intensity and urgency.[35] If we tailor the gospel to fit the expectations of the consumer, we have forgotten what the gospel sounds like on the lips of Jesus. When I was on the staff of a megachurch, the seven-member pastoral team met once a week for breakfast. We were always on the lookout for what might hold the attention of a restless audience. Sermons were built on a humorous anecdote or an emotional story. The designated refrain for the anecdotes and jokes that were good enough for prime time preaching was "That'll preach!" What was often missing in our preaching was any sense of "Thus says the Lord."

The first angel delivers his message to unbelieving earth dwellers in a last-ditch effort to turn their hearts to God and away from their infatuation with the devil and his cohorts. There is still time, but the opportunity is closing fast. The angel's proclamation recalls Jesus' pronouncement in his Sermon on the End of the World: "This gospel of the kingdom will be preached in the whole world as a testimony to all the nations, and then the end will come."[36]

The second angel announces judgment: "Fallen! Fallen is Babylon the Great, which made all the nations drink the maddening wine of her adulteries." This second part of the three-point gospel sermon echoes Isaiah's prophecy, "Babylon has fallen, has fallen!" and alludes to Nebuchadnezzar's boastful confidence in the great city of Babylon.[37] The great city intoxicates the world into bowing before the goddess of success. Rome's global economy was built on oppressive power and exploitation, producing a spirituality based on idolatry that glorified the state and the pagan gods. The angel's announcement leaves no doubt as to the failure of the great city. The striving and struggling of humanity for power and success will end in complete collapse. The last word on judgement is pronounced with finality.

The third angel shouts in a great voice, "If anyone worships the beast, if anyone worships its image, if anyone receives its mark on their

33. Heb 4:7; see Ps 95:7, 8.

34. Matt 5:24–27; 8:12; 10:12f.; 11:21–24; 12:30–32; 12:39–45; 13:40–43; 13:47–50; 21:42–44; 23:13–39.

35. Jas 4:7–10.

36. Matt 24:14.

37. Isa 21:9; Dan 4:30.

forehead, if anyone receives its mark on their hand, then they too will drink of the wine of God's fury." The conditional clause applied four times points back to the power of the beast to control humanity, but it also leaves room for people to respond.[38] The implicit message is this: it's not too late. If you are in this position, repent right now—don't wait another moment. The third angel drives the sermon home with a graphic description of judgment. Those who refuse to respond will drink up the wrath of God at its full strength. The ungodly "will be tormented with burning sulfur in the presence of the holy angels and of the Lamb. And the smoke of their torment will rise for ever and ever." Their suffering will be intense and enduring. They will languish in the presence of the Lamb, aware of their culpability and mindful of their refusal to respond to the call of God. Their hell is too horrible to be either self-imposed or self-perpetuated, but it is self-selected due to their rejection of the Lamb and their loyalty to the beast. They will come to know in the presence of the Lamb and his holy angels that they chose this path, and for the first time they will see it for what it is—hell.

Believers have a responsibility to proclaim this message of judgment. But the mobility and magnitude of the angelic message does not justify a "fire and brimstone" pulpit-pounding harangue. We must hear this message for ourselves. We do not stand apart from this word of warning.[39] We stand under this judgment, with the only hope of salvation found in the grace of Christ. Secondly, we must deliver this message of warning and judgment with love and compassion. We are like a caring doctor informing a vulnerable patient that he or she has cancer. When I was eighteen an oncologist sat down and looked me in the eye and said, "I'm sorry. I have some bad news. You have non-Hodgkin's lymphoma." My doctor promised to do everything he could to help me through the experience. My cancer became his challenge, and I remember his devotion to my healing. He entered into my struggle as if it were his war to fight. It is that kind of empathy and heartfelt concern that ought to accompany the preaching of judgment.

Church historian James Bradley underscores this necessary tension between "seriousness of purpose" and "affection for people" when he writes:

38. Rev 13:4, 8, 12, 15–17.
39. 1 Pet 4:17.

> The gravity of the message of the Gospel must be united with a warm love for people, because seriousness by itself tends to turn legalistic and mean, while affection alone may become sentimental and indulgent, and indulgence in the ministry is dangerous. . . . When we no longer believe that people are truly lost without Christ, or that the Gospel is important but not infinite in implication, then we will also lose the ultimate meaning of grace and love.[40]

The purpose of this sermon is to bring people to Christ; it is to preach the gospel truth in a lost and evil world. It is not intended to scare people or frighten them into the kingdom of God. Nevertheless it is a serious life-and-death matter—an eternal life-and-death matter. The ungodly can foolishly dismiss it as bellicose and bullying, but its intention is to deliver the truth with authority, and without coercion or manipulation. We do not dismiss the report of the physician who diagnoses cancer as meaningless drivel. We do not ridicule the lifeguard for warning of dangerous riptides. If we are going to hell, shouldn't someone stand in our way and offer the gospel? Three angels preach a three-point salvation message to "every nation, tribe, language and people," because the Lord is patient, "not wanting anyone to perish, but everyone to come to repentance."[41]

The Response

The message of judgment is hard to accept. John doesn't say, "This calls for celebration." He says, "This calls for patient endurance on the part of the people of God, who keep his commands and remain faithful to Jesus." This message sobers everyone: the ungodly who refuse to forsake their idolatrous ways as well as the godly, lest they be seduced into following the ways of the beast.[42] Based on the prayers of the saints, Craig Keener sees the sermon assuring "oppressed Christians of their coming

---

40. Bradley, "Future Judgment in Doctrine and Ministry," 6, as quoted in Bruner, *The Gospel of John*, 395.

41. 2 Peter 3:9.

42. Beale, *Revelation*, 765. Beale argues that the impact of this sermon on the believer is the main reason for the sermon: "Now an exhortation is given to true saints to persevere through temporary suffering inflicted on them because of their loyalty to Christ, so that they might avoid the eternal consequences of loyalty to the beast and receive an eternal reward (14:13). The warning in vv 6–11 is intended to motivate believers to persevere. Therefore, v 12 is the main point of vv 6–12, as with the similar exhortations in 13:10 and 13:18" (*Revelation*, 765).

vindication."[43] He writes, "For those of us who generally face a much lesser level of oppression, the image may not strike us as cause for celebration. To fully capture the spirit of the text, we need to enter into the sufferings of our oppressed brothers and sisters elsewhere in the world. . . . This text may remind us that judgment often comes as vindication of those who have been wronged."[44] Keener's pastoral concern to identify with our persecuted brothers and sisters in Christ is important, but the challenge to faithfulness outweighs the assurance of vindication. The saints called out in a loud voice, "How long, Sovereign Lord, holy and true, until you judge the inhabitants of the earth and avenge our blood?"[45] They were not told that their persecutors would be judged. They were told "to wait a little longer, until the full number of their fellow servants and brothers and sisters were killed just as they had been."[46]

The sermon ends on a note of benediction. John writes, "Then I heard a voice from heaven say, 'Write: Blessed are the dead who die in the Lord from now on.'" The Lord himself offers a blessing and John writes it down. The blessing subsumes the victory over Satan and the vindication of the saints under their abiding relationship with the Lord; there is no greater joy than belonging to the Lord. As Jesus said to his disciples when they returned home, "I saw Satan fall like lightning from heaven. I have given you authority to trample on snakes and scorpions and to overcome all the power of the enemy; nothing will harm you. However, do not rejoice that the spirits submit to you, but rejoice that your names are written in heaven."[47] The challenge to believers remains—stand firm. The apostles are inspired to give the same spiritual direction. "Let nothing move you. Always give yourselves fully to the work of the Lord, because you know that your labor in the Lord is not in vain."[48]

---

43. Rev 6:9–11; 8:3–5.
44. Keener, *Revelation*, 380.
45. Rev 6:10.
46. Rev 6:11.
47. Luke 10:18–20.
48. 1 Cor 15:58.

24

The Wrath of God

⌣· Revelation 14:14—16:21 ·⌣

[**14:14–20**] *I looked, and there before me was a white cloud, and seated on the cloud was one like a son of man with a crown of gold on his head and a sharp sickle in his hand. Then another angel came out of the temple and called in a loud voice to him who was sitting on the cloud, "Take your sickle and reap, because the time to reap has come, for the harvest of the earth is ripe." So he who was seated on the cloud swung his sickle over the earth, and the earth was harvested.*

Another angel came out of the temple in heaven, and he too had a sharp sickle. Still another angel, who had charge of the fire, came from the altar and called in a loud voice to him who had the sharp sickle, "Take your sharp sickle and gather the clusters of grapes from the earth's vine, because its grapes are ripe." The angel swung his sickle on the earth, gathered its grapes and threw them into the great winepress of God's wrath. They were trampled in the winepress outside the city, the blood flowed out of the press, rising as high as the horses' bridles for a distance of 1,600 stadia.

THERE HAS TO BE an end to evil. The wars, killings, rapes, and abortions must come to an end. The gang violence, the school massacres, the threat of nuclear annihilation, and the trading in human cargo must end. The adultery, abandonment, abuse, and divorce must end. The plagues, epi-

222

demics, malignancies, and deformities must end. The earthquakes, floods, tsunamis, and famines must end. The volcanos, tornadoes, hurricanes, and droughts must end. The lies, slander, deception, and manipulation must end. The fraud, greed, bribes, and kickbacks must end. The addictions, obsessions, fixations, and perversions must end. The gluttony and starvation must end. If we itemized every sin, every crime, every disease, every form of deviancy and perversion, would there ever be an end to evil? But we know all evil will end one day. The Apostle John announces this end, and plays it out live on the stage of our praying imagination so we can feel the drama of the cataclysmic end of evil. If you don't want evil to end, you won't like his script.

The eternal gospel of salvation and judgment is preached boldly, throughout the world, to every nation, tribe, language, and people. People are given a real opportunity to respond positively and "worship him who made the heavens, the earth, the sea and the springs of water." Their adamant refusal to repent and receive the mercy of God and to turn from their idolatrous worship of the unholy trinity proves their insistence on their own evil ways. John envisions "one like a son of man" coming in judgment, burning up the chaff and trampling the bad grapes. He sees seven angels coming from heaven "with the seven last plagues—last, because with them God's wrath is completed."[1] Their coming is celebrated by "those who have been victorious over the beast and its image and over the number of its name."[2] The seven angels emerge from "the tabernacle of testimony," dressed in clean, shining linen with golden sashes. One of the four living creatures, who is stationed at the throne of God, commissions them by giving each angel "golden bowls filled with the wrath of God."[3] They are commanded, "Go, pour out the seven bowls of God's wrath on the earth."[4] Instead of pouring out bowls of incense before the altar, symbolizing prayer, these angels robed like priests pour out judgment on the earth. The plagues are modeled after the Egyptian plagues, and parallel the series of judgments announced by the trumpets. But the impact of the bowls is devastatingly universal. Each plague progressively intensifies the severity of the judgment. The sixth bowl incites the battle of Armageddon, and the seventh bowl brings it all to an end. "God

1. Rev 15:1.
2. Rev 15:2.
3. Rev 15:7.
4. Rev 16:1.

remembered Babylon the Great and gave her the cup filled with the wine of the fury of his wrath."[5]

The end of evil will not come about through legal reform or advances in education or a thriving global economy or international efforts for world peace. Evil will only come to an end in God's final judgment. The will to power and the weapons of this world will not achieve the end of evil. With that said, the Christian is called to be salt and light in a decaying, dark world, not because of the promise of reform, but because of the promise of salvation. The world needs help. Decay and darkness are realities, not surprises! Jesus intended for his followers to penetrate their culture the way salt was rubbed into meat to prevent it from going bad. Jesus does not say, "You are the sugar of the earth" or "You are the honey of the world." German theologian Helmut Thielicke speaks of the biting quality of true Christian witness, saying that there is a natural temptation for Christians "to sweeten and sugar the bitterness of life with an all too easy conception of a loving God."[6] Jesus expected his followers to be an essential preservative in a culture bent on evil. We enter into this mission for the good of the world, knowing that the evil of the world will not end until God's wrath is poured out. The Apostle John turns next to a description of the final judgment.

The Great Winepress of God's Wrath

John's vision of "one like a son of man" seated on a white cloud recalls Daniel's experience: "In my vision at night I looked, and there before me was one like a son of man, coming with the clouds of heaven. He approached the Ancient of Days and was led into his presence."[7] John heard Jesus use this same image in his Sermon on the End, when he said, "At that time the sign of the Son of Man will appear in the sky, and all the peoples of the earth will mourn. They will see the Son of Man coming on the clouds of heaven, with power and great glory."[8] The gold crown is a metaphor for the royal rule of Christ. The sickle signifies judgment.[9]

5. Rev 16:19.
6. Thielicke, *Life Can Begin Again*, 28.
7. Dan 7:13.
8. Matt 24:30.
9. Dan 7:13–14; Ezek 39:17–20; Ps 110:4–5; Jer 51:33; Isa 63:3; Lam 1:15; Hos 6:11; Joel 3:13; Matt 13:30, 40–42; Rev 19:15.

The reaping is authorized directly from the temple, indicating a divine edict. An angel "came out of the temple and called in a loud voice to him who was sitting on the cloud, 'Take your sickle and reap.'" The earth is harvested—that is to say, judged—with a single swing of the sickle. Then another angel came out of the temple with a sickle and still another angel came out with fire from the altar, calling the first angel with a sickle to gather the earth's grapes and throw them in the winepress of God's wrath. The imagery recalls Joel's vision of the Day of the Lord, when the Lord gathers all the nations and judges them in the Valley of Jehoshaphat.

> Swing the sickle, for the harvest is ripe. Come, trample the grapes, for the winepress is full and the vats overflow—so great is their wickedness! Multitudes, multitudes in the valley of decision! For the day of the Lord is near in the valley of decision.[10]

Joel developed the theme of God's ultimate judgment and applied the certainty of God's justice to his own day. He looked to the day of the Lord when God would gather all nations and "bring them down to the Valley of Jehoshaphat."[11] He expanded the horizon of his vision and enlarged the sphere of God's ultimate judgment to take in all the nations. "Proclaim this among the nations: Prepare for war!"[12] The language he used to describe this judgment shows up in the teachings of Jesus and in the Apostle John's vision of the end.[13] In Joel's prophecy there is no mention of blood, but in John's vision, blood, not wine, gushes from the winepress—a river of blood, flowing as high as a horse's neck for 184 miles. However, a literal number misses the meaning John intended: 1,600 stadia symbolically stands for completeness ($4 \times 4 \times 10 \times 10 = 1,600$); the numbers four and ten signify the completeness of worldwide judgement. The end of evil is accomplished.

The Seven Angels With Seven Plagues

[15:1–8] *I saw in heaven another great and marvelous sign: seven angels with the seven last plagues—last, because with them God's wrath is completed. And I saw what looked like a sea of glass glowing with fire and,*

10. Joel 3:13–14.
11. Joel 3:2.
12. Joel 3:9.
13. See Mark 4:29.

standing beside the sea, those who had been victorious over the beast and its image and over the number of its name. They held harps given them by God and sang the song of God's servant Moses and of the Lamb: "Great and marvelous are your deeds, Lord God Almighty. Just and true are your ways, King of the nations. Who will not fear you, Lord, and bring glory to your name? For you alone are holy. All nations will come and worship before you, for your righteous acts have been revealed." After this I looked, and I saw in heaven the temple—that is, the tabernacle of the covenant law— and it was opened. Out of the temple came the seven angels with the seven plagues. They were dressed in clean, shining linen and wore golden sashes around their chests. Then one of the four living creatures gave to the seven angels seven golden bowls filled with the wrath of God, who lives for ever and ever. And the temple was filled with smoke from the glory of God and from his power, and no one could enter the temple until the seven plagues of the seven angels were completed.

Seven angels with the seven last plagues are introduced beside a calm sea glowing with fire. The sovereign Lord has calmed the sea of cosmic evil with the fire of judgment. Beside the sea stand all those who had been "victorious over the beast and its image and over the number of its name" and they sing "the song of God's servant Moses and of the Lamb." The new song is in the tradition of the Exodus victory, but it has been transposed into a higher key by the righteous victory of the Lamb. The militant and nationalistic fervor of Moses' original song has been reworked in the light of redemption.[14] The appearance of these seven angels with the seven last plagues stands for the completion of God's wrath. They are wearing priestly robes that recall the appearance of the Son of Man in the first vision of Christ. This may imply that they serve as his representatives. They are about to pour out the seven golden bowls filled with the wrath of God. The momentous nature of the occasion is signified by the manifestation of the glory and power of God in the temple. All of this is a sign that the end of evil is in sight.

The Seven Bowls of God's Wrath

[16:1–21] *Then I heard a loud voice from the temple saying to the seven angels, "Go, pour out the seven bowls of God's wrath on the earth." The first angel went and poured out his bowl on the land, and ugly, festering sores*

14. See Ps 111:2, 3; Deut 32:4; Jer 10:7; Ps 86:9–10; 98:2.

broke out on the people who had the mark of the beast and worshiped its image. The second angel poured out his bowl on the sea, and it turned into blood like that of a dead person, and every living thing in the sea died. The third angel poured out his bowl on the rivers and springs of water, and they became blood. Then I heard the angel in charge of the waters say: "You are just in these judgments, you who are and who were, the Holy One, because you have so judged; for they have shed the blood of your people and your prophets, and you have given them blood to drink as they deserve." And I heard the altar respond: "Yes, Lord God Almighty, true and just are your judgments."

The fourth angel poured out his bowl on the sun, and the sun was allowed to scorch people with fire. They were seared by the intense heat and they cursed the name of God, who had control over these plagues, but they refused to repent and glorify him. The fifth angel poured out his bowl on the throne of the beast, and its kingdom was plunged into darkness. People gnawed their tongues in agony and cursed the God of heaven because of their pains and their sores, but they refused to repent of what they had done.

The sixth angel poured out his bowl on the great river Euphrates, and its water was dried up to prepare the way for the kings from the East. Then I saw three evil spirits that looked like frogs; they came out of the mouth of the dragon, out of the mouth of the beast and out of the mouth of the false prophet. They are demonic spirits that perform signs, and they go out to the kings of the whole world, to gather them for the battle on the great day of God Almighty.

"Look, I come like a thief! Blessed are those who stay awake and keep their clothes on, so that they may not go naked and be shamefully exposed." Then they gathered the kings together to the place in Hebrew is called Armageddon. The seventh angel poured out his bowl into the air, and out of the temple came a loud voice from the throne, saying, "It is done!" Then there came flashes of lightning, rumblings, peals of thunder and a severe earthquake. No earthquake like it has ever occurred since the human race has been on earth, so tremendous was the quake. The great city split into three parts, and the cities of the nations collapsed. God remembered Babylon the Great and gave her the cup filled with the wine of the fury of his wrath. Every island fled away and the mountains could not be found. From the sky huge hailstones, each weighing about a hundred pounds, fell on people. And they cursed God on account of the plague of hail, because the plague was so terrible.

The bowls are modeled on the Exodus plagues:

Bowl 1 — malignant sores (Exod 9:8)
Bowl 2 — the seas become blood (Exod 7:17–21)
Bowl 3 — the rivers become blood (Exod 7:17–21)
Bowl 4 — the sun scorches people with fire (Exod 9:22)
Bowl 5 — the throne of beast is darkened (Exod 10:21)
Bowl 6 — the Euphrates dries up (Exod 8:2)
Bowl 7 — the final earthquake (Exod 9:22–25)

Finally, after this long build up, a loud voice from the temple announces to the seven angels, "Go, pour out the seven bowls of God's wrath on earth." The first three angels pour out their bowls onto the land, sea, and rivers, causing painful sores on the followers of the beast, wiping out all aquatic life, and poisoning the water supply. This outpouring of wrath corresponds to the trumpet blasts of judgment, only intensified and universal. The agents of judgment are in complete unanimity with divine justice, and the saints under the altar add their affirmation as well: "Yes, Lord God Almighty, true and just are your judgments."[15]

Everyone involved in the execution, including those who had prayed long and hard for judgment, are in agreement that this is the right thing to do. The fourth angel pours out his bowl of the sun's scorching heat and people respond by cursing the name of God, "who had control over these plagues." They refuse to repent and glorify God. The fifth angel pours out his bowl and plunges "the throne of the beast, and its kingdom" into utter darkness.[16] Once again, the judgment is met with the people's adamant refusal "to repent of what they had done." The sixth bowl of wrath dries up the Euphrates, which is a figurative way of saying that the influence of Babylon dries up.[17] The world order is coming apart; it has been plunged into darkness and its power has evaporated.

Benediction

The final judgment scenarios are interrupted by a benediction from King Jesus. In the midst of these evil-ending judgments the followers of the

15. Rev 6:9.
16. Matt 8:12; 22:13; 25:30.
17. Rev 17:1.

Lamb are given only a brief word of spiritual direction. The voice is un-identified, but the first person singular makes the identity of the speaker certain. It is Christ himself, warning and admonishing his followers. The Lord says, "Keep watch! I come unannounced, like a thief. You're blessed if, awake and dressed, you're ready for me. Too bad if you're found run-ning through the streets, naked and ashamed."[18] The message is consis-tent with Jesus' pointed challenge in the Olivet discourse, "Stay alert!"[19]

The staccato imperative "Keep your clothes on" may strike us as a bit odd at first. But clothing has been an important metaphor throughout the Revelation. It signifies purity and righteousness. To their shame, many in the church in Sardis had soiled their clothes, but a few had not, and Christ promised that "They will walk with me, dressed in white, for they are worthy."[20] Nakedness signifies exposure and shame. To be clothed in compassion, kindness, humility, gentleness, and patience is the best defense against being caught "shamefully exposed."[21] To put off the old self and to put on the full armor of God is the best way to be prepared for any and every eventuality in a world that would love to expose the Chris-tian.[22] As we have seen, the witnessing church is clothed in sackcloth, signifying repentance and genuine humility.[23]

Armageddon

As a last-ditch effort the dragon and the beasts rally the troops for Ar-mageddon.[24] They sound like croaking frogs as they gather the nations to wage war against almighty God. This battle is called "the war of the great day of God," which is another way of saying that evil is about to come to an end in a final and climactic war.[25] The seventh angel flings his bowl into the air and all hell breaks loose. The "ruler of the kingdom of

---

18. Rev 16:15, *The Message*.

19. Matt 24:36–51; see Luke 12:39; 1 Thess 5:2; 2 Pet 3:10.

20. Rev 3:4.

21. Col 3:12.

22. Eph 4:22; 6:11–17.

23. Rev 11:3.

24. Beale, *Revelation*, 840. Beale writes, "Armageddon in Hebrew means 'mount of Megiddo'" (*Revelation*, 840). It is where the Israelites were attacked. Deborah refers to the kings and forces arrayed against the people of God (Judg 5:19).

25. Joel 2:11; 3:9–12; Zeph 1:14–16.

the air" is powerless to prevent a world-ending catastrophic earthquake.[26] The great city splits into three parts and the cities of the nations collapse. Babylon the Great drinks "the wine of the fury of [God's] wrath." One-hundred-pound hailstones slam into earth, pummeling and smashing people whose only response is to curse and blaspheme God. The end of evil is signified by the disappearance of every island and every mountain. The end of evil is not a pretty picture. Did we think evil would end without a bloody fight? The adamant refusal to repent coupled with a demonic insistence on cursing God will persist right up to the end. The dragon and his beasts will continue to croak until they are forever silenced. But make no mistake, evil has to end.

God's Grace

We "all have sinned and fallen short of the glory of God."[27] As much as we might resist the idea, we are by nature deserving of wrath. This is offensive to some and confirms their worst fears of "fire and brimstone" old-time religion. C. S. Lewis observed:

> Speak about beauty, truth and goodness, or about a God who is simply the indwelling principle of these things, speak about a great spiritual force pervading all things, a common mind of which we are all parts, a pool of generalized spirituality to which we can all flow, and you will command friendly interest. But the temperature drops as soon as you mention a God who has purposes and performs particular actions, who does one thing and not another, a concrete, choosing, commanding, prohibiting God with a determinate character. People become embarrassed or angry. Such a conception seems to them primitive and crude and irreverent."[28]

But to argue that the wrath of God is obsolete would be to argue against the teaching of the Bible, the nature of God, and even the moral sensibilities of what it means to be human. Miroslav Volf asks us to imagine giving a lecture in a war zone to people "whose cities and villages have been first plundered, then burned and leveled to the ground, whose daughters and sisters have been raped, whose fathers and brothers have had their

---

26. Eph 2:2; Dan 12:1; Hag 2:6–7; Zech 14:4; Heb 12:25–29.

27. Rom 3:23.

28. Lewis, *Miracles*, 83–84.

throats slit." The subject is "a Christian attitude toward violence" and the thesis is that "the practice of nonviolence requires a belief in divine vengeance." Volf, himself a Croatian who lived and taught in Croatia during the war in former Yugoslavia, argues that non-retaliation and the possibility of reconciliation is grounded in the reality of God's judgment. If there is no divine accountability for sin and evil, it is impossible to live out the gospel of Christ. To deny the wrath of God often means that one has not experienced the horrors of war and the tragedy of evil.[29] Let's be clear on the meaning of wrath: wrath does not mean "the intemperate outburst of an uncontrolled character. It is rather the temperature of God's love, the manifestation of his will and power to resist, to overcome, to burn away all that contradicts his counsels of love."[30] The wrath of God is not an embarrassment, but a blessing.

I remember one time in particular when I provoked the wrath of my father. I had convinced my younger brother that it would be fun to set our model cars on fire by pouring gasoline over them. The smell of burnt plastic must have traveled farther than we thought, because my father came out to the garage to check on the odor. He caught us in the act, uncapped gasoline can and matches in hand. He exploded in anger; he never touched me, but I felt his wrath. At first I wondered why he was making such a big deal about it, but that only made my father angrier. I pictured a little mischief, some harmless fun. He pictured my brother and me in a burn treatment ward. Before the afternoon was over I had gotten the picture; now I can't look at a red gasoline can without thinking of that incident and my father's wrath.

The wrath of God means that there are consequences for evil. There is real accountability and judgment. Eliminate the wrath of God and you eliminate the need for the gospel. The wrath of God provokes the necessity for the gospel. This is why C. S. Lewis said, "The hardness of God is kinder than the softness of men, and His compulsion is our liberation."[31] The stark contrast between sin and salvation heightens our appreciation for the necessity and reality of God's grace. The intervention of God's grace is "set in contrast to the bankruptcy and doom of a humanity left to itself, left to what it is 'by nature.'"[32]

29. Volf, *Exclusion and Embrace*, 304.

30. Barth, *Ephesians*, 231–32.

31. Lewis, *Surprised By Joy*, 183.

32. Lincoln, *Ephesians*, 104.

25

The Beautiful Side of Evil

⤳ Revelation 17:1—18:24 ⤲

[17:1–18] *One of the seven angels who had the seven bowls came and said to me, "Come, I will show you the punishment of the great prostitute, who sits by many waters. With her the kings of the earth committed adultery, and the inhabitants of the earth were intoxicated with the wine of her adulteries." Then the angel carried me away in the Spirit into a wilderness. There I saw a woman sitting on a scarlet beast that was covered with blasphemous names and had seven heads and ten horns. The woman was dressed in purple and scarlet, and was glittering with gold, precious stones and pearls. She held a golden cup in her hand, filled with abominable things and the filth of her adulteries. This title was written on her forehead: Mystery, Babylon The Great, The Mother Of Prostitutes, and of the Abominations of the Earth. I saw the woman was drunk with the blood of God's people, the blood of those who bore testimony to Jesus. When I saw her, I was greatly astonished. Then the angel said to me: "Why are you astonished? I will explain to you the mystery of the woman and of the beast she rides, which has the seven heads and ten horns. The beast, which you saw, once was, now is not, and will come up out of the Abyss and go to its destruction. The inhabitants of the earth whose names have not been written in the book of life from the creation of the world will be astonished when they see the beast, because it once was, now is not, and yet will come. This calls for a mind with wisdom. The seven heads are seven hills on which the woman* sits. *They are also seven kings. Five have fallen, one is, the other has not yet come; but when he does come, he must remain for a little while. The beast who once was, and now is not, is an eighth king. He belongs to the seven and is going to his destruction.*

The ten horns you saw are ten kings who have not yet received a king-dom, but who for one hour will receive authority as kings along with the beast. They have one purpose and will give their power and authority to the beast. They will make war against the Lamb, but the Lamb will triumph over them because he is Lord of lords and King of kings—and with him will be his called, chosen and faithful followers."

Then the angel said to me, "The waters you saw, where the prostitute sits, are peoples, multitudes, nations and languages. The beast and the ten horns you saw will hate the prostitute. They will bring her to ruin and leave her naked; they will eat her flesh and burn her with fire. For God has put it into their hearts to accomplish his purpose by agreeing to give the beast their power to rule, until God's words are fulfilled. The woman you saw is the great city that rules over the kings of the earth."

HATE AND SELF-DESTRUCTION ARE at the core of civilization, because our culture has turned away from God. The "mystery of the woman and of the beast she rides" is really no mystery at all. God lets evil run its course through its long history of antichrist resistance. Regimes come and go, but the dominant world system remains bent on waging war against the Lamb. John's lengthy description of the fall of Babylon the Great and the intense grief felt by those who invested everything in her success is paralleled in heaven by "the roar of a great multitude" shouting "Hallelujah!"[1] There is tremendous joy in heaven over the destruction of the great city.

Following the four stanza hallelujah anthem in heaven, the final judgment is described for the final time. The King of kings and Lord of lords destroys the beast, the false prophet and all those who fought against God. The final end of this protracted description of the end comes when Satan is thrown into the lake of fire. This is followed by the great white throne judgment that assigns all those whose names are not written in the Book of Life to the lake of fire.

One of the themes running through John's description of the end is the refusal of men and women to repent and turn to Christ. They would

1. Rev 19:1.

rather wear the mark of the beast and worship his image than turn to God and follow the Lamb. Even confronted by all-out judgment, they continue to curse God. They are adamant in their refusal to repent and glorify God. Instead of allowing the consequences of evil to drive them to repentance and the mercy of God, they dig in their heels and resist God. Let the truth be known, God is patient, "not wanting anyone to perish, but everyone to come to repentance. But the day of the Lord will come like a thief. The heavens will disappear with a roar; the elements will be destroyed by fire, and the earth and everything in it will be laid bare."[2] The description of evil and the analysis of the present world's culture follows the certain knowledge of its destruction.

The Two Sides of Evil

There are two sides to evil. The Apostle John's audit of evil is only half done. He has traced the ugly side of evil to its specific and distinctive source. He has described the unholy trinity, the enormous red dragon seeking to devour the church, the beast of the sea with its power to make war against the saints, and the beast of the earth that looks like a lamb and talks like a dragon. He has evil's number, pulled up its file, and knows its account: 666. Now he turns his attention to the great prostitute and the great city.

The two-sided description of evil is graphic. The Apostle John makes no effort to tone down his description with examples of God's common grace. The goodness of God is implied in the descriptions of music, craftsmanship, weddings, and commerce, all of which are lost in the great city's doom.[3] John's analysis focuses on the culture of evil that is doomed to destruction. He is like an oncologist treating a malignancy. The culture of evil, no matter how pervasive and popular, is terminal. The only healing available is through the blood of the Lamb.

The Revelation portrays a way of life that is antithetical to God. John fixes a vivid image in our minds of "a woman sitting on a scarlet beast" that is "covered with blasphemous names." She is "dressed in purple and scarlet, and [is] glittering with gold, precious stones and pearls. She [holds] a golden cup in her hand, filled with abominable things and the filth of her adulteries."

2. 2 Pet 3:9–10.
3. Rev 18:22–23.

The Beauty Queen

Evil's hideous strength is not only fearsome and tyrannical, it is also thrilling and beautiful. There is a seductive side to evil that the inhabitants of the earth find attractive and compelling. The beautiful side of evil is personified in the great prostitute, who is "drunk with the blood of God's people, the blood of those who bore testimony to Jesus." She seduces the world with the intoxicating wine of her abominations and adulteries. Another word that could be used for this intoxication is addiction. "We become ensnared by our spiritual idols in much the same way that people are snared by drink and drugs."[4] Sitting on top of the beast she wears her title proudly. We almost forget that the angel's purpose is to show John "the *punishment* of the great prostitute." We get caught up in this magnificent pictorial layout of glitz and glamor. Even John seems a bit enamored with the Babylonian woman. Quite possibly, he was "awestruck."[5] Sometimes evil comes charging at us like the four horses of the apocalypse, threatening to trample us under foot by conquest, terror, starvation, and death. And at other times, evil comes to us as a seductress, riding a scarlet beast, representing a counterfeit glory and symbolizing the gorgeous and glamorous allure of evil.

Chaste Bride	Prostitute
21:2, 9 fidelity	immorality 17:1–2; 18:9
21:24 submission to God's rule	submit to Babylon 17:18
21:24–26 worship	wealth 18:12–17
21:8, 27 moral purity	moral chaos 17:4–5; 18:23
22:1–2 healing and life	persecution of the saints 17:6; 18:24
22:14 safety for the saints	separation of the saints 18:4
21:2 the glory of God	self-glorifying pride 18:5
21:6 the bridal city forever	the great city destroyed 16:17–18
22:4 marked in Christ	marked in Satan 17:5
21:3 dwelling place for God	dwelling place of demons 18:2

4. Keller, *Center Church*, 128.
5. Beale, *Revelation*, 863.

The contrast between the beauty of the queen of Babylon and that of the bride of Christ is striking. When we describe the great prostitute as beautiful we do so within a particular aesthetic tradition. The Greek notion of beauty resided in "the autonomy of form and the purity of the aesthetic experience."[6] An object of beauty was someone or something that stood apart and detached from the observer, to be applauded by the spectator. The beauty of the great prostitute is visual and visceral. She has an allure of romance and excitement. She incites lust, not love. The Hebrews looked for beauty in the integration of life and meaning: gray hair on an old man, a mother surrounded by her children. Beauty is not observed as an object over and against oneself; beauty is beheld in the midst of life. The Hebrew notion of beauty was more comprehensive and integrated.[7]

The "beauty queen" of Babylon has nothing to do with the quality of beauty sought by the psalmist when he seeks "to gaze on the beauty of the Lord and to seek him in his temple."[8] The great prostitute and the great city are one in the same, and they stand for a culture that makes "war against the Lamb." This beauty queen is the polar opposite of the bride of Christ, the wife of the Lamb, who will be described later.[9] First the parody, but this is no *Saturday Night Live* satirical skit, it is deadly serious. There is no humor here. She is the world's greatest celebrity, surrounded by paparazzi 24/7. With her golden cup of opportunity and pleasure, the great prostitute invites the world to her party, even as the bride of Christ invites believers to the wedding supper of the Lamb. She *is* the great city, with all of its attractions and achievements. She offers an attractive, aesthetically appealing culture. We see a beautiful, richly-attired woman, possessing exquisite taste, surrounded by luxury, and adorned with expensive jewelry. Instead of decay, decadence, pain, and suffering, we see perfection and wealth. Conspicuous consumption abounds; impoverishment remains hidden. The four horses of the apocalypse are not on the cover of *Vogue*. The great prostitute uses her perch of privilege to seduce and beguile the world. She holds the golden cup of opportunity, a symbol of pleasure and success. From John's position in the wilderness, he is able to see her clearly. She is the epitome of the human quest for self-fulfillment and the cult of self-worship. The "Mother of Prostitutes,"

6. Dyrness, "Aesthetics in the Old Testament," 421–32.

7. Ibid., 430.

8. Ps 27:4.

9. Rev 21:9–14.

the great hooker, is the goddess of bodily perfection and the ultimate icon of consumption. She proudly sits atop the beast.

One of the angels of judgment explained to John "the mystery of the woman and of the beast she rides, which has the seven heads and ten horns." This beast is the devil embodied in a monster. He is identified mockingly by three phrases: it "once was, now is not, and will come out of the abyss and go to destruction." This negative parody recalls the description of the Alpha and Omega, the Lord God, "who is, and who was, and who is to come, the Almighty."[10] The seven heads and the seven hills signify the oppressive world system. The obvious adaptation of Daniel's prophecy allows John to translate what is said of Babylon to Rome. The image of the beast is not limited to the current political power but represents all those sovereignties that challenge the lordship of Jesus Christ, both ancient and modern.

There is no need to identify the ten horns with particular Roman emperors. It is not John's purpose to survey Roman political history. The seven names, seven hills, seven kings, and ten horns all signify the comprehensiveness of the opposition against Christ. When John says that "five have fallen, one is, the other has not yet come," he is saying we are nearing the end.[11] Evil reaches its climax in an eighth king who is "the beast who once was, and now is not." The number eight suggests a vain attempt by the beast who has come up from the abyss to mimic the risen Christ. Eight is the symbolic number for Christ, who commences a new creation on the eighth day following his resurrection. John's description of the eighth beast is important: "He belongs to the seven and is going to his destruction." The climax of evil is nothing more than what believers have weathered before; it is more of the same. The manifestation of evil is what the followers of the Lamb have experienced all along. The eighth beast "is not some new outbreak of invincible, demonic power."[12]

10. Rev 1:8; 4:8; 11:16; 16:5.

11. Bauckham, *The Climax of Prophecy*, 406. Bauckham: "Revelation's first readers knew perfectly well who the sixth head, the reigning emperor, was, and did not need to work it out.... Even John did not need to discover that there were to be seven emperors by counting them: he knew there had to be seven because that is the number of completeness.... All that 17:10 is intended to tell his readers is how far they are from the end of the sequence of seven, that is, of the full sequence of emperors of Rome. It tells them there is only one short reign to go before the end of Roman imperial dominance of the world. It tells them, as Revelation frequently does, that the end is near" (*Climax*, 406).

12. Beale, *Revelation*, 876.

The beast knows that it has already been defeated by the cross of Christ and has been assigned to the abyss. Its antagonism against the church will be intense, but in line with what has come before. John advises the "called, chosen and faithful followers" of the Lamb that the beast will turn on the prostitute and destroy her—the beast will strip her naked and begin to eat her flesh. Evil will be inspired by God to turn on the great city and begin the process of self-destruction. This is the extreme manifestation of God giving the world up to its own sinful desires, shameful lusts, and depraved mind.[13] The ultimate consumer society will begin to consume itself.

Given what has been said about the dragon and the beasts, we would expect to find hell on earth, but instead we see a parody of heaven on earth. We behold a great city of power and luxury, riches and splendor, commerce and capitalism. No mention is made here of the underside of evil. Nothing is said of poverty, homelessness, destitution, abandonment, abortion, disease, addiction, violence, and crime. Although all of these evils still exist in their most virulent form, the prevailing image of the great city is money, sex, and power.

I used to think the Lord would not come again because the world was not bad enough yet. But John places the beautiful side of evil right alongside the horrors of it's ugly side. The devil's influence is felt not only in violent acts of terrorism, but in skyrocketing sales of pharmaceuticals and warheads as well. The oppressive world system legitimizes abortions on demand and turns children into immortality symbols. Evil is in the dark alley mugging and evil is in the corporate windfall. There is a bull market on Wall Street and poverty runs rampant. The streetwise pimp and the corporate CEO have something in common. I realize now that the pervasiveness of evil and the universal sweep of idolatry fits the Apostle John's vision of the end.

> A world of nice people, content in their own niceness, looking
> no further, turned away from God, would be just as desperately
> in need of salvation as a miserable world—and even might be
> more difficult to save.[14]

---

13. Rom 1:24–29.

14. Lewis, *Surprised by Joy*, 181.

The Greatest City in the World

[18:1–8] *After this I saw another angel coming down from heaven. He had great authority, and the earth was illuminated by his splendor. With a mighty voice he shouted:*

"Fallen! Fallen is Babylon the Great! She has become a dwelling for demons and a haunt for every evil spirit, a haunt for every unclean bird, a haunt for every unclean and detestable animal. For all the nations have drunk the maddening wine of her adulteries. The kings of the earth committed adultery with her, and the merchants of the earth grew rich from her excessive luxuries." Then I heard another voice from heaven say: "Come out of her, my people, so that you will not share in her sins, so that you will not receive any of her plagues; for her sins are piled up to heaven, and God has remembered her crimes. Give back to her as she has given; pay her back double for what she has done. Pour her a double portion from her own cup. Give her as much torment and grief as the glory and luxury she gave herself. In her heart she boasts, 'I sit enthroned as queen. I am not a widow; I will never mourn.'

Therefore in one day her plagues will overtake her: death, mourning and famine. She will be consumed by fire, for mighty is the Lord God who judges her."

The great city of Babylon has its roots in the Tower of Babel culture described in Genesis, and is named after the city that Nebuchadnezzar built to honor the glory of his majesty.[15] It was Sodom in Abraham's day, Egypt in Moses' day, and Jerusalem in Jesus' day.[16] For John the great city was Rome. For you it may be San Diego or New York or Moscow or Beijing. The great city is where the Lord was crucified and where people turn away from God. The great city continues to be the world's marketplace, trading in precious metals, fine fashions, luxury products, and every conceivable commodity, including " people's bodies and souls." The world is the ultimate consumer society, and no one appears to be asking, "What good will it be for someone to gain the whole world, yet forfeits their soul? Or what can anyone give in exchange for their soul?"[17] John observes the great city at the end of time, in the twilight of human civilization. "After

15. Gen 11; Dan 4:30.
16. Rev 11:8.
17. Matt 16:26.

this" refers to the progression of images in John's vision, not the actual chronological order of history.[18] The description of the world system that follows overlaps with the description of the woman who sits on the beast. The great city is set in contrast with the new Jerusalem. There is a "clear parallelism," although the description of the fallen city is more complex and involved.[19] The great city has all the conveniences and refinements anyone could imagine: fine dining, beautiful music, luxury living, skilled craftsmanship, and powerful people. But John calls it "a dwelling for demons and a haunt for every evil spirit," and finishes his description of the great city by saying, "In her was found the blood of prophets and of God's people, of all who have been slaughtered on the earth."[20] As it turns out, evil is great for the economy and the arts, but awful for God's people. The merchants trade in the "bodies and souls of men" and martyr the saints. John's description of the great city is a funeral eulogy, because it has already been split apart and destroyed. The city has drunk the wine of the fury of God's wrath. This account amounts to a retrospective look on what the great city was and is no longer.

The followers of the Lamb are warned, "Come out of her, my people, so that you will not share in her sins, so that you will not receive any of her plagues; for her sins are piled up to heaven, and God has remembered her crimes." This is an ominous warning that is said without immediate qualifications.[21] When this kind of separation was called for in Isaiah's prophecy, it meant a physical departure, but the prophet was careful to qualify his warning: "Depart, depart, go out from there! Touch no unclean thing! . . . But you will not leave in haste or go in flight; for the Lord will go before you, the God of Israel will be your rear guard."[22]

There is plenty of evidence throughout the Revelation that the followers of the Lamb are in the thick of culture, bearing gospel witness. The timing of the end has been set by the number of martyrs "who keep God's commands and hold fast their testimony about Jesus."[23] The followers of

---

18. Rev 18:1.

19. Bauckham, *The Climax of Prophecy*, 339. See Rev 17:1–19; 21:9—22:9.

20. Rev 18:2, 24.

21. Beale, *Revelation*, 903. Beale writes, "The church must beware of trusting in economic security lest its members be judged along with the world. This is especially the case in Laodicea, whose church said, 'I am rich and have become wealthy, and I have need of nothing' (3:17)" (*Revelation*, 903).

22. Isa 52:11–12.

23. Rev 6:11; 12:11, 17.

the Lamb remain easy prey for the devil and his beasts for the sake of Christ. They are in the world, but not of the world.[24] The call for separation from this oppressive world system relieves believers of the mistaken notion that they must fight to control the destiny of the great city. John's vision of the end of the world corresponds with a hell-bent culture: abortion and infanticide are practiced, the poor are exploited and oppressed, the family is broken, sexual anarchy is rampant, gay marriages are sanctioned, the military-industrial complex dominates, greed drives the economy, conspicuous consumption is glorified, and entertainment glorifies violence. Christ never intended his followers to impose on the great city his moral order. It is not their place to copy the Muslims in their quest to institute sharia law.

James Hunter argues that culture is generated through a multitude of power networks and various spheres of influence. It is a complex, dynamic system, the product of history, institutions, and elites. Change is nearly always from the top down and controlled by elites "who have a lopsided access to the means of cultural production."[25] Christians are called to be faithful and to bear witness to the gospel. They have not been called to change the world, but to be transformed by Christ in the world. Do they have impact? Yes! But even an army of Martin Luther Kings and William Wilberforces could not end evil. No sooner is racism suppressed in one place than it pops up in another. Win the war against poverty and society breaks out into greed. Liberate the oppressed, *as we must*, but observe how quickly the oppressed become oppressors. Hunter's thesis is in keeping with the Apostle John's understanding of culture.

> The most humane understandings of personhood, relationships, community, time, space, freedom, obligation, material wealth, cannot be established or recovered through a five-year plan or even in a generation—certainly not through politics, not through social reform, and not even in revival. In this light, the call to this generation of Americans to repent and pray for revival to renew values of the national culture may be welcome, but no one should be under any illusion about its capacity to fundamentally transform the present cultural order at its most rudimentary level.[26]

24. Rev 16:6; 17:6; 18:24.
25. Hunter, *To Change the World*, 41.
26. Ibid., 46–47.

We might expect Hunter to challenge believers to seek influential positions of leadership and decision making in the various spheres of power
that shape culture. On the contrary, Hunter argues that elitism, "a dis-
position and relationality of superiority, condescension, and entitlement
by social elites," is "abhorrent for the Christian." "By its very nature, elitism is exploitative. So far as I can tell, elitism for believers is despicable
and utterly anathema to the gospel they cherish."[27] Hunter reasons, "The
worst possible conclusion, then, is that what Christians need is a new
strategy for achieving and holding on to power in the world—at least in
any conventional sense. Such a conclusion is not only wrong on its own
terms, it is wrong because Christians operate with an understanding of
power that is derived from the larger and dominant culture of the late
modern world."[28]

This conclusion is freeing, even invigorating. Instead of buying into
the lobbying strategies and tactics of the world, Christians are freed up to
establish a faithful presence wherever the Lord has called and gifted them
to serve. Biblical insight and sociological research converge to dispel the
false notion that cultural change comes about by changing hearts and
minds and lobbying for political power.

Hyperpower and the Global Economy

[18:9–20] *When the kings of the earth who committed adultery with her
and shared her luxury see the smoke of her burning, they will weep and
mourn over her. Terrified at her torment, they will stand far off and cry:
"Woe! Woe to you, great city, you mighty city of Babylon! In one hour your
doom has come!" The merchants of the earth will weep and mourn over her
because no one buys their cargoes anymore—cargoes of gold, silver, precious
stones and pearls; fine linen, purple, silk and scarlet cloth; every sort of
citron wood, and articles of every kind made of ivory, costly wood, bronze,
iron and marble; cargoes of cinnamon and spice, of incense, myrrh and
frankincense, of wine and olive oil, of fine flour and wheat; cattle and sheep;
horses and carriages; and human beings sold as slaves.*

*They will say, "The fruit you longed for is gone from you. All your
luxury and splendor have vanished, never to be recovered." The merchants
who sold these things and gained their wealth from her will stand far off,*

27. Ibid., 94.
28. Ibid., 99–100.

terrified at her torment. They will weep and mourn and cry out: "Woe! Woe
to you, great city, dressed in fine linen, purple and scarlet, and glittering
with gold, precious stones and pearls! In one hour such great wealth has
been brought to ruin!" Every sea captain, and all who travel by ship, the
sailors, and all who earn their living from the sea, will stand afar off. When
they see the smoke of her burning, they will exclaim, "Was there ever a city
like this great city?" They will throw dust on their heads, and with weeping
and mourning cry out: "Woe! Woe to you, great ity, where all who had
ships on the sea became rich through her wealth! In one hour she has been
brought to ruin!" Rejoice over her, you heavens! Rejoice, you people of God!
Rejoice, apostles and prophets! For God has judged her with the judgment
she imposed on you.

The seductive power of political and military might, famously known as
the Pax Romana, dominated John's culture. The metaphors of the great
prostitute and the great city merge into one seemingly all-encompassing
dark reality—imperial Rome. "The political religion of Rome was the
worst kind of false religion, since it absolutized Rome's claim on her
subjects and cloaked her exploitation of them in the garb of religious
loyalty."[29] "John sees a connection between Rome's economic affluence,
Rome's idolatrous self-deification, and Rome's military and political
brutality."[30] Her power and wealth are the product of her ruthless world
domination, and John's prophetic critique extends not only to the persecution of Christians and the idolatry of the imperial cult, but to all the
evils that have shaped the culture of Rome.

The list of twenty-eight imported cargoes represents Rome's global
economy. Professor Bauckham's research reveals that these twenty-eight
products (note the significance of 4 x 7) provides a comprehensive picture of the economic exploitation and global reach of Rome. Anyone
who argues that the New Testament knows nothing of modern financial
systems and today's market economy ought to examine John's description
of Rome's market economy. Gold and silver from Spain, precious stones
from India, pearls from the Persian Gulf, and fine linen from Egypt represent Rome's quest for luxury; all of these products epitomized it. Purple
linen was one of the most enduring status symbols, because the expensive
dye was extracted from shellfish.[31] Silk from China and all kinds of citrus

29. Bauckham, *The Climax of Prophecy*, 348.
30. Ibid., 349.
31. Ibid., 354.

wood from north Africa were shipped to Rome. Tables made from Moroccan citrus wood and furniture made of ivory were status symbols of the luxurious life. Bronze art from Corinth, steel swords and cutlery from Spain, and marble imported from Africa, Egypt, and Greece displayed Rome's hunger for conspicuous consumption. Cinnamon and spices from south Asia and incense and other sweet-smelling ointments from Yemen and Somalia were "typical features of the good life in imperial Rome."[32] Expensive wines from Spain and Sicily were more profitable to grow for the market in Rome than grain, leading to local food shortages. Olive oil from Italy, fine flour from Africa, and wheat and corn were all shipped in abundance by thousands of ships from across the Mediterranean. Imported cattle, sheep, and horses were brought in mainly for breeding purposes. Special silver-plated chariots were shipped from Gaul. The final cargo listed by John was slaves. The market for attractive slaves, that is, "human persons," among the Roman rich was so competitive that it drove up the price and turned slaves into luxury items. To end the list by making this critical distinction between products and persons suggests that John is not only making a comment on the slave trade, but judging that "the whole of Rome's prosperity and luxury rests" on "inhuman brutality," greed, "contempt for human life," and an "addiction to consumption."[33] "Give her as much torment and grief as the glory and luxury she gave herself."[34]

John portrays the bright side of an affluent, sophisticated culture, where musicians and artists have their privileged place.[35] Craftsmen are kept busy; merchants are happy; the people are entertained. But now the whole thing is gone. Its citizens are in mourning. Their three-stanza song of "Woe! Woe" on earth contrasts with the four-stanza hallelujah anthem in heaven.[36] Those who lament the fall of the great city cannot get over

32. Ibid., 360–61.

33. Ibid., 371, 368.

34. Rev 18:7.

35. Bauckham, *The Climax of Prophecy*, 343. Bauckham writes, "The whole of chapter 18 is closely related to Old Testament prophecies of the fall of Babylon and the fall of Tyre. . . . John has created a fresh prophecy of considerable literary skill, which appears especially in the vivid portrayal of the three groups of mourners for Babylon (18:9–19). This is inspired by and borrows phrases from Ezekiel's prophecies of the fall of Tyre, which includes dirges sung for Tyre by two different groups of mourners (Ezek 26:15–18; 27:29–36) and also a catalogue of the merchandise from various lands in which Tyre traded (Ezek 27:12–24)" (*Climax*, 343).

36. Rev 19:1–8.

the fact that such wealth and power and luxury could all be destroyed in an hour! All the buying and selling, entertaining and creating, investing and celebrating is brought to a halt in an hour. The great city crashes without warning, like a house of cards. Evil turns on itself and the culture implodes. The beast ends up hating the prostitute and together they self-destruct. "In one hour such great wealth has been brought to ruin!" "In one hour she has been brought to ruin."[37]

These little masters of the universe, who craved luxury and power, are in mourning. The merchants who bought low and sold high and the shippers who risked life and limb to make a living are devastated. But how did John's seven congregations recieve this lament for Babylon? Did they mourn right along with the kings, merchants, and sea captains? "Any reader who finds himself sharing the perspective of Rome's mourners—viewing the prospect of the fall of Rome with dismay—should thereby discover, with a shock, where he stands, and the peril in which he stands."[38] The Apostle John's purpose in describing the end of Roman commerce was to shock and convict believers. He sought to lead believers in Thyatira and Laodicea to repentance for participating in and prospering from an oppressive economic system. John's greatest concern was for the vitality and integrity of the church's witness. He hoped that his critique of Rome would challenge the complicity of the church and its idolatrous compromise with Rome's commerce and cult. What was true for the believers in Rome is true for believers in America. If we have any hope of redeeming our witness, we will have "to disentangle the life and identity of the church from the life and identity of American society." James Davison Hunter continues,

> For conservatives and progressives alike, Christianity far too comfortably legitimates the dominant political ideologies and far too uncritically justifies the prevailing macroeconomic structures and practices of our time. . . . The moral life and everyday social practices of the church are also far too entwined with the prevailing normative assumptions of American culture. . . . Christianity has uncritically assimilated to the dominant ways of life in a manner dubious at the least. Even more, these assimilations arguably compromise the fundamental integrity of its witness to the world.[39]

37. Rev 18:17, 19.
38. Bauckham, *The Climax of Prophecy*, 376.
39. Hunter, *To Change the World*, 184–85.

The mighty angel is unsympathetic. He does not mourn with the mourners. He does not share their grief. Instead, he calls for a joyous celebration.
He shouts out three times, "Rejoice!" The idolatry and the oppression, the
persecution and the suffering are over. This is the prelude that ushers in
the hallelujah chorus: "Rejoice over her, you heavens! Rejoice, you people
of God! Rejoice, apostles and prophets! For God has judged her with the
judgment she imposed on you."[40]

The Day the Music Died

[18:21–24] *Then a mighty angel picked up a boulder the size of a large
millstone and threw it into the sea, and said: "With such violence the great
city of Babylon will be thrown down, never to be found again. The music of
harpists and musicians, pipers and trumpeters, will never be heard in you
again. No worker of any trade will ever be found in you again. The sound of
a millstone will never be heard in you again. The light of a lamp will never
shine in you again. The voice of bridegroom and bride will never be heard
in you again. Your merchants were the world's important people. By your
magic spell all the nations were led astray. In her was found the blood of
prophets and of God's people, all of who have been slaughtered on the earth."*

A mighty angel picks up a huge stone and throws it into the sea as a
dramatic object lesson of judgment. As the boulder-sized millstone hits
the water he says, "With such violence the great city of Babylon will be
thrown down, never to be found again." The description recalls Jesus'
words, "If anyone causes one of these little ones—those who believe in
me—to stumble, it would be better for them if a large millstone were
hung around their neck and they were drowned in the depths of the sea.
Woe to the world because of the things that cause people to stumble!"[41]
   The lament for Babylon concludes with a lyrical portrait of a society
at its best. Gone are the images of glamour, luxury, and violence. The
angel eulogizes the beauty of the symphony and the sound of the craftsmen hard at work. He recounts what will be no more. "The light of the
lamp will never shine in you again. The voice of bridegroom and bride
will never be heard in you again." The angel is aware of the goodness God
intended for the city and the beauty of ordinary life lifted up to God.

40. Rev 18:20.
41. Matt 18:6–7.

But everyday life is tragically sabotaged by an idolatrous and oppressive economic system. "Your merchants were the world's important people. By your magic spell all the nations were led astray." The beauty of normal everyday life has concealed the hidden tragedy of martyrdom and all kinds of persecutions: "In her was found the blood of prophets and of God's people, of all who have been slaughtered on the earth."

This description fits the American ideal. The beauty of the arts, the productivity of labor, and the tranquility of domestic life rests on a principle that people have the right to pursue happiness. Americans are united in their respect for individual freedom. The US Constitution sought to depoliticize religion and defend religious freedom, but America has evolved under the pressure of radical pluralism and secularism. Faithful Christians belong to a beleaguered minority whose convictions contradict society's prevailing ideological commitments. When the angel says, "By your magic spell all the nations were led astray," he captured the spirit of the prevailing cultural ideology that narrows the sphere of Christ's influence to the sanctuary and a private faith. In society we worship the imperial self and the Christian is coerced, under penalty of ostracization or persecution, to bow the knee to a new kind of Caesar.

From Hosanna to Hallelujah!

In contrast to evil's complexity and power, John's Spirit-inspired spiritual direction remains simple and straightforward. John says, "This calls for patient endurance and faithfulness on the part of God's people."[42] John has nothing new to add that we haven't already heard from Jesus. Faithfulness embraces prayer and obedience, worship and witness, purity and truth-telling. Perseverance involves staying alert, not letting our guard down, and being ready for action.[43] True maturity means cultivating the mind of Christ in a mindless world. The evil agents of the beast "will make war against the Lamb," but we can count on the fact that "the Lamb will triumph over them because he is Lord of lords and King of kings— and with him will be his called, chosen and faithful followers."[44] The call to faithfulness opens up immense possibilities for the followers of the Lamb. We need to pray through the implications of what Jesus meant

42. Rev 13:10.

43. Rev 16:10.

44. Rev 17:14.

when he said to his followers, "I am sending you out like sheep among wolves. Therefore be as shrewd as snakes and as innocent as doves."[45]

First, we set our sights on real hope. We "recognize that all social organizations exist as parodies of eschatological hope." James Davison Hunter writes,

> . . . The city is a poor imitation of heavenly community; the modern state, a deformed version of the *ecclesia*; the market, a distortion of consummation; modern entertainment, a caricature of joy; schooling, a misrepresentation of true formation; liberalism, a crass simulacrum of freedom; and the sovereignty we accord to the self, a parody of God himself. As these institutions and ideals become ends in themselves, they become the objects of idolatry.[46]

Reflecting on the truth that Jesus Christ will come again to rule and reign, Karl Barth commented on how Christians ought to speak to non-Christians. We need courage and confidence. If we are fearful and angry, we betray the peace of Christ. Barth challenged believers to understand the world's hopes and fears in order to communicate to the world true hope and true faith.

> We must not sit among them like melancholy owls, but in a certainty about our goal, which surpasses all other certainty. Yet how often we stand ashamed beside the children of the world, and how we must understand them if our message will not satisfy them. He who knows that "my times are in your hands" (Psalm 31:15) will not haughtily regard the [people] of the world, who, in a definite hope that often shames us, go their way; but he will understand them better than they understand themselves. He will see their hope as a parable, a sign that the world is not abandoned, but has a beginning and a goal. We Christians have to put the right Alpha and Omega into the heart of this secular thought and hope. But we can only do so if we surpass the world in confidence.[47]

Second, we practice loving resistance. We study the cultural engagement of the Lord Jesus and the apostles. We follow the example of their loving resistance, regardless of the provocation and persecution. In the Spirit, we become resilient saints in community, who know the difference

45. Matt 10:16.

46. Hunter, *To Change the World*, 234–35.

47. Barth, *Dogmatics in Outline*, 132.

between Christlike resistance and worldly resentment. The way forward is through incarnational identification and sacrificial love. This can be said so simply, but it takes one's whole life in faithful determination and utter dependence upon the Lord to live this way. There is plenty of repentance and confession along the way, and we never arrive. But the aim is clear: "The Jesus way wedded to the Jesus truth brings about the Jesus life."[48]

Third, the followers of the Lamb "seek first [Christ's] kingdom and his righteousness" without running after all the things pagans do.[49] We reject the privileges of status and the approval of the world. We extend hospitality to the stranger and seek to meet the needs of the poor, whether or not they are willing to follow Jesus. As Christ reached out to the lost, we do as well. Instead of blaming the culture, we seek to live as God's called-out community within the culture. God's plan is for the world to grasp Christ's cosmic supremacy through God's new society: the church. From a humanistic point of view, the "plan of him who works out everything in conformity with the purpose of his will" may appear obscure and hidden, but to the apostles, the mystery of Christ and the manifold wisdom of God, "which for ages past was kept hidden in God," is now being made known through the church "to the rulers and authorities in the heavenly realms."[50]

This high view of the church and its impact in the world echoes Jesus' authoritative pronouncement in the Sermon on the Mount, when he declared to his disciples, "You are the salt of the earth," and "You are the light of the world."[51] That is to say, Beatitude-based believers possess God's kingdom, experience God's comfort, and will inherit God's earth. They have been blessed with God's righteousness and they are defined by God's mercy and vision. What more could God give them? They have it all, and for that reason they are salt and light. "'You folks *are*' not 'You folks *ought* to be,' the most significant people on the planet."[52]

John sees the great prostitute sitting on a scarlet beast, a symbol of world domination, but he remembers Jesus riding into Jerusalem on a borrowed donkey, deliberately distancing himself from any sign of worldly prestige and power. Jesus intentionally chose to make his entrance

48. Peterson, *The Jesus Way*, 4.

49. Matt 6:32–33.

50. Eph 1:11; 3:11.

51. Matt 5:13, 14.

52. Bruner, *The Churchbook: Matthew 1–12*, 188.

on a young donkey, a sign of humility and gentleness. The never-before-ridden colt, the festive crowd of families, children shouting "hosanna," and the elderly praising God create a wonderful picture of peace and joy. God continues to approach us in humility and gentleness with his gift of salvation. The real tragedy is that anyone would turn down his invitation for the allure of the whore working the streets of the great city. The picture in Revelation of the white horse whose rider is called Faithful and True is yet to come.[53] The approach of God will be as fearsome and devastating in the end as it was gentle and humble in the beginning. Those who have spurned his love and rejected his salvation will be struck down. The Lord, who is faithful and true, comes to us with grace and mercy. Christ's journey to the cross fulfills Zechariah's prophecy.

> Rejoice greatly, Daughter Zion! Shout, Daughter Jerusalem! See, your king comes to you, righteous and having salvation, lowly and riding on a donkey, on a colt, the foal of a donkey.[54]

53. Rev 19:11–16.
54. Zech 9:9.

26

Salvation and Judgment

⌐· Revelation 19:1–21 ·⌐

[**19:1–10**] *After this I heard what sounded like the roar of a great multitude in heaven shouting: "Hallelujah! Salvation and glory and power belong to our God, for true and just are his judgments. He has condemned the great prostitute who corrupted the earth by her adulteries. He has avenged on her the blood of his servants." And again they shouted: "Hallelujah! The smoke from her goes up for ever and ever." The twenty-four elders and the four living creatures fell down and worshiped God, who was seated on the throne. And they cried: "Amen, Hallelujah!" Then a voice came from the throne, saying: "Praise our God, all you his servants, you who fear him, both great and small!" Then I heard what sounded like a great multitude, like the roar of rushing waters and like loud peals of thunder, shouting: "Hallelujah! For our Lord God Almighty reigns. Let us rejoice and be glad and give him glory! For the wedding of the Lamb has come, and his bride has made herself ready. Fine linen, bright and clean, was given her to wear." (Fine linen stands for the righteous acts of God's holy people.) Then the angel said to me, "Write: Blessed are those who are invited to the wedding supper of the Lamb!" And he added, "These are the true words of God." At this I fell at his feet to worship him. But he said to me, "Don't do that! I am a fellow servant with you and with your brothers and sisters who hold to the testimony of Jesus. Worship God! For it is the Spirit of prophecy who bears testimony to Jesus."*

THE SPIRALING INTENSITY OF salvation and judgment are reaching their zenith. The sounds of silence are eclipsed by "the roar of a great multitude in heaven shouting: 'Hallelujah!'" We are moving to the end. The eerie silence of the once-great city is contrasted with the pulsating praise of heaven. The mournful melancholy of the funeral dirge gives way to the exuberant sounds of praise encircling the throne and encompassing everyone in heaven. The social critic cannot imagine anything like this exhilarating praise and absolute certainty. This description of worship is strange. "We will never find what we are looking for in the things we pick up along the way," writes Craig Barnes. "Not even the religious things. Not even important things like relationships. All of these things will leave our souls empty if we try to force them to satisfy our thirst. The true object of our search is nothing less than an encounter with the Holy One."[1] The eternal gospel that inspires the symphony of "Hallelujahs!" strikes the world as foolishness.

Almost the End

The span of the end runs from Jesus' seventh statement from the cross, "It is finished!" to the glorious announcement from the throne, "It is done!"[2] The Revelation has led us to the end repeatedly, only to find that there is more to the great day of God's wrath than we realized. God keeps putting off the painful finality of judgment. He moves toward the end, offering redemption and mercy, "not wanting anyone to perish, but everyone to come to repentance."[3] Nevertheless, God's justice is inevitable, and the momentum of his salvation history is irreversible. There is nothing new in this book that has not been said before in God's word; nothing of critical importance in the book that is not repeated over and over again. The Apostle John meant for us to be caught up in the dynamic interplay between worship and judgment.

The slow ending is a sign of God's mercy. Those who love God suffer a seemingly interminable delay for the sake of God's universal offer of salvation, but they also maintain a courageous and compelling witness. The followers of the Lamb are clearly marked out. They persist in proclaiming the truth of God against overwhelming opposition and persecution.

1. Barnes, *Sacred Thirst*, 24.
2. John 19:30; Rev 16:17.
3. 2 Pet 3:9.

They entrust themselves to the providence of God and remain undefiled and unbowed. In that day, there will be two kinds of people: mourners and worshipers. The world weeps and mourns and cries out, "Woe! Woe, O great city!" while heaven shouts "Hallelujah!"[4] "Salvation and glory and power belong to our God, for true and just are his judgments." The spiraling intensity has reached a crescendo. Having heard the language of judgment, we are thrilled to hear the shout of adoration. For every "Woe!" there is a "Hallelujah!" The beast is as good as gone, never to return, and the Lord God almighty, who was and is and is to come, will rule and reign forever.

Worship is the reward for witnessing the opening of the seals, hearing the trumpet blasts of judgment, and patiently enduring the outpouring of God's bowls of wrath. The saints are all those who have overcome the power of evil by the precious blood of the Lamb. They waited a long time for this moment of jubilant praise. This is the worship John anticipated from the beginning. The opening doxology set the tone: "To him who loves us and has freed us from our sins by his blood, and has made us to be a kingdom and priests to serve his God and Father—to him be glory and power for ever and ever!"[5] And the song from the throne establishes the theme: "Worthy is the Lamb, who was slain, to receive power and wealth and wisdom and strength and honor and glory and praise!"[6]

The four-stanza hallelujah hymn comes at just the right time. Heaven bursts into song after the seven bowls of wrath have been poured out, the great prostitute has been destroyed, and the great city has been destroyed—judgment is complete. The final stanza sets up a vivid contrast between the great prostitute and the bride of Christ. Marriage is John's chosen metaphor for salvation, in keeping with God's intention from the beginning. John is not inventing a metaphor out of thin air. He is using a tried-and-true analogy to capture the union and fulfillment of God's people. "For the wedding of the Lamb has come, and his bride has made herself ready."

John uses a double-edged metaphor. He employs the image of the great prostitute and the bride of Christ to project two destinies. His Spirit-inspired vision uses sexual intimacy to portray the range of human

4. *Halal* (to praise) and *Yah* (abbreviated form of the divine name, Yahweh) combine to denote admiration, adulation, and rejoicing; it stands as a recognized shout of praise.

5. Rev 1:5–6.

6. Rev 5:12.

response to God, from blasphemy to blessing, damnation to doxology. The essence of life is pictured as either an orgy or a liturgy. We are either drinking from the golden cup filled with abominable things and the filth of the great prostitute's adulteries, or celebrating the Eucharist in the body of Christ. John pushes these images as far as they can possibly go: we are either drinking up the blood of the saints or saved by the blood of the Lamb. Our choice in life is between the brothel or the household of faith; the strip joint or the sanctuary; seduction or salvation. According to John, there are only two kinds of people: mournful earth dwellers and God-glorifying worshipers.

Write!

John is instructed to write: "Blessed are those who are invited to the wedding supper of the Lamb!" Can there be a more important invitation than this one? This is what the soul has been yearning for all along, but who hasn't failed to understand the true nature of this longing? In a world of seduction and deception, blasphemy and bluster, manipulation and intimidation, we are invited into God's real presence. Presidents, popes, and celebrities are nothing compared to this presence. Then the angel adds, "These are the true words of God," as if to say, "Listen carefully; these are God's words!" The all-out admonition is clear: "Worship God. For the testimony of Jesus is the spirit of prophecy." John is given definitive instructions. "The testimony of Jesus" deserves to be written down and shared freely. This witness deserves a hearing everywhere: in the lecture hall, on the shop floor, in the corner office, on the playing field. Wherever people gather, "the testimony of Jesus" deserves a hearing. The commission to write covers the full range of witnessing possibilities. The hallelujah anthem is not the finale but the prelude to John's final Advent vision. John carries us forward into a future that many of us may feel is too good to be true. But John is here to announce, "Believe it! It's true!"

The Wedding Supper

The wedding invitation has been sent. "Blessed are those who are invited to the wedding supper of the Lamb!" The bride of Christ "has made herself ready. Fine linen, bright and clean, was given her to wear." "Fine linen stands for the righteous acts of God's holy people." The followers of the

Lamb are transformed by the grace of Christ. The bride of Christ becomes holy because she has been made holy. The nature of this holy interplay is explicit in Leviticus: "Consecrate yourselves and be holy, because I am the Lord your God. Keep my decrees and follow them. I am the Lord, who makes you holy."[7] The Prophet Isaiah prepares the church for this beautiful metaphor: "I delight greatly in the Lord; my soul rejoices in my God. For he has clothed me with garments of salvation and arrayed me in a robe of his righteousness."[8]

John's wedding invitation recalls Jesus' parable of the wedding banquet: "The kingdom of heaven is like a king who prepared a wedding banquet for his son. He sent his servants to those who had been invited to the banquet to tell them to come, but they refused to come."[9] The parable intensifies the juxtaposition of marriage and militancy, hospitality and hostility. The spurned rejection provokes war and the enraged king sends out his army to wipe out those who mistreated his servants. This parallels John's description of the wedding supper of the Lamb and the great supper of God. Jesus merged his images in a single parable. John positions his images of wedding and war, salvation and judgment, side by side. In Jesus' parable the king confronts a wedding guest, who "was not wearing wedding clothes." "Friend," he asked, "how did you get in here without wedding clothes?" Then, the king ordered his servants, "Tie him hand and foot, and throw him outside, into the darkness, where there will be weeping and gnashing of teeth." Jesus adds an ominous note: "For many are invited, but few are chosen."[10] The warning is picked up by John in his description of "the great supper of God."

The "supper of the Lamb" signifies the beauty and intimacy of our relationship with Christ. There is a deep connection between The Last Supper and the wedding supper of the Lamb. On the night that Jesus was betrayed, he served as host to three meals in one (the Passover, the Last Supper, and a farewell meal). He ate this family meal in anticipation of the glorious reunion at the marriage supper of the Lamb. "Blessed are those who are invited to the wedding supper of the Lamb!"

In the transition between the wedding supper of the Lamb and the great supper of God, John acted inappropriately. He fell at the angel's feet "to worship him." The angel immediately and emphatically reprimanded

7. Lev 20:7-8; see Phil 2:12-13.
8. Isa 61:10.
9. Matt 22:2-3.
10. Matt 22:11-14.

John. "Don't do that!" he said. "I am a fellow servant with you and with your brothers and sisters who hold to Jesus' testimony. Worship God! For the testimony of Jesus is the Spirit of prophecy." The incident reminds us that it only takes a thoughtless moment to falsify true worship. Deep feelings of sincerity notwithstanding, we can become confused and revere the messenger instead of Christ. If the thrust of John's "whole prophecy is the distinction between true worship and idolatry," then he draws the issue out personally in this revealing moment.[11] In the midst of heightened spiritual excitement, even John had trouble discerning true worship. He shows "how easy it is to fall into idolatry."[12] The angel's words must have had their true impact on John, because he uses these very words to identify himself at the beginning of the Revelation. The fact that John faced this same experience again serves only to heighten the warning.[13] The "subtlety of mistaken identity of the true object of worship" is an ongoing danger.[14]

The Prince of Peace Makes War

[**19:11–21**] *I saw heaven standing open and there before me was a white horse, whose rider is called Faithful and True. With justice he judges and makes war. His eyes are like blazing fire, and on his head are many crowns. He has a name written on him that no one knows but he himself. He is dressed in a robe dipped in blood, and his name is the Word of God. The armies of heaven were following him, riding on white horses and dressed in fine linen, white and clean. Coming out of his mouth is a sharp sword with which to strike down the nations. "He will rule them with an iron scepter." He treads the winepress of the fury of the wrath of God Almighty. On his robe and on his thigh he has this name written: King of kings and Lord of lords.*

And I saw an angel standing in the sun, who cried in a loud voice to all the birds flying in midair, "Come, gather together for the great supper of God, so that you may eat the flesh of kings, generals, and the mighty, of horses and their riders, and the flesh of all people, free and slave, great and small." Then I saw the beast and the kings of the earth and their armies

11. Bauckham, *The Climax of Prophecy*, 135.
12. Beale, *Revelation*, 946.
13. Rev 22:8–9.
14. Beale, *Revelation*, 947.

gathered together to make war against the rider on the horse and his army. But the beast was captured, and with him the false prophet who had performed the signs on this behalf. With these signs he had deluded those who had received the mark of the beast and worshiped his image. The two of them were thrown alive into the fiery lake of burning sulfur. The rest were killed with the sword coming out of the mouth of the rider on the horse, and all the birds gorged themselves on their flesh.

The thunderous roar of the great multitude shouting "Hallelujah!" introduces the Apostle John's sixth vision of the Son of Man and the final description of the end of evil. John saw "heaven standing open," signifying a divine perspective of salvation and judgment. In a dramatic contrast to the symbolism of the Lamb, John envisions a white horse coming forth. The identity of the rider is made certain in three ways. First, he is identified by four names. The rider is called by a dual name, Faithful and True, along with the Word of God, and the King of Kings and Lord of Lords. Second, he is identified by four attributes. His eyes are like blazing fire; his head is crowned with many crowns; he has a name that no one knows but himself; and his robe is dipped in blood. Third, he is identified by four actions: he leads the armies of heaven, strikes down the nations with a sharp sword, rules the nations with an iron scepter, and "treads the winepress of the fury of the wrath of God Almighty."

John's original hearers understood the imagery right away. Blazing eyes stand for penetrating and purifying, soul-searching wisdom. The crowned head signifies sovereign authority over all creation. The unknown name represents his independence and transcendence ("in light inaccessible hid from our eyes"). The bloodstained robe stands for divine judgment justly executed.[15] The identity of the one who is Faithful and True stands in sharp contrast to the idolatrous beast who opposes the living God. The heavenly warrior makes himself known by name, by character, and by action.

The humble Messiah who rode into Jerusalem on a young donkey, heading for the cross, is now the victorious Messiah, riding into history on a white stallion, leading the armies of heaven. These two realities converge in the one who is Faithful and True. The robe dipped in blood signifies judgment and vengeance. His enemies are slain by a sharp sword coming out of his mouth. Christ is the agent of judgment, but he does

15. Isa 63:1–6.

not wage war in a protracted campaign. There is no literal military battle to be fought, because as Luther put it, "one little word shall fell him."[16] All God needs to do is speak and the conflict is over before it starts. The Judge pronounces sentence and administers justice with an iron scepter. Miroslav Volf writes:

> The violence of the Rider is the righteous judgment against this system of the one called "Faithful and True." Without such judgment there can be no world of peace, of truth, of justice: terror (the "beast" that devours) and propaganda (the "false prophet" that deceives) must be overcome, evil must be separated from good, and darkness from the light. These are the causes of violence, and they must be removed if a world of peace is to be established.[17]

The followers of the Lamb cannot afford to be squeamish at the sight of blood—neither the shed blood of martyrs nor the spilt blood of those who "make war against the rider on the horse and his army." Miroslav Volf argues that the prejudice against divine judgment belongs to those who have only known "the quiet of a suburban home." To protest that it is unworthy of a loving, long-suffering God "to wield the sword" is to presume to dictate to God how his love should work. "A 'nice' God is a figment of liberal imagination." Such a toothless theory cannot stand up against the reality of evil and injustice. "In a scorched land, soaked in the blood of the innocent, it will invariably die." "If God were not angry at injustice and deception and did not make the final end to violence," concludes Volf, "God would not be worthy of our worship." The strategy of the Lamb on this side of eternity "requires a belief in divine vengeance."[18]

Carnage

One moment all the armies are gathering and the next moment vultures are swooping down on the vast carnage of fallen humanity. John's description of "the great supper of God" is commentary on Psalm 2: "Why do the nations conspire and the peoples plot in vain? The kings of the earth rise up and the rulers band together against the Lord and against

16. Luther, "A Mighty Fortress Is Our God," st. 3, in *Hymns for the Living Church*, 11.

17. Volf, *Exclusion and Embrace*, 296.

18. Ibid., 304.

his anointed, saying, 'Let us break their chains and throw off their shackles.' The One enthroned in heaven laughs; the Lord scoffs at them. He rebukes them in his anger and terrifies them in his wrath, saying, 'I have installed my king on Zion, my holy mountain.'"[19]

The Messiah "treads the winepress of the fury of the wrath of God Almighty" and then presides over a feast that consumes "the flesh of kings, generals, and the mighty, of horses and their riders, and the flesh of all people, free and slave, great and small." Graphic images of utter and irrevocable destruction are stacked on top of one another. Evil is consumed in the great supper of God. John draws his horrific image of slaughter from the Prophet Ezekiel, who prophesied the judgment of Gog and Magog.[20] Two radically different feasts, the wedding supper of the Lamb and the great supper of God, are portrayed as contrasting and competing destinies, painting a vivid picture of salvation and judgment. "You have your choice; either you can go to the Lamb's supper as *guests*, friends of the bride (better, *members* of the bride), or you can go to this other supper as part of the *menu*, food for the vultures."[21]

Once again we arrive at the end of evil. The beast and the kings of the earth gather together to fight the rider on the horse and his army. But there is no fight. The beast and the false prophet are captured and "thrown alive into the fiery lake of burning sulfur." Satan's reign of terror winds down to a finale. The age of deception is over and the fury of evil's final fling is finished in a flaming ball of fire. This is the sixth description of the end of evil. We have seen the end many times before. We have seen it in the devastating earthquake, when "the kings of the earth, the princes, the generals, the rich, the mighty, and everyone else, both slave and free, hid in the caves. . . . They called to the mountains and the rocks, 'Fall on us and hide us from the face of him who sits on the throne and from the wrath of the Lamb!'"[22] We have seen it in the devastating plague of the sixth trumpet blast, when those who were not killed refused to repent.[23] We have seen it in the severe earthquake that brought down a tenth of the city and killed seven thousand people.[24] We have seen it in the swing of the sharp sickle as it harvested the earth in judgment and as

19. Ps 2:1–6.

20. Ezek 39:1–6.

21. Eller, *The Most Revealing Book of the Bible*, 177.

22. Rev 6:12, 15–17.

23. Rev 9:13–21.

24. Rev 11:13.

it gathered the clusters of grapes for the winepress of God's wrath.[25] We have seen it in the judgment of the seventh bowl, when the great city split apart and the nations collapsed.[26] How can we interpret these repeated and intensifying "ends" as anything but the certainty of divine judgment? With this reality firmly understood, the equally convincing truth of the good news of salvation shines through. Since salvation and judgment are absolute finalities, Christians are challenged and empowered to persevere. Evil will end and the saints will rejoice forever.

25. Rev 14:14–20.
26. Rev 16:17–21.

27

Millennial Martyrs

∼· Revelation 20:1–6 ·∼

[20:1–6] *And I saw an angel coming down out of heaven, having the key to the Abyss and holding in his hand a great chain. He seized the dragon, that ancient serpent, who is the devil, or Satan, and bound him for a thousand years. He threw him into the Abyss, and locked and sealed it over him, to keep him from deceiving the nations anymore until the thousand years were ended. After that, he must be set free for a short time.*

I saw thrones on which were seated those who had been given author-ity to judge. And I saw the souls of those who had been beheaded because of their testimony about Jesus and because of the word of God. They had not worshiped the beast or his image and had not received his mark on their foreheads or their hands. They came to life and reigned with Christ a thousand years. (The rest of the dead did not come to life until the thousand years were ended.) This is the first resurrection. Blessed and holy are those who have part in the first resurrection. The second death has no power over them, but they will be priests of God and of Christ and will reign with him for a thousand years.

WE COME TO ONE of the most hotly contested passages in the whole book, but if we have been paying attention to the Apostle John's one act drama, this text is not as difficult to interpret as we have been led to believe.

The redemptive interlude between judgments emphasizes the beauty and dignity of the witnessing church. Whenever an angel comes down out of heaven, John sees what is happening on earth from heaven's perspective.[1] The earth is illuminated by the angel's splendor and the truth is declared by his mighty voice. The beautiful side of evil is attractive and compelling; if it were not for heaven's take on evil we might not see past the glitz and glamour. We could be seduced into thinking that the great city is truly great. We might not hear the warning to stay alert, or heed the angel's command, "Come out of her, my people."[2] The vision emboldens believers and gives them the courage to stand for Christ.

John's prophecy might have segued from predatory birds gorging themselves on the flesh of evil combatants to the final battle scene of Armageddon, but John consistently juxtaposes judgment and witness. The theme of judgment is interrupted with a redemptive interlude. After each description of "the wrath of the Lamb," we are reminded that the church is "signed, sealed, and delivered." The description of the 144,000 and the two witnesses reminds the church of its inherent witnessing nature.[3] God keeps putting off the painful finality of judgment. The fact that the end does not come quickly is a sign of God's mercy. Those who love God suffer a seemingly interminable delay for the sake of God's universal offer of salvation.[4] During this delay believers remain courageous, their witness compelling. The testimony of the 144,000 is powerful, persistent, undefiled, and unbowed.[5] The Lord God moves toward the end in mercy, "not wanting anyone to perish, but everyone to come to repentance."[6]

A Merciful Millennium

John used numbers to signify meaning. One thousand is a symbolic number. It holds no previous statistical or symbolic value other than to stand for God's perfect timing: the psalmist says, "A thousand years in your sight are like a day that has just gone by, or like a watch in the

---

1. Rev 10:1; 18:1; 20:1.
2. Rev 18:4.
3. Rev 7:1–8; 11:1–12.
4. Rev 6:10.
5. Rev 11:1–12; 13:9–10; 14:4–5; 20:4–6.
6. 2 Pet 3:9.

night."[7] The apostle says, "But do not forget this one thing, dear friends: With the Lord a day is like a thousand years, and a thousand years are like a day."[8] The number 1,000 was not to be taken literally, but symbolically, to affirm the perfection of God's mercy and the extended opportunity people have to respond to the gospel. During this time the followers of the Lamb maintain a courageous and compelling witness.

Satan's doom is part of the good news, but before his story can be completed, the church of martyrs (witnesses) is described. For a thousand years the church has born witness to the redemptive power of the Lamb. During that time "the dragon, that ancient serpent, who is the devil, or Satan," has been bound and kept from "deceiving the nations." This doesn't mean that the devil is literally in solitary confinement without influence or power. It is a figurative way of saying the devil's power is curtailed and limited. The Apostle John used the same word for binding Satan that Jesus used to describe the binding of the strong man.[9] Satan's power was curtailed because of the presence of the Incarnate One. Jesus said to his disciples, "I saw Satan fall like lightning from heaven."[10] "Now is the time for judgment on this world," Jesus said; "now the prince of this world will be driven out. But I, when I am lifted up from the earth, will draw all people to myself."[11] The spirit of the antichrist pervades the world, but as John reminds us, "greater is he that is in you than he that is in the world."[12] The crucified and risen Lord has "disarmed the powers and authorities . . . triumphing over them by the cross."[13]

There is a thematic parallel between chapter twelve and chapter twenty. In both texts, Satan is called by four names: great dragon, ancient serpent, devil, and Satan. In chapter twelve Satan is defeated by the blood of the Lamb and cast down to earth; in chapter twenty Satan is bound and cast into the abyss. "The casting of the dragon into the abyss, therefore, we understand as coinciding with his being cast down from heaven as previously recorded in 12:7–9."[14]

---

7. Ps 90:4.
8. 2 Pet 3:8.
9. Matt 12:29.
10. Luke 10:18.
11. John 12:31–32.
12. 1 John 4:4.
13. Col 2:15.
14. Hughes, *Revelation*, 210.

12:7–11	20:1–6
1. heavenly scene 7	1. heavenly scene 1
2. angelic battle against Satan 7–8	2. presupposed angelic battle with Satan 2
3. Satan cast to earth 9	3. Satan cast into the abyss 3
4. fourfold description 9	4. fourfold description 2-3
5. Satan's great wrath 12	5. Satan released 3
6. Satan's fall/Christ's rule 10–11.	6. Satan's fall/Christ's rule 4
7. Saints rule based on Satan's fall, Christ's victory and their faithfulness 11	7. Saints rule based on Satan's fall, Christ's rule and their faithfulness 4

Before the incarnation, the nations remained in darkness "induced by Satan's deception."[15] They walked in their own ways.[16] But now, God's salvation is "prepared in the presence of all peoples."[17] The power of Satan over the nations is broken by the power of the gospel: "The people living in darkness have seen a great light; on those living in the land of the shadow of death a light has dawned."[18]

As Jesus said when challenged by the Pharisees, the strong man must first be bound before plundering his home.[19] When the seventy-two return, rejoicing in their power over the demons, Jesus said, "I saw Satan fall like lightning from heaven."[20] Jesus said, "Now is the time for judgment on this world; now the prince of this world will be driven out. And I, when I am lifted up from the earth, will draw all people to myself."[21] The binding of Satan means that the church is free to "make disciples of all nations."[22] Satan's power is checked by the spirit of Christ; his demonic influence is curtailed. Nevertheless, Peter warns, "Be alert and of sober mind. Your enemy the devil prowls around like a roaring lion looking for someone to devour. Resist him."[23]

15. Ibid., 209.
16. Acts 14:16.
17. Luke 2:30–32.
18. Matt 4:16; Isa 9:1–2.
19. Matt 12:29; Mark 3:27.
20. Luke 10:18.
21. John 12:31–32.
22. Matt 28:18–20.
23. 1 Pet 5:8–9.

The Beautiful Side of Witness

The Revelation reveals two sides to evil: the ugly side of evil and the beautiful side of evil. One side is horrific and repulsive, the other attractive and seductive. These two versions of evil are synergistic. They play off of one another, and both types of evil appear to increase and intensify right up to the end. Together, they shape the evil of the world in its many varied forms. But as we have seen, divine judgment is inevitable and absolute; evil will one day end in the second death.

The Apostle John's vision reveals two sides to the witness of the church. There is a painful side, involving persecution and suffering; but there is also a beautiful side of witness that belongs to believers in this life. Salvation is assured and absolute. Life—the resurrection life of Christ—is the gift of grace. The two sides of witness interface so closely that "to be absent from the body, [is] to be present with the Lord."[24] The followers of the Lamb live with the assurance that "If we die with him, we will also live with him. If we endure hardship, we will reign with him."[25] This means that even in the throes of living out a difficult and costly witness, disciples experience the joy of their salvation. Everlasting life begins on this side of eternity. The costly and beautiful sides of witness converge in the Christian's life.

The millennial promise is in keeping with the strategy of the Lamb. During the curtailment of the devil's deception the church remains an embattled church of martyrs. Yet the church thrives on the promise of Christ: "I will build my church, and the gates of Hades will not overcome it." The witness of the church points forward to the new creation and the beauty of the sacramental life. The church turns "the keys of the kingdom of heaven" and opens the door on a new reality.[26] In the tension between the already and the not yet, the church humbly lives in two worlds—the one that is dying, and the one that groans for the new birth.

The church exists to point people to Christ. Her appeal is not in anything that the world puts stock in, but in the deep attributes of goodness and life that resonate with what it means to be made in God's image. The church is not competing for power and influence. Her energy goes into showing the love of Christ. To be filled with the spirit of Christ is very

24. 2 Cor 5:8.
25. 2 Tim 2:11–12.
26. Matt 16:18–19.

different from being in control in any worldly sense. Lesslie Newbigin describes the impact of the witnessing church thusly:

> It follows that the visible embodiment of this new reality is not a movement which will take control of history and shape the future according to its own vision, not a new imperialism, not a victorious crusade. Its visible embodiment will be a community that lives by this story, a community whose existence is visibly defined in the regular rehearsing and reenactment of the story which has given it birth, the story of the self-emptying of God in the ministry, life, death, and resurrection of Jesus.[27]

The church of millennial martyrs knows that its testimony is not enhanced by becoming impressive in the eyes of the world. The cross of Christ destroys any sense of moral merit or ethnic privilege or pride of race. In Christ, one new humanity is created. There is no basis for any person, group, race, tribe, or nation to feel superior. When the gospel of peace is present the crisis of history deepens, Newbigin writes:

> The gospel calls us back again and again to the real clue, the crucified and risen Jesus, so that we learn that the meaning of history is not immanent in history itself, that history cannot find its meaning at the end of a process of development, but that history is given its meaning by what God has done in Jesus Christ and by what he has promised to do; and that the true horizon is not at the successful end of our projects but in his coming to reign. One may say, therefore, that missions are the test of our faith.[28]

The momentum of the millennium carries John's prophecy to the end. "When the thousand years are over, Satan will be released from his prison and will go out to deceive the nations in the four corners of the earth." A limited period of time in which the influence of a defeated Satan intensifies right before the end is represented by forty-two months; 1,260 days; a time, times and half a time.[29] The grim reality and bitter finality of hell is also part of the good news. John describes hell in contrast to the picture of the new heaven and new earth and is consistent with other biblical references to hell.[30] The Bible uses extreme images to depict the grim reality and utter finality of hell. The final destiny of the wicked is

---

27. Newbigin, *The Gospel in a Pluralistic Society*, 120.

28. Ibid., 126.

29. Rev 11:2–3; 12:6, 14; 13:5.

30. Matt 3:12; 5:22; 8:12; 13:50; 18:8; 23:33; 25:41; 2 Pet 2:17; Jude 1:13.

punishment, destruction, privation, exclusion, and banishment. Torment and destruction are combined. The very nature of the imagery invites the use of our imagination to understand the unimaginable horror of life apart from God.

A Messianic Millennium

We may have to change our perspective on the millennium the way the Jews had to change their understanding of the messiah. They expected a political and nationalistic conqueror, not the suffering servant. Some believers expect the reign of Christ to be tribulation free. But John pictures martyred saints "under the altar" crying out, "How long, Sovereign Lord, holy and true, until you judge the inhabitants of the earth and avenge our blood?"[31] And he pictures witnessing saints (the two lampstands and the two olive trees) who continue to witness. He describes both those on earth and those in heaven as fully alive in the presence of God. All those who experience the new birth participate in the first resurrection. This is why the voice from heaven tells John to write, "Blessed are the dead who die in the Lord from now on." And the Spirit confirms the testimony by adding, "Yes . . . they will rest from their labor, for their deeds will follow them."[32]

Throughout the Revelation witness has come in pairs. The antiphonal response to the 144,000 is the great multitude with white robes. John eats the little scroll and the two witnesses herald the gospel. When the 144,000 are reintroduced, the three angels preach the word of God. This collaborative double witness may also be found in the two groups described in chapter twenty. The saints who have gone before are millennial martyrs; they form one group. But a second group of millennial martyrs—witnesses—remain undefiled and uncompromising until Christ returns. The 144,000 and the millennial martyrs are two different ways of describing the saints who are signed, sealed, and delivered. They have been "faithful, even to the point of death," and have received the crown of life.[33] They are victorious and bear the seal of the living God.[34] They "have come out of the great tribulation; they have washed their robes and made

31. Rev 6:9–10.
32. Rev 14:13.
33. Rev 2:10.
34. Rev 3:21; 7:2.

them white in the blood of the Lamb."[35] Their names are written in the Lamb's Book of Life.[36] They accept God's call for their lives and respond with patient endurance and faithfulness.[37] "They follow the Lamb wherever he goes. . . . No lie was found in their mouths; they are blameless."[38] They are invited to the wedding supper of the Lamb.[39] They have been raised in the newness of Christ's resurrection life.

35. Rev 7:14.
36. Rev 13:8.
37. Rev 13:10.
38. Rev 14:4–5.
39. Rev 19:9.

28

The Second Death

⌐· Revelation 20:7–15 ·⌐

[20:7–15] *When the thousand years are over, Satan will be released from his prison and will go out to deceive the nations in the four corners of the earth—Gog and Magog—and to gather them for battle. In number they are like the sand on the seashore. They marched across the breadth of the earth and surrounded the camp of God's people, the city he loves. But fire came down from heaven and devoured them. And the devil, who deceived them, was thrown into the lake of burning sulfur, where the beast and the false prophet had been thrown. They will be tormented day and night for ever and ever.*

Then I saw a great white throne and him who was seated on it. The earth and the heavens fled from his presence, and there was no place for them. And I saw the dead, great and small, standing before the throne, and books were opened. Another book was opened, which is the book of life. The dead were judged according to what they had done as recorded in the books. The sea gave up the dead that were in it, and death and Hades gave up the dead that were in them, and everyone was judged according to what they had done. Then death and Hades were thrown into the lake of fire. The lake of fire is the second death. All whose names were not found written in the book of life were thrown into the lake of fire.

The actual reality of hell sounds barbaric to many. Talk of divine judgment for our misdemeanors and mistakes sounds excessive. Evil ought to be reserved for a select group who are truly bad, while the rest of us struggle with wrongs that the culture blames on demographics or education or parenting. A minimalist view of sin belittles the judgment of God and the redemptive provision of his grace. The Revelation corrects this travesty of truth and realigns humanity's fallen condition.

The Bible spends no time on the psychology of Satan. Evil's backstory remains a mystery. We can explore the nature and scope of evil, but we cannot get behind its reality or fully comprehend its cosmic reach. We can surmise that evil is much worse than any of us could ever imagine. Human depravity alone defies description, but when it is combined with demonic evil it is beyond our calculation. We should be careful not to prejudge the judgment of God, because the malignancy of evil is far worse than we can imagine. Understandably, we want to avoid the subject of hell, but now is not the time for mistrust or cowardice—theology requires courage. Dante's exploration of sin provides insight into the nature and experience of sin. Passing through the gate of hell in his quest to understand evil, Dante reads the inscription posted above the gate: "I am the way into the doleful city, I am the way into eternal grief, I am the way to a forsaken place. Justice it was that moved my great creator; divine omnipotence created me, and highest wisdom joined with primal love. Before me nothing but eternal things were made, and I shall last eternally. Abandon every hope, all who enter." Dante says to his guide, "These words I see are cruel." His guide, speaking from experience, says, "Now here you must leave all distrust behind; let all your cowardice die on this spot."[1]

The Militant Horde

The dynamic synergy of the ugly and beautiful sides of evil converge in one great international assembly of nations. Satan experiences a surge of power, one final demonic thrust of deception. The surreptitious commander and chief of the hordes of humanity has finally come into his own. His massive, militant army, so vast that it is like "the sand on the seashore," will march in lockstepp conformity across "the breadth of the earth and surround the camp of God's people, the city he loves." The

---

1. Dante, *The Portable Dante*, 14 (Canto III, 1–15).

Apostle John has brought us to this point twice before.[2] He recapitulates the battle narrative a third time to emphasize the climactic nature of the event. The symphony has played this theme before and John brings it to a crescendo. This demonically inspired movement of "antagonistic peoples throughout the earth" has been building for a long time.[3] John draws on the language of Ezekiel, Zechariah, and Zephaniah to describe this universal event.[4] The freedom and power of this militant and malevolent force is demonstrated in their strategic advantage over "the camp of God's people, the city he loves." The evil hordes are poised to wipe out the goodness and justice of God once and for all. The camp of saints is cornered and trapped. Surrounded by evil, they are on the verge of being annihilated. Their life-threatening vulnerability is the costly price for the divine patience that longs to extend mercy—wants no one to perish, "but everyone to come to repentance."[5] "But the day of the Lord will come like a thief," wrote the Apostle Peter. "The heavens will disappear with a roar; the elements will be destroyed by fire, and the earth and everything in it will be laid bare."[6]

Evil runs so deep that even the dire consequences of judgment provide no motivation to repent. Trumpet blasts announce judgment and bowls of wrath are poured out, but people prefer death to repentance. What was meant to soften hearts has only hardened hearts and strengthened evil's opposition. In the face of evil's resistance, the imperative remains. Don't be deceived, distracted, or confused. Don't become fearful, complacent, or lazy. Preach the gospel; live the Jesus way. Stay awake and keep your clothes on!

What may be most surprising about this battle narrative is that the battle itself never occurs. No fight scene is reported. Fire comes down from heaven and the war is over before it begins. In the presence of almighty God, Satan is the defeated foe. There is no heroic last stand, nothing worth reporting. The end of evil comes down to this: the garbage has to be taken out and tossed in the fire. The consequences are eternal. "They will be tormented day and night for ever and ever."

In *Paradise Lost*, English poet John Milton imagines Satan longing to be as far from God as possible. The mournful gloom of hell is preferred

---

2. Rev 16:13–14, 16; 19:17–19.
3. Beale, *Revelation*, 1024.
4. Ezek 38:2–8; 39:2; Zech 12–14; Zeph 3.
5. 2 Pet 3:9.
6. 2 Pet 3:10.

over the celestial light of heaven. Satan contends that any place, even hell, is better than heaven, if it means freedom from the will of God.

> To do aught good never will be our task, but ever to do ill our sole delight, as being the contrary to his high will. Whom we resist. If then his Providence out of our evil seek to bring forth good, our labor must be to pervert that end, and out of good still to find means of evil; which oft-times may succeed, so as perhaps shall grieve him.[7]

Milton captures the perversity of evil that adamantly refuses to yield to what is right and true. This evil will always persist to plot and rage against eternal justice. Satan is forever defiant:

> All is not lost; the unconquerable Will, and study of revenge, immortal hate, and courage never to submit or yield: and what is else not to be overcome? That Glory never shall his wrath or might extort from me.[8]

When Satan is released to pursue "his own dark designs," his actions only serve to "heap on himself damnation." But even then God's goodness prevails. Satan's malice only brings out the good in God: "Infinite goodness, grace and mercy."[9] Evil's dreadful freedom resists God's goodness and love and insists that "farthest from him is best." Satan boasts, "Farewell happy fields where Joy for ever dwells: hail horrors, hail infernal world, and thou profoundest hell. Receive thy new Possessor: One who brings a mind not to be changed by place or time. The mind is its own place, and in itself can make a Heaven of Hell, a Hell of Heaven."[10] Milton imagines Satan preferring hell over heaven because hell allows Satan to be himself: "Better to reign in Hell, than serve in Heav'n."[11]

Milton is only imagining Satan's feelings about hell; he cannot know. The Bible is silent on the psychology of demonic beings, but if Milton is right, "freedom" will be the theme that inspires the masses, because it is Satan's theme. The compelling cry will be for freedom—the freedom of the manipulated masses and the freedom of the willful self. The psalmist gives us a sense of their battle cry: "The kings of the earth rise up and the rulers band together against the Lord and against his anointed, saying,

7. Milton, *Complete Poems*, bk. 1, lines 159–67.
8. Ibid., bk. 1, lines 106–11.
9. Ibid., bk. 1, line 218.
10. Ibid., bk. 1, lines 159–69, 245–55.
11. Ibid., bk. 1, lines 256–63.

'Let us break their chains and throw off their shackles.'"[12] The Revelation puts a halt to any speculation about the "freedom" Satan will experience in hell; no one, much less Satan, will be "reigning" in hell. Hell is not some sin haven or a paradise for people who love evil. Hell is where death and hell itself go to die the second death. We have no idea what Satan thinks of hell, and God doesn't care—God couldn't give a damn.

The Great White Throne Judgment

The judgment of humanity follows the judgment of Satan. It is a double climax signifying the absolute end of all evil. These two simultaneous events are held up as a two-fold witness to the finality of evil. The scene moves from the battlefield to the courtroom, but there is no contest in either arena. No army is needed in the first scene and no jury is needed in the second. Fire comes down and devours the massive militant hordes and the earth and heavens flee from the presence of God. Catastrophic events are described in simple, short sentences. In both judgment scenes all attention is given to the outcome—the end of evil. This is the seventh throne scene. We are drawn back to Daniel's description of the throne of God.[13] Humanity is gathered around the throne; everyone who has ever lived is present before God. "And I saw the dead, great and small, standing before the throne, and books were opened. Another book was opened, which is the book of life. The dead were judged according to what they had done as recorded in the books." The two books are symbolic, one a record of human deeds, the other a record of the redeemed. They signify God's unfailing memory.[14] The whole matter is adjudicated without delay. There is no debate or pleading—justice is served. Evil is ended once and for all. "Then death and Hades were thrown into the lake of fire. The lake of fire is the second death." This is a remarkable description. Death dies the second death. Hell itself dies in hell. Everything about evil is finally gone. The Apostle Paul's quote from Isaiah and Hosea comes to mind: "Death has been swallowed up in victory. Where, O death, is your victory? Where, O death, is your sting?"[15]

12. Ps 2:2–3.

13. Dan 7:9–10; Rev 4:1—5:14; 7:9–17; 8:1–4; 11:15–19; 16:17; 19:1–8; 20:11–15.

14. Beale, *Revelation*, 1033.

15. 1 Cor 15:54–55; Isa 25:8; Hos 3:14.

The full title for the Book of Life is The Lamb's Book of Life.[16] The Lamb who was slain before the creation of the world is responsible for saving all whose names are written in the book. Their identification with the righteousness of the Lamb spares them the second death. "They do not suffer judgment for their evil deeds because he has already suffered it for them: he was slain on their behalf."[17]

Jesus on Hell

Eternal torment and the lake of fire are not popular subjects in our day. "There is no doctrine which I would more willingly remove from Christianity than this, if it lay in my power," wrote C. S. Lewis. "But it has the full support of Scripture and, specially, of Our Lord's own words . . . "[18] Lewis was right; Jesus spoke of hell often. A quick review of his teaching ministry captures the highlights. Jesus repeatedly promised that on the day of judgment those who rejected the gospel would suffer a worse fate than Sodom and Gomorrah.[19] He observed that in the days of Solomon the Queen of Sheba responded to what light she had and the people of Nineveh responded to the preaching of Jonah. Only a wicked generation, Jesus insisted, rejects the one greater than Solomon. Only hardened sinners refuse to hear the preaching of one greater than Jonah. The people of Nineveh and the Queen of Sheba will rise up at the judgment and condemn a generation that had every advantage to receive the gospel but stubbornly refused.[20] Jesus stated plainly, "There is a judge for those who reject me and do not accept my words; the very words I have spoken will condemn them at the last day."[21] "Repent or perish" was a refrain that ran through his ministry.[22] Any generation that rejects the gospel is guilty of the blood of all the prophets.[23] Jesus lashed out, "You snakes! You brood of vipers! How will you escape being condemned to hell?"[24]

16. Rev 13:8; 21:27.
17. Beale, *Revelation*, 1037; Rev 1:5; 5:9; 13:8.
18. Lewis, *The Problem of Pain*, 118.
19. Matt 10:15; 11:21–24; Luke 10:12–15.
20. Luke 11:29–32.
21. John 12:48.
22. Luke 13:2–5.
23. Luke 11:50–51.
24. Matt 23:33.

When the Pharisees accused Jesus of working for the devil, he said that their refusal to accept him amounted to blasphemy against the Holy Spirit; they would not be forgiven in the age to come. Jesus was emphatic: "But I tell you that people will have to give account on the day of judgment for every empty word they have spoken. For by your words you will be acquitted, and by your words you will be condemned."[25] Jesus warned that even if a person gained the whole world, what good would it be if he lost his soul?[26] To be ashamed of Jesus and his gospel was to identify with an "adulterous and sinful generation" and to invite a reciprocal response: "the Son of Man will be ashamed of you when he comes in his Father's glory with the holy angels."[27] Jesus warned, "Do not be afraid of those who kill the body but cannot kill the soul. Rather, be afraid of the One who can destroy both the soul and body in hell."[28]

Jesus described judgment in graphic and violent language. Hell is outer darkness, a place of weeping and gnashing of teeth.[29] Jesus warned, "Anyone who says, 'You fool!' will be in danger of the fire of hell."[30] And again, "If your hand or your foot causes you to stumble, cut it off and throw it away. It is better for you to enter life maimed or crippled than to have two hands and two feet and be thrown into eternal fire."[31] Jesus offers these words of condemnation at the final judgment: "Depart from me, you who are cursed, into the eternal fire prepared for the devil and his angels."[32] On the theme of judgment, the language of Jesus and the language of the Revelation draw on the same truth. "The Son of Man will send out his angels, and they will weed out of his kingdom everything that causes sin and all who do evil. They will throw them into the blazing furnace, where there will be weeping and gnashing of teeth. Then the righteous will shine like the sun in the kingdom of their Father. Whoever has ears, let them hear."[33]

25. Matt 12:35–37.
26. Matt 16:26.
27. Mark 8:36–38; Luke 9:23–26.
28. Matt 10:28.
29. Matt 22:13; 24:51; 25:30; Luke 13:28.
30. Matt 5:22.
31. Matt 18:8–9.
32. Matt 25:41.
33. Matt 13:41–43.

The Narrow Door and the Great Banquet

Someone asked Jesus, "Lord, are only a few people going to be saved?" Jesus responded, "Make every effort to enter through the narrow door, because many, I tell you, will try to enter and will not be able to."[34] Jesus implied that religious insiders will end up as outsiders and outsiders will be insiders. And by the time that truth sinks in, it will be too late. Jesus said to his listeners, "Then you will say, 'We ate and drank with you, and you taught in our streets.' But he will reply, 'I don't know you or where you come from. Away from me you evildoers!'" Those who thought they were home free will be thrown out. Meanwhile, those who are far off will be brought near and embraced. "People will come from east and west and north and south, and will take their places at the feast in the kingdom of God. Indeed there are those who are last who will be first, and first who will be last."[35] Jesus was talking to the very people who thought salvation history was all about them. But instead of bolstering their confidence he challenged their salvation. Jesus spoke to religious people who thought they were home free whether they responded to him or not. What he said applies to people who place their confidence in themselves or in their tradition, and not in the mercy of God in Christ.

In the parable of the great banquet, the same message comes through; those who thought they belonged in heaven were heading for hell. Jesus was trying to impress upon his hearers the seriousness of their rejection. Jesus exposed self-designated insiders as being outsiders because they were foreigners to the mercy and grace of God. When Luke wrote his Gospel he set the Pharisee's dinner and Jesus' parable of the great banquet in direct conflict. The worldly banquet and the great banquet have nothing in common. In the parable, Jesus made it clear: "For everyone who exalts himself will be humbled, and he who humbles himself will be exalted." He reiterated the message, "the last will be first and the first will be last."[36] Jesus said, in effect, "Wait a minute! Watch out! Those who assume they are *in* are in perilous danger of being *out*!"

Jesus told the parables of the narrow door and the great banquet in an atmosphere of suspicion and silently seething disapproval. He was not received well. His religious audience didn't respond with joyful anticipation, but rather with evident disdain and disapproval. They thought they

34. Luke 13:23–24.
35. Luke 13:26–30.
36. Luke 14:1–35.

had an inside track on salvation, but Jesus showed them otherwise. The Jews thought they were *in* because of their heritage. Many today, Jews and Gentiles alike, think they are *in* because God would never exclude them from salvation—but Jesus taught otherwise. We can choose to make excuses or we can choose to receive Christ's invitation. The gospel is inclusive, but we choose exclusion. We have that freedom.

The Apostle John pictures Jesus entreating professing believers to open up and let him in: "Here I am! I stand at the door and knock. If anyone hears my voice and opens the door, I will come in and eat with them, and they with me. To those who are victorious, I will give the right to sit with me on my throne, just as I was victorious and sat down with my Father on his throne. Whoever has ears, let them hear what the Spirit says to the churches."[37] We can offer excuses, or we can receive the embrace of the risen Lord Jesus Christ. "In all discussions of hell," C. S. Lewis reminds us, "we should keep steadily before our eyes the possible damnation, not of our enemies nor our friends (since both disturb the reason) but of ourselves. This is not about your wife or son, nor about Nero or Judas Iscariot; it is about you and me."[38]

Optimal Grace

"I would pay any price to be able to say truthfully 'All will be saved,'" writes Lewis. "But my reason retorts, 'Without their will, or with it?' If I say 'Without their will' I at once perceive a contradiction; how can the supreme voluntary act of self-surrender be involuntary? If I say 'With their will,' my reason replies 'How if they will not give in?'"[39] The doctrine of hell sounds barbaric to the world, but no greater price could be paid to remove the doctrine of hell than the one already paid. Lewis exclaimed, "I could not pay one-thousandth part of the price that God has already paid to remove the fact. And here is the real problem: so much mercy, yet still there is Hell."[40]

We may think of many reasons why an all-loving and all-powerful God should simply override stubborn human objections and rescue humanity from the second death whether they want to be rescued or not.

37. Rev 3:20–22.
38. Lewis, *The Problem of Pain*, 128.
39. Ibid., 118.
40. Ibid., 120.

If it was up to us we might take away freedom and conscript people into heaven in spite of their objections. "It is for your own good," we'd be tempted to say. "You will thank us later." We cherish the dream of everyone living happily ever after. Hell violates our utopian instincts. But the living triune God is not like us, and we cannot fathom perfect love and perfect justice. We either come to him by way of mercy and love or we don't come at all. We either accept his free gift of grace and respond to the Christ-light we have or we don't. The mystery of salvation and judgment may be stated that clearly—that simply. Knowing what we know of the mercy of God, a case can be made for optimal grace.[41] The heavens declare the glory of God loudly enough, and the human conscience knows the law of God deeply enough.[42] By divine grace people have the God-given wherewithal to repent and turn to God for his mercy. "People can be in a saving relationship with God if they respond in a positive way to whatever level of light and grace that is available to them." But the question remains, will they? Kyle Blanchette and Jerry Walls are skeptical:

> Would not optimal grace virtually guarantee universalism, the view that all will be saved? We think not. While optimal grace does ensure that in the long run everyone is put in circumstances that are maximally conducive to their receiving saving grace, God nevertheless must leave the dimension of moral trial in place in order to preserve our free will. Consequently, it must always be possible for us to resist God's grace at every juncture. And the more we resist God's grace and cling to our sin, the less likely it becomes that we will repent in the future, for our characters become increasingly formed in opposition to God and the good.[43]

Hell may be opposed by those who claim "that the ultimate loss of a single soul means the defeat of omnipotence." But C. S. Lewis countered,

---

41. Blanchette and Walls, "God and Hell Reconciled," 258. Blanchette and Walls write, "The criterion for ultimate salvation and damnation is not arbitrary but quite fitting and reasonable. God takes into account our search for truth and goodness. Those who continue on that search will eventually find the fullness of truth in the Christian gospel, and if they embrace it and persist in it, they will be saved. Moreover, no one is lost simply due to geographical or situational accident; God takes into account the light and grace available to us, and he judges us accordingly. In fact, God's perfect love necessarily moves him to grant optimal grace to all, such that damnation is only reserved for those who decisively reject his overtures of salvation and stubbornly cling to their evil" ("God and Hell," 258).

42. Ps 19; Rom 2:15.

43. Blanchette and Walls, "God and Hell Reconciled," 250, 252.

"What you call defeat, I call miracle: for to make things which are not Itself, and thus to become, in a sense, capable of being resisted by its own handiwork, is the most astonishing and unimaginable of all the feats we attribute to Deity." He continues,

> I willingly believe that the damned are, in one sense, successful, rebels to the end; that the doors of hell are locked on the inside. . . . They enjoy forever the horrible freedom they have demanded, and are therefore self-enslaved. . . . In the long run the answer to all those who object to the doctrine of hell is itself a question: "What are you asking God to do?" To wipe out their past sins and, at all costs, to give them a fresh start, smoothing every difficulty and offering every miraculous help? But He has done so, on Calvary. To forgive them? They will not be forgiven. To leave them alone? Alas, I am afraid that is what He does.[44]

44. Lewis, *The Problem of Pain*, 128.

29

All Things New

⌁· Revelation 21:1–5 ·⌁

[21:1–5] *Then I saw "a new heaven and a new earth," for the first heaven and the first earth had passed away, and there was no longer any sea. I saw the Holy City, the new Jerusalem, coming down out of heaven from God, prepared as a bride beautifully dressed for her husband. And I heard a loud voice from the throne saying, "Look! God's dwelling place is now among the people, and he will dwell with them. They will be his people, and God himself will be with them and be their God. He will wipe every tear from their eyes. There will be no more death or mourning or crying or pain, for the old order of things has passed away." He who was seated on the throne said, "I am making everything new!" Then he said, "Write this down, for these words are trustworthy and true."*

WE HAVE A HARD time imagining heaven. We live in a culture where most people believe that death ends all and the best that can be said at a funeral is that the memory of the deceased lives on. Life is like the scene in *Castaway* where the main character, played by Tom Hanks, digs a shallow grave to bury the dead pilot who has washed up on shore. His two-word eulogy sums it up: "That's that." Many have a hard time believing in life after death, let alone a whole new order of creation. John's vision of the new heaven and the new earth corresponds with the Apostle Paul's vision of the new, glorified, resurrected body. Without the resurrection, the gospel of the Lamb not only doesn't make sense, it is in fact dishonest and deceptive. If there is no resurrection from the dead then death ends all and "that's that." If Jesus Christ is not "the firstborn from the dead" then there is no hope of heaven.[1] If the bones of Jesus disintegrated in a Palestinian tomb, the Christian faith dissolves in a sad delusion. But Jesus was "not abandoned to the realm of the dead, nor did his body see decay."[2] On this side of eternity, bodily death is part and parcel of biological living. It factors into everything, from reproduction to digestion to circulation. But in the new creation, bodily existence will be characterized by life, not death. Life as we know it is characterized by death and dying, grief and humiliation, frailty and weakness—but a new day is coming when the key to life will not be death but life. The inevitability of decay, shame, and weakness will be eliminated by the life, glory, and power of the resurrection. And this new, glorified, resurrected body will surpass the limitations of a natural body. It will embrace the fullness of personal identity and experience the richness of community life. This risen body will include the whole person and will be nothing like the Greek notion of a bodiless, immortal soul or the modern idea of the spirit of a person living on in people's memory. The spiritual body will be no less real than the natural body. The resurrection of Jesus is the "firstfruits" of a whole new harvest; it is the key that unlocks the door to a whole new order. There are no humanistic resources that can transform the natural life into the spiritual life and triumph over death. "I declare to you, brothers and sisters, that flesh and blood cannot inherit the kingdom of God, nor does the perishable inherit the imperishable."[3] Christian hope lies in understanding that we were meant to move from death-defining natural life to death-defying spiritual life. If the wonderful diversity of creation points to the power of God to create an entirely new mode of existence, then the message of salvation history declares that there is much more to life than the old Adam. The first Adam stands for sin and death; he represents the fallen human condition. The last Adam stands for salvation and life; he represents the "firstfruits" of the new creation.

1. Rev 1:5.
2. Acts 2:31, 36.
3. 1 Cor 15:50.

A New Heaven

When Jesus entered the old order to fully embrace our humanity, he brought nothing with him—he emptied himself. He transcended his transcendence for the sake of our redemption. When he returns, he will bring a new heaven and a new earth. He will rule and reign over a whole new created order. John writes, "I saw the Holy City, the new Jerusalem, coming down out of heaven from God, prepared as a bride beautifully dressed for her husband." Anticipation is not based on our achievement. New, glorified, resurrected bodies in a new heaven on a new earth are entirely the work of God. The emphasis throughout the Revelation has been on faithfulness, not accomplishment. We are not building Christ's kingdom on earth. We are called to wait, pray, witness, and stay alert. By the grace of God it is our responsibility to be a faithful presence for Christ and his kingdom wherever he has placed us. We are to be vigilant and faithful.

The gospel is a countercultural movement that will remain a voice crying in the wilderness of an evil and broken culture. The church will not—nor should it expect to—be a controlling voice of culture. The church's vision for human flourishing is always going to be different from the prevailing culture's vision for success. The world will never fulfill our dreams for human flourishing. The faithful presence of Christians can hopefully make the world more liveable, but the synergy of the beautiful and ugly sides of evil will only continue to intensify and fight against the church. To misread this is inevitability to be misled and eventually disillusioned. In the final analysis, the church is always offering the world something the culture as a whole rejects.

The Holy City and the Beautiful Bride

"See, I will create new heavens and a new earth. The former things will not be remembered, nor will they come to mind. But be glad and rejoice forever in what I will create, for I will create Jerusalem to be a delight and its people a joy. I will rejoice over Jerusalem and take delight in my people; the sound of weeping and crying will be found in it no more."[4]

The convergence of these two images brings together everything that is important. The apparent contradictory metaphors are necessary to

4. Isa 65:17–19.

capture the fullness of the presence of God and what it means for God to dwell among his people. These two metaphors establish an inclusion that runs from the intensity of relational intimacy to the full extent of human flourishing in community. John's vision of the New Jerusalem is deeply personal and fully relational. What comes down out of heaven is not just a place, but a people. As the great prostitute was synonymous with the great city, so the Holy City is synonymous with the bride of Christ. Once again the relational impact of the Holy City dominates John's description.

The presence of God and the absence of evil are the two controlling realities of this new order of existence. John identifies two kinds of people: those who hunger and thirst for righteousness and those who don't. The former have finally found their place and the latter are categorically and eternally out of place.[5] When John first sees the Holy City coming down out of heaven he likens it to a bride beautifully dressed for her husband. But when he is invited to see the bride of the Lamb he sees the Holy City, Jerusalem, "coming down out of heaven from God."[6] There is a perfect match between people and place. Faith will give way to sight. Heaven is not a mythical carrot on the end of a stick. Heaven is very real and visible and down-to-earth. It is not a state of mind, but a place to live. Heaven and earth are united, merged into one God-filled reality. Because of the Incarnate One, we are destined to experience the inauguration of God's society. The followers of the Lamb are citizens in this new reality, not spectators. We are participants in a new social order. Heaven is the grace-filled invasion of the garden city of God. The hallmark of this city is not escapism, but engagement. Our earthly sojourn is inspired by our citizenship in heaven. "And we eagerly await a Savior from there, the Lord Jesus Christ, who, by the power that enables him to bring everything under his control, will transform our lowly bodies so that they will be like his glorious body."[7]

The New Order

John hears a loud voice from the throne saying, "I am making everything new!" We will let the theologians debate whether the old order is

5. Rev 21:6–8.
6. Rev 21:10.
7. Phil 3:20–21.

regenerated and restored or whether it is entirely recreated from scratch.[8] In any case, the old is gone and the new has come.[9] This qualitatively new order is defined negatively by what is no longer present. There is no sea, no death, no mourning, no crying, and no pain. The new order is defined positively by the real presence of God. John announces that there will no longer be any sea. If you are an ocean lifeguard who loves surfing and can't imagine living away from the beach, heaven may not look like such a cool place. It is important to understand that John never intended for us to read our first impressions into these metaphors. The meaning of the sea has to be drawn from what John meant throughout his prophecy.[10] What is missing in the new order is any hint of evil or the threat of tribulation. To develop the metaphor we might say that what is missing in the new order are drownings, storms, and shark attacks. What remains are beautiful ocean vistas, great swells, and a sea teeming with God's creation. We can hardly even imagine what life will be like without pain and suffering, grief and mourning. Since our only experience has been life based on death, how can we begin to fathom life based on life? This great reversal is beyond our ability to grasp; but then, there is a great deal in our immediate natural world that seems beyond our comprehension. Life based on life instead of death is consistent with the new order of things.

Do we dare live our lives on the promise of the new order? The followers of the Lamb are either delusional from the start or truly perceptive of the most real world. "If only for this life we have hope in Christ, we are to be pitied more than all others. But Christ has indeed been raised from the dead, the firstfruits of those who have fallen asleep."[11] Life's true vantage point allows us to look beyond the brevity of life to eternity and inspires faithfulness, not fatalism. "From everlasting to everlasting the Lord's love is with those who fear him."[12]

---

8. See Matt 19:28; Acts 3:21; Rom 8:18–21; 2 Pet 3:13.

9. 2 Cor 5:17.

10. Beale, *Revelation*, 1042. Beale summarizes five identifications of the sea: "(1) the origin of cosmic evil (see 4:6; 12:18; 13:1; 15:2), (2) the unbelieving, rebellious nations who cause tribulation for God's people (2:18; 13:1; 17:1; Isa 57:20), (3) the place of the dead (20:13), (4) the primary location of the world's idolatrous trade activity (18:10–19), (5) a literal body of water, sometimes mentioned together with 'the earth,' used as a synecdoche in which the sea as a part of creation represents the totality of it (5:13; 7:1–3; 8:8–9; 10:2, 5–6, 8; 14:7; 16:3)" (*Revelation*, 1042).

11. 1 Cor 15:19–20.

12. Ps 103:17.

In response to the Sadducees, who were trying to put him on the spot, Jesus said that marriage is a temporary provision for life on this side of eternity. They had posed the most complicated relational scenario they could think of: A woman had been married in turn to seven brothers. Each time a brother died, the next brother in line married his widow according to Old Testament law. Their question was simple: "Now then, at the resurrection, whose wife shall she be of the seven, since all of them were married to her?" Jesus replied, "You are in error, because you do not know the Scriptures or the power of God. At the resurrection people will neither marry nor be given in marriage; they will be like the angels in heaven."[13] In other words, "If you think you're going to take your broken, sin-damaged relationships into heaven, forget it!"

The simplicity on the other side of our complex world will be characterized not by our mixed motives and hardness of heart, but by the truth and power of God. Eternity with God opens up a whole new realm of relational fulfillment that is only hinted at in the best of human friendships and loving marriages. On this side of eternity, at times, we can hardly imagine a love deeper and more fulfilling than that of our beloved. We feel like the couple in the Song of Songs who are passionately in love. Who could possibly imagine anything better than this? But the answer comes back: God can. Our expectations are too low. "'No eye has seen, no ear has heard, and no mind has imagined what God has prepared for those who love him.' But it was to us that God revealed these things by his Spirit."[14]

We should not imagine heaven as a place that is in any way less satisfying relationally than our friendships and marriages on this side of eternity. I am confident that we will one day laugh about such thoughts, wondering how we could have been so skeptical about heaven's fulfillment. What if in eternity all of our friendships are like the very best friendship we ever experienced—only better? What if heaven is not so much minus marriage but all marriage? I expect that the intimacy, companionship, and fidelity that we desire in a good marriage is but a prototype of all relationships in heaven. The very imagery God's word uses to describe the day of Christ—the marriage supper of the Lamb—anticipates a day when all loves will be empowered by the wisdom, purity and holiness of our beloved Lord. Followers of the Lamb anticipate that day with earnest expectation.

13. Matt 22:28–30.
14. 1 Cor 2:9–10.

30

The Garden City of God

⤳ Revelation 21:6—22:21 ⤳

[21:6–27] *He said to me: "It is done. I am the Alpha and Omega, the Beginning and the End. To the thirsty I will give water without cost from the spring of the water of life. Those who are victorious will inherit all this, and I will be their God and they will be my children. But the cowardly, the unbelieving, the vile, the murderers, the sexually immoral, those who practice magic arts, the idolaters and all liars—they will be consigned to the fiery lake of burning sulfur. This is the second death."*

One of the seven angels who had the seven bowls full of the seven last plagues came and said to me, "Come, I will show you the bride, the wife of the Lamb." And he carried me away in the Spirit to a mountain great and high, and showed me the Holy City, Jerusalem, coming down out of heaven from God. It shone with the glory of God, and its brilliance was like that of a very precious jewel, like a jasper, clear as crystal. It had a great, high wall with twelve gates, and with twelve angels at the gates. On the gates were written the names of the twelve tribes of Israel. There were three gates on the east, three on the north, three on the south and three on the west. The wall of the city had twelve foundations, and on them were the names of the twelve apostles of the Lamb.

The angel who talked with me had a measuring rod of gold to measure the city, its gates and walls. The city was laid out like a square, as long as it was wide. He measured the city with the rod and found it to be 12,000 stadia in length, and as wide and high as it is long. He measured its wall and it was 144 cubits thick, by human measurement, which the angel was using. The wall was made of jasper, and the city of pure gold, as pure as glass. The foundations of the city walls were decorated with every kind of precious stone. The first foundation was jasper, the second sapphire, the third agate, the fourth emerald, the fifth onyx, the sixth ruby, the seventh chrysolite, the eighth beryl, the ninth topaz, the tenth turquoise, the eleventh jacinth, and the twelfth amethyst. The twelve gates were twelve pearls, each gate made of a single pearl. The great street of the city was of gold, as pure as transparent glass. I did not see a temple in the city, because the Lord God Almighty and the Lamb are its temple. The city does not need the sun or the moon to shine on it, for the glory of God gives it light, and the Lamb is its lamp. The nations will walk by its light, and the kings of the earth will bring their splendor into it. On no day will its gates ever be shut, for there will be no night there. The glory and honor of the nations will be brought into it. Nothing impure will ever enter it, nor will anyone who does what is shameful or deceitful, but only those whose names are written in the Lamb's book of life.

THE DESCENT OF THE Holy City depends on the word of God. "And God said" defines creation, and the Word made flesh defines redemption. "It is done" defines the whole new order. Only "the Alpha and the Omega, the Beginning and the End" has the power to say, "I am making everything new!" and then to add, "It is done." We are not the masters of the universe we thought we were. We cannot save our souls or plot our destinies. Only he who said from the cross, "It is finished!" can say from the throne, "It is done."

Fulfilled Promises to the Overcomers:

Tree of life — 2:7; 22:2
New Temple — 3:12; 21:22ff
Citizens of the New Jerusalem — 3:12; 21:2,10
Marked by the Name of God — 3:12; 22:4
Name written in the Book of Life — 3:5; 21:27
Bright garments — 3:5; 21:2ff.; cf 19:7–8.
Bright stone — 2:17, 28; 21:11, 18–21, 23; 22:5, 16
Reign with Christ — 2:26–27; 3:21; 22:5
Exclusion from Second Death — 2:11; 21:7–8

Salvation is pictured in a metaphor drawn from Isaiah. "To the thirsty I will give water without cost from the spring of the water of life."[1] The image of living water recalls Jesus' promise to the Samaritan woman: "If you knew the gift of God and who it is that asks you for a drink, you would have asked him and he would have given you living water."[2] The "water of life" and the inheritance pledged to all "those who are victorious" fulfills the promises given to the overcomers in the seven churches. The symbolic description of the Holy City corresponds to the rewards promised to the churches. John's vision expands on the phrase "all this," which is both cryptic and comprehensive of all that God's presence means for those whose names are in the Book of Life. The third and climactic benefit, in addition to the water of life and the abundant inheritance, is a simple promise: "I will be their God and they will be my children." There is no greater truth—no greater gift.

These salvation promises are followed by a jarring description of those who "will be consigned to the fiery lake of burning sulfur."[3] These include "the cowardly, the unbelieving, the vile, the murderers, the sexually immoral, those who practice the magic arts, the idolaters and all liars." A similar statement interrupts the positive description of the city of God. John writes, "Nothing impure will enter it, nor will anyone who does what is shameful or deceitful, but only those whose names are written in the Lamb's book of life." And then finally in the epilogue, a third statement is given: "Outside are the dogs, those who practice magic arts, the sexually immoral, the murderers, the idolaters and everyone who loves and practices falsehood." Even after fully describing the end of all evil, including the judgment of Satan and the great white throne judg-

1. Rev 21:6; Isa 55:1–3; 49:10.

2. John 4:10.

3. Charles, *The Revelation of St. John*, vol. 2. 144–54. Charles argues that the biblical text as it stands is "incoherent and self-contradictory." He reasons that since "the final condemnation and destruction of all evil" has been accomplished, then there would be no point of speaking of evil practices (Charles, *Revelation*, vol. 2, 144–45). "How is it that we are told that, outside the gates of the Holy City which has come down from God to the new earth, there are 'the dogs and the sorcerers, and the fornicators, and the murderers, and the idolaters, and every one that loveth and maketh a lie' (22:15)? A greater contradiction in thought and statement is hardly conceivable" (Charles, *Revelation*, vol. 2, 146). What Charles does not accept is that John is committed to delivering his prophetic warning right up to the end. Moreover, to say that something does not exist in and is excluded from the Holy City is another way of underscoring the true meaning of the new heaven and the new earth.

ment, John is still preaching to any and all who might be tempted to turn their backs on Christ. No matter how positive his vision of the Holy City is, the Apostle John cannot forget the importance of a prophetic warning. G. K. Beale suggests that the "catalog of sins," with its concluding emphasis on liars and those who practice deceit and falsehood, may focus on professing Christians who were tempted to betray the faith.[4]

The New Jerusalem

From every angle the Holy City is complete and whole; from relationships to rest, from aesthetics to politics. Everything about the place is awesome in the fullest sense of the word. The one seated on the throne sums it up: "I am making everything new!" And the description that follows gives commentary on Jesus' promise, "I am going there to prepare a place for you. . . . And if I go and prepare a place for you, I will come back and take you to be with me that you also may be where I am."[5]

In John's poetic revelation, four key metaphors converge: the bride of the Lamb, the Holy City, the river of the water of life, and the tree of life. These four images describe the wonder of living in the presence of God. This soul-crafted poem takes these deeply rooted biblical images and narrates an experience that is meant to inspire faithfulness and patient endurance. It is fitting that one of the seven angels who executed the bowls of wrath comes to John and says, "Come, I will show you the bride, the wife of the Lamb." There is no dark side to God's will. Everything about the divine will is redemptive in ways that we can hardly imagine. Judgment and salvation belong together in the mind of God. John sought to impress upon his congregations the theological symmetry between the descriptions of Babylon and Jerusalem.[6] The clash of splendors pits the beautiful and seductive side of evil against the beauty and glory of God's presence.

The beauty and brilliance of the Holy City offers a theological aesthetic to Christ's followers. The glory of God is mediated through metaphor and revealed in a series of biblical images drawn from salvation history. Aaron's emerald-studded breastplate is translated into dazzling city walls made out of jasper and decorated with every kind of precious

---

4. Beale, *Revelation*, 1060. See Rev 14:5; 21:8, 27; 22:15.

5. John 14:2–3.

6. Rev 17:1–3; 21:9–10.

stone.[7] The city's twelve gates are guarded by twelve angels and named after the twelve tribes of Israel. The wall stands for "the inviolable nature of fellowship with God" and rests on the twelve foundations named after the twelve apostles.[8] The dimensions of the city are laid out like a square. Previously, John had been given a reed to measure the community of the faithful followers of Christ, but now the angel measures the city with a rod of gold.[9] The measurements are symbolic: twelve thousand stadia stands for perfection—12,000 = 3 x 4 x 1,000; 3 stands for the triune God, 4 for the north, south, east, and west of the world, and 1,000 for completeness. The largeness of the number may also symbolize the entire Hellenistic world.[10] The thickness of the wall is 144 cubits and signifies perfection (12 x 12).[11] To render these measurements literally describes a wall that is 1,500 miles high and only 216 feet thick—an engineering disaster. John is using numbers symbolically to describe salvation's spacious security, a perfect setting for human flourishing. "The cubical shape is a sign of the city's perfection, its inherent harmony and order, not only in architectural but in political and economic terms: 'A city that is bound firmly together,' enjoying peace within its borders."[12]

The description of the Holy City recalls the measurement of Ezekiel's temple, but now the entire city is the temple, because there is no need for a temple.[13] The holy of holies in Solomon's temple measured 20 cubits x 20 cubits x 20 cubits and formed a perfect cube.[14] Its interior was overlaid with pure gold. The whole city is a perfect cube encompassing the entire civilized world. The streets are paved with pure gold. Everything is included in the holy of holies; the walls are as holy as Aaron's breastplate and the foundations are as sure as the apostle's gospel. Covenant access is unlimited through gates that never close (Rev 21:25). The luminosity of God's truth shines everywhere. Nothing is dull; everything is brilliant. Light is refracted through precious stones into perpetual rainbows. The

7. Exod 28:17–20; 39:8–14.

8. Beale, *Revelation*, 1068.

9. Rev 11:1.

10. Beale, *Revelation*, 1074.

11. The number 144 recalls the earlier number of 144,000 signifying the totality of the people of God (7:4–9; 14:1–5).

12. Mangina, *Revelation*, 241. Ps 122:3, 7.

13. Ezek 42:15–20; 45:2.

14. 1 Kgs 6:20.

glory of God encompasses the nations, including "only those whose names are written in the Lamb's book of life."

The city of *shalom* is laid out twelve by twelve. There are twelve gates, twelve angels at each gate, and on each gate the names of the twelve tribes of Israel. There are three gates on each side of the city adding up to twelve gates. There are twelve foundations, and on each foundation the name of one of the twelve apostles. The length, width, and height of the city is 12,000 stadia. The wall's width is 12 x 12 cubits and it is made of twelve kinds of precious stones. The twelve gates are made of twelve pearls. The tree with its twelve crops of fruit, yielding its fruit every month, completes the picture of twelve twelves.

John crafts a portrait of the New Jerusalem using the qualities of an ancient city. The high walls symbolize strength and security. These walls do not confine, but contain in a vast wholeness the people of God. The priceless building materials do not symbolize excessive luxury, but limitless glory and brilliance. Who ever heard of building a wall out of jasper or paving a street with gold or a pearl large enough to drive a camel through? Nothing can match the glory of this city. The twelve precious stones that adorned the high priest's breastplate now decorate the foundations of the Holy City. Redemption and reconciliation are the foundation of this city. The light of the Lamb illuminates the city for ever and ever. The old competing values have been integrated beautifully in the glory of God. When precious gold has become the new urban asphalt you know something has changed! Relationships can be fully appreciated without becoming idolatrous. The self is finally itself without becoming self-centered. When Jesus walked out of the Jerusalem temple for the final time, he had his sights fixed on the New Jerusalem.[15] John's vision of the new heaven and the new earth perfectly reflects the theology of Jesus. The is the city of the Lamb, built by the blood of Lamb, filled with the followers of the Lamb, drawn from every nation, tribe, language, and people, whose names are written in the Lamb's Book of Life.

Central Park

[22:1-5] *Then the angel showed me the river of the water of life, as clear as crystal, flowing from the throne of God and of the Lamb down the middle of the great street of the city. On each side of the river stood the tree of*

---

15. Matt 24:1-2.

life, bearing twelve crops of fruit, yielding its fruit every month. And the leaves of the tree are for the healing of the nations. No longer will there be any curse. The throne of God and of the Lamb will be in the city, and his servants will serve him. They will see his face, and his name will be on their foreheads. There will be no more night. They will not need the light of a lamp or the light of the sun, for the Lord God will give them light. And they will reign for ever and ever.

The Holy City has perfect security, unsurpassed splendor, and an unceasing water supply. The angel shows John the river of life, as clear as crystal, flowing from the throne of God and of the Lamb, "down the middle of the great street of the city."[16] The river of life and the tree of life offer a pastoral picture of fruitful provision and peace. The Genesis curse is finally reversed—salvation is complete. The beauty of Eden is recalled in a picture of abundance and fertility. The followers of the Lamb will not have to choose between urban life and rural life. The river runs through the city center, with the fruit-bearing tree of life on either side of the river and always in season.[17] The followers of the Lamb will have the best of both worlds. At long last we will be free from the curse. There will be everlasting joy and peace. No more curse means no more suffering or scarcity or strife. The healing of the nations will be experienced around the throne of God and of the Lamb. There will be no more night, because the Lord God will be its light. No more curse means the full restoration of face-to-face fellowship with God. We will no longer feel the need to hide from God.[18] No more curse means that whatever we do, "whether in word or deed, [we] do it all in the name of the Lord Jesus, giving thanks to God the Father through him."[19] Skeptics may say this is way too good to be true, but this is the goodness we were made to experience. This is the home we have longed for. C. S. Lewis observed:

> We are very shy nowadays of even mentioning heaven. We are afraid of the jeer about "pie in the sky," and of being told that we are trying to "escape" from the duty of making a happy world here and now into the dreams of a happy world elsewhere. But either there is a "pie in the sky" or there is not. If there is not, then Christianity is false, for this doctrine is woven into its

16. Ezek 47:1–9; Zech 14:8; Joel 3:18.
17. Ezek 47:12.
18. Gen 3:8.
19. Col 3:17.

whole fabric. If there is, then this truth, like any other, must be faced, whether it is useful . . . or not. Again, we are afraid that heaven is a bribe."[20]

If we immerse ourselves in John's prophecy we will soon lose that shyness and begin to live in the present in the light and life of our future home. To embrace this destiny is to experience the sacramental life.

A Sacramental View of Life

There is more to life than meets the eye. C. S. Lewis was convinced that one of the best ways to present the truth about life was through the imagination. Lewis reasoned that when he became a man he put away childish things, one of which was the fear of being childlike. He cultivated the capacity of wonder. He took his Lord seriously: "Truly I tell you, unless you change and become like little children, you will never enter the kingdom of heaven."[21] All of life is of God and belongs to God. Creation and redemption converge to infuse life with sacred significance. "He is before all things, and in him all things hold together" and all things are reconciled through him, "by making peace through his blood, shed on the cross."[22] The divine purpose—bringing unity to all things in heaven and on earth in Christ—overcomes the great divorce between our fallenness and our fulfillment. In Christ, the physical and the spiritual, the temporal and the eternal, the mundane and the devotional, are united. Redemptive love rescues romantic love, integrates truth and beauty, unifies families and races, and infuses meaning into ordinary daily life. This unity depends on the absolute singularity of Christ. The sacramentalist takes comfort in knowing the center of life personally. In Christ we have the lens through which we can examine life from every angle, without fear of meaninglessness—without the dread of nothingness. Harry Blamires writes, "The Christian Faith presents a sacramental view of life. It shows life's positive richness as derivative from the supernatural. It teaches us that to create beauty or to experience beauty, to recognize truth or to discover truth, to receive love or to give love, is to come into contact with realities that express the Divine Nature. At a time when Christianity is so widely misrepresented as life-rejecting rather than life-affirming, it

20. Lewis, *The Problem of Pain*, 145.

21. Matt 18:3.

22. Col 1:17, 20.

is urgently necessary to right the balance."[23] We believe that "if anyone is in Christ, the new creation has come: The old has gone, the new is here!"[24] Redemption means the evolution of a whole new person. "People often ask when the next step in evolution—the step to something beyond man—will happen. But on the Christian view, it has happened already."[25] In Christ the new kind of person has already arrived.

The Lamb of God

We finish the body of John's prophecy by drawing attention to the fact that John persists in using the metaphor of the lamb even when he is describing the new heaven and the new earth. We might think that the symbol has served its purpose and ought to be succeeded by metaphors that represent the rule and reign of Christ. But if anything, John uses the image of the Lamb with greater emphasis at the end than he does at the beginning. In this section he uses the metaphor of the lamb seven times. The bride of Christ is "the wife of the Lamb" and inscribed on the twelve foundations of the wall of the Holy City are "the names of the twelve apostles of the Lamb."The reason there is no temple is because "the Lord God Almighty and the Lamb are its temple," and the reason the city does not need the sun or the moon to shine on it is because "the glory of God gives it light, and the Lamb is its lamp." Only those whose names are written in "the Lamb's book of life" are able to enter the Holy City, and the river of life flows "from the throne of God and of the Lamb." At the center of the city is "the throne of God and of the Lamb."[26]

John reminds the followers of the Lamb that the new heaven and the new earth depend entirely on the centrality of the sacrifice of Christ. Even in heaven's glory the humility of God is always front and center, and the words of Jesus are never forgotten: "For even the Son of Man did not come to be served, but to serve, and to give his life as a ransom for many."[27] The triumph of the Lamb is never triumphalist, and those who follow the Lamb never forget the testimony of Jesus. There is no arrogance or ego at the throne of God—only the sacrificial humility

23. Blamires, *The Christian Mind*, 173.

24. 2 Cor 5:17.

25. Lewis, *Mere Christianity*, 60, 63–64.

26. Rev 21:9, 22–24, 27; 22:1, 3.

27. Mark 10:45.

that extends redemption to a lost and dying world. The Lamb that was slain extends his invitation through his Spirit and the bride of Christ, saying, "Let those who are thirsty come; and let all who wish to take the free gift of the water of life."[28]

"I Am Coming Soon!"

[22:6–21] *The angel said to me, "These words are trustworthy and true. The Lord, the God who inspires the prophets, sent his angel to show his servants the things that must soon take place." "Look, I am coming soon! Blessed are those who keep the words of the prophecy in this scroll."*

I, John, am the one who heard and saw these things. And when I had heard and seen them, I fell down to worship at the feet of the angel who had been showing them to me. But he said to me, "Don't do that! I am a fellow servant with you and with your fellow prophets and with all who keep the words of this scroll. Worship God!"

Then he told me, "Do not seal up the words of the prophecy of this scroll, because the time is near. Let those who do wrong continue to do wrong; let those who are vile continue to be vile; let those who do right continue to do right; and let those who are holy continue to be holy."

"Look, I am coming soon! My reward is with me, and I will give to everyone according to what they have done. I am the Alpha and the Omega, the First and the Last, the Beginning and the End. Blessed are those who wash their robes, that they may have the right to the tree of life and may go through the gates into the city. Outside are the dogs, those who practice magic arts, the sexually immoral, the murderers, the idolaters and everyone who loves and practices falsehood.

"I, Jesus, have sent my angel to give you this testimony for the churches. I am the Root and the Offspring of David, and the bright Morning Star." The Spirit and the bride say, "Come!" And let those who hear say, "Come!" Let those who are thirsty come; and let all who wish take the free gift of the water of life. I warn everyone who hears the words of the prophecy of this scroll: If any one of you adds anything to them, God will add to you the plagues described in this scroll. And if any one of you takes words away from this scroll of prophecy, God will take away from you your share in the tree of life and in the Holy City, which are described in this scroll. He who

---

28. Rev 22:17.

testifies to these things says, "Yes, I am coming soon." Amen. Come, Lord Jesus. The grace of the Lord Jesus be with God's people. Amen.

The conclusion of the main body of John's prophetic vision ends with the sentence, "And they will reign for ever and ever." But like the encore to a well-performed symphony, there is more. The epilogue to John's one act drama is a final liturgical exhortation to obedience. The followers of the Lamb are to trust in these trustworthy words. They are to "keep the words of the prophecy" and "continue to be holy." They are to act according to this word, wash their robes, and keep "the words of the prophecy" without adding or subtracting from them. The authority of God's word is assumed; the emphasis lies on living into this truth—under its authority and by its power—until Christ comes again.

Embracing this climactic prophecy from the prologue to the epilogue has a way of unsettling and radicalizing the believer. John's Spirit-inspired linguistic fire has intensified the Christian life. The professorial tone of much of our theology seems cool and detached compared to John's white-hot passion for Christ. We are often in the company of academics and scholars, but John invites us into the fellowship of the prophets. The exiled apostle has nowhere to go but to the word of God. He is immersed in its description of evil and in its hope for redemption. He conveys a heightened concern for idolatry and a deepening concern for witness. The analytical mind unpacks the truth and breaks it down into logical lists and neat propositions; the apocalyptic mind writes out the truth in the vortex of spiraling worship and judgment. John's Spirit-inspired prophecy sets the mind and heart on fire. If the Revelation does not quicken our spiritual pulse and enliven our obedience, chances are nothing will.

The Conversation

The epilogue is a lively conversation between the angel, the Lord Jesus, and the Prophet John. The dialogue takes place in our hearing and for our benefit. The exhortations to faithfulness and holiness are meant for John and for believers who have ears to hear what the Spirit says to the churches. Jesus speaks seven times in the first person singular:

> I am coming soon! Blessed are those who keep the words of the prophecy of this scroll.

I am coming soon! My reward is with me, and I will give to everyone according to what they have done.

I am the Alpha and the Omega, the First and the Last, the Beginning and the End.

I, Jesus, have sent my angel to give you this testimony for the churches.

I am the Root and the Offspring of David, and the bright Morning Star.

I am coming soon.

Throughout the Revelation we have never been very far from the vision and voice of Christ. In his presence, we are constantly reminded that this entire experience is deeply personal. Jesus said, "I am the way, the truth, and the life."[29] We are not called to merely defend a system of ideas or doctrinal tenets, but to follow the Lamb. The propositional truth of biblical revelation has always required an abiding personal relationship with Christ.

In the presence of Christ and the angel, John is disoriented. He appears to be overwhelmed, and once again he honestly conveys to his hearers his own weakness and fallibility.[30] In confusion, John falls down to worship at the feet of the angel. And for a second time, the angel immediately explains, "Don't do that! I am a fellow servant with you and with your fellow prophets and with all who keep the words of this scroll. Worship God!" We are warned along with John of making too much of the holy servants who declare God's word. There is no place for idolatry or hero worship or Christian celebrities. The solid truth of the priesthood of all believers, the shared gifts of the Spirit, and the universal call to salvation, service, sacrifice, and simplicity cautions against showing undue deference and honor to any of Christ's servants. The words of the angel to John rules out kissing the signet ring of the bishop or putting the charismatic pastor on a pedestal.

The reason we are so vulnerable to this well-intentioned but misguided deception is that it is always "easier to indulge in ecstasies than

29. John 14:6.
30. Rev 19:10.

to engage in obedience."[31] We might wish that some of our influential Christian leaders were as quick as the angel to say, "Don't do that! I am a fellow servant, too." The corrective to this common sinful practice of making too much of influential disciples is simple and straightforward: "Worship God!" The hallmark of the spiritual direction in the Revelation is its down-to-earth simplicity. Over and against John's description of the intricacies, subtleties, and complexities of evil is always his uncomplicated prescription for obedience. We can insist on making a mystery of discipleship or we can wake up, keep watch, stay alert, and worship the Lamb. It's that simple.

"Do Not Seal Up"

Unlike Daniel, John is told by the angel, "Do not seal up the words of the prophecy of this scroll, because the time is near." Daniel's seventh-century-BC prophecy was meant to be confidential: "But you, Daniel, close up and seal the words of the scroll until the time of the end."[32] But that which Daniel was told to seal up, the Apostle John was now told to open up. Since the time of the end commenced with the coming of Christ—his life, death and resurrection—the meaning of John's prophecy was immediately applicable. In Christ, that which was far off in Daniel's day had become near in John's.

The angel's next exhortation is meant to relieve disciples of any self-imposed pressure to change the world. "Let those who do wrong continue to do wrong; let those who are vile continue to be vile; let those who do right continue to do right; and let those who are holy continue to be holy."[33] The angel's observation recalls the sober reality presented to Daniel when he was told that "Many will be purified, made spotless and refined, but the wicked will continue to be wicked."[34] The lines of thought between Daniel and the Revelation run parallel. History will show that the world is not becoming any more open to the gospel and is, in fact, more resistant as time goes on. The church is responsible for maintaining its faithful witness—for continuing to be holy. But the church should not expect to win the world for Christ; it is what it is. Holiness is key. Stay

31. Peterson, *Reversed Thunder*, 186.

32. Dan 12:4.

33. Rev 22:11

34. Dan 12:10.

alert. Pray earnestly. Let no one use their dreams of success to manipulate the church into claiming victory over Babylon. It's not going to happen, so don't waste your time and energy trying to Christianize the world. The sober line in Daniel needs to be recalled: "When the power of the holy people has been finally broken, all these things will be completed."[35] This does not render the faithful witness of the followers of the Lamb null and void, but it does remind the church that everything depends on the Lord coming soon!

There may be a third line of thought drawn from Daniel's concluding chapter that fits Revelation's epilogue and applies to Christians today. "The man clothed in linen," who appears to be the same person as the Son of Man, tells Daniel, "As for you, go your way till the end. You will rest, and then at the end of the days you will rise to receive your allotted inheritance." In other words, "Go about your business without fretting or worrying. Relax. When it's all over, you will be on your feet to receive your reward."[36] The application for those who follow the Lord Jesus is as plain and simple as it is costly. Don't let the end times distract you from going and making disciples. Don't let the free reign of evil prevent you from loving your neighbor and being salt and light. Don't let a hostile world discourage you from resting in the sovereign, saving care of your Lord and Savior Jesus Christ. "Let those who are holy continue to be holy."

"Look, I am coming soon!"

Christ himself interjects intensity into this concluding exhortation. His loving humility continues to woo the bride of Christ. The intensity of the Revelation is consistent with the feeling of urgency that pervades the entire prophecy. We are in the end times that are about to end and we are exhorted to keep the words of the prophecy to the end. This prevailing sense of immediacy belongs to the believer even though the generations may come and go. The fact that John wrote two thousand years ago does not change the fact "that these things must soon take place." The note of urgency remains, as Jesus promises three times, "Look, I am coming soon!" The promised reward for faithfulness is delivered by none other than "the Alpha and Omega, the First and the Last, the Beginning and the End." What is our *doing* compared to his *being*? Nothing, absolutely

35. Dan 12:7.
36. Dan 12:13, *The Message.*

nothing by human standards and merit, but by God's grace our sanctified actions mean a great deal—to God. Life is redeemable and our actions are rewardable. Sacred purposes sanctify our ordinary humdrum lives and infuse life with praise to God. Three familiar images of redemption fill the dialogue. "Blessed are those who wash their robes, that they may have the right to the tree of life and may go through the gates into the city."

Christ himself defines who is on the outside, not because there is any doubt as to who is on the inside, nor any question about the final judgment, but because the prophetic witness endures to the end. This is confirmation that the Apostle John has been faithful in both the "yes" and "no" of the gospel. The wicked are excluded, but not because of any deficiency in God's mercy. In his own words, Christ affirms what his apostles have been saying all along.[37]

Christ himself is responsible for this message. "I, Jesus, have sent my angel to give you this testimony for the churches." The Apostle John has only delivered what he was authorized and entrusted to deliver by the one who identifies himself as "the Root and Offspring of David, and the bright Morning Star."[38] In response to Christ's invitation and promise, the Holy Spirit says, "Come!" And the bride of Christ says, "Come!" Not surprisingly, the invitation of the gospel of Christ remains mercifully open: "Let those who are thirsty come; and let all who wish take the free gift of the water of life." Christ is still wooing the unredeemed; the Spirit is still calling the lost; the bride is still giving the invitation. There is still time, but there is an urgency about this moment that must not be denied. There is a redemptive antiphonal response in John's liturgical epilogue. Christ's threefold exclamation, "I am coming soon!" is met with the Spirit's and bride's exuberant "Come!" But what is not lost in the eager expectation of Christ's coming is the open invitation to the lost, to the thirsty, to come to Christ. "Let all who wish take the free gift of the water of life." Jesus said to the woman at the well, "If you knew the gift of God and who it is that asks you for a drink, you would have asked him and he would have given you living water."[39]

The open and positive invitation to the lost in the light of Christ's imminent return is juxtaposed with a dire warning against professing Christians who are in danger of apostasy. Whatever concerns were evident in the letters to the seven churches, John saw fit to remind his readers

37. Titus 2:11–14.
38. Isa 11:1; 2 Pet 1:17–19.
39. John 4:10.

of them again. The prophetic edge persists right up to the last word. The final words are reminiscent of the Lord's command in Deuteronomy, calling for obedience to the whole counsel of God: "Do not add to what I command you and do not subtract from it, but keep the commands of the Lord your God that I give you."[40] John delivers a warning:

> I warn everyone who hears the words of the prophecy of this scroll: If any one of you adds anything to them, God will add to you the plagues described in this scroll. And if any one of you takes words away from this scroll of prophecy, God will take away from you your share in the tree of life and in the Holy City, which are described in this scroll.

For a third and final time, Jesus says, "Yes, I am coming soon," to which John replies, "Amen. Come, Lord Jesus," followed by a simple benediction: "The grace of the Lord Jesus be with God's people." "The last word in worship is Amen, the Yes, to all that God has done. It is the worshiping affirmation to the God who affirms us. God says *yes* to us. We respond to his *yes* by saying, *Yes, Amen*."[41] We join the Apostle John in worship, saying, "Amen. Come, Lord Jesus." We say "Yes" to the Spirit's urging and the bride's shout of "Come!" We say "Yes" to Jesus' invitation to all those who are thirsty to come. We join the followers of the Lamb in prayer, and say *Maranatha*, "Come, Lord!"[42] Our "Yes" is a response to God's "Yes" to us. "Yes, I am coming soon."

40. Deut 4:2.

41. Peterson, *Reversed Thunder*, 68.

42. 1 Cor 16:22.

Bibliography

Baldwin, Joyce G. *Daniel: Tyndale Old Testament Commentary*. Downers Grove, IL: InterVarsity, 1978.

Barna, George. *Revolution: Finding Vibrant Faith Beyond the Walls of the Sanctuary*. Carol Stream, IL: Tyndale House, 2006.

Barnes, Craig. *Sacred Thirst*. Grand Rapids: Zondervan, 2001.

Barth, Karl. *The Christian Life: Church Dogmatics*, vol. 4. Translated by Geoffrey Bromiley. Grand Rapids, MI: Eerdmans, 1981.

———. *Dogmatics in Outline*. New York: Harper & Row, 1959.

Barth, Markus. *Ephesians: The Anchor Bible*, vol. 34. New York: Doubleday, 1974.

Bauckham, Richard. *The Climax of Prophecy: Studies on the Book of Revelation*. London: T. & T. Clark, 1993.

———. *The Theology of the Book of Revelation*. Cambridge: Cambridge University Press, 1993.

Beale, G. K. *The Book of Revelation*. Grand Rapids: Eerdmans, 1999.

Beale, G. K., and D. A. Carson, eds. *Commentary on the New Testament Use of the Old Testament*. Grand Rapids: Baker Academic, 2007.

Bell, Rob. *Love Wins: A Book About Heaven, Hell, and the Fate of Every Person Who Ever Lived*. New York: HarperOne, 2012.

Bergen, Doris L. *Twisted Cross: The German Christian Movement in the Third Reich*. Chapel Hill: The University of North Carolina Press, 1996.

Blamires, Harry. *The Christian Mind*. London: SPCK, 1963.

Blanchette, Kyle, and Jerry L. Walls. "God and Hell Reconciled." In *God and Evil*, edited by Chad Meister and James K. Dew, Jr., 243–58. Downers Grove, IL: InterVarsity, 2013.

Bonhoeffer, Dietrich. *The Cost of Discipleship*. New York: Macmillan, 1970.

———. *Creation and Fall: A Theological Interpretation of Genesis 1–3*. New York: Macmillan, 1971.

———. *A Testament To Freedom*. Edited by Geffrey Kelly and Burton Nelson. San Francisco: HarperCollins, 1995.

Boring, Eugene M. *Revelation*. Louisville: John Knox, 1989.

Boorstin, Daniel. *The Discoverers*. New York: Random House, 1983.

Bradley, James. "Future Judgment in Doctrine and Ministry." The SEMI, May 12, 2008, 6.

Brauch, Manfred T. *Hard Sayings of Paul*. Downers Grove, IL: InterVarsity, 1989.

Brown, Brené. "The Power of Vulnerability." Filmed June 2010. TED video, 20:19. https:www.ted.com/talks/brene_brown_on_vulnerability.

Bruner, Frederick Dale. *The Churchbook: Matthew*, vol. 1–2. Grand Rapids: Eerdmans, 2004.

————. *The Gospel of John*. Grand Rapids: Eerdmans, 2012.

Bryson, Bill. *A Short History of Nearly Everything*. New York: Broadway, 2004.

Burch, George Bosworth. *Alternative Goals in Religion*. Montreal: McGill-Queens University Press, 1972.

Caird, G. B. *The Revelation of Saint John: Black's New Testament Commentary*. Peabody, MA: Hendrickson, 2006.

Carlson, Lois. *Monganga Paul*. New York: Harper & Row, 1966.

Carson, Donald A., and Douglas J. Moo. *An Introduction to the New Testament*. Grand Rapids: Zondervan, 2005.

Carson, Donald A., "Three Books on the Bible: A Critical Review," *Ref21* (blog). www.reformation21.org/shelf-life/three-books-on-the-bible-a-critical-review.php.

Charles, R. H. *The Revelation of St. John*, vol 1–2. Edinburgh: T. & T. Clark, 1980.

Chesterton, G. K. *Orthodoxy*. New York: Image, 1959.

Crouch, Andy. "Steve Jobs: The Secular Prophet." *The Wall Street Journal*, October 8, 2011.

Dante. *The Portable Dante*. Edited by Mark Musa. New York: Penguin, 1995.

Darby, J. N. *The Collected Writings of J. N. Darby*. Ecclesiastical no. 3, vol. 14. Edited by William Kelly. Oak Park, IL: Bible Truth, 1972.

Delbanco, Andrew. *The Real American Dream: A Meditation on Hope*. Cambridge, MA: Harvard University Press, 1999.

Dinwiddie, Richard D. "The God Who Sings." *Christianity Today*, July 15, 1983, 21–23.

Douthat, Ross. *Bad Religion: How We Became a Nation of Heretics*. New York: Simon & Schuster, 2010.

Dreyfus, Hubert, and Sean Dorrance Kelly. *All Things Shining: Reading the Western Classics to Find Meaning in a Secular Age*. New York: Free Press, 2011.

Durant, Will. *Caesar and Christ: A History of Roman Civilization and of Christianity from Their Beginnings to A.D. 325*. New York: Simon & Schuster, 1972.

Dubay, Thomas. *The Evidential Power of Beauty*. San Francisco: Ignatius, 1999.

Dyrness, William A. "Aesthetics in the Old Testament: Beauty in Context." *JETS* 28, no. 4 (December 1985): 421–32.

Edwards, Jonathan. "Sinners in the Hands of an Angry God." In *The Sermons of Jonathan Edwards: A Reader*, edited by Wilson H. Kimnach, Kenneth P. Minkema, and Douglas Sweeney, 49–65. New Haven, CT: Yale University Press, 1999.

Eller, Vernard. *The Most Revealing Book of the Bible: Making Sense Out of Revelation*. Grand Rapids: Eerdmans, 1974.

Ellul, Jacques. *Apocalypse: The Book of Revelation*. Translated by George W. Schreiner. New York: Seabury, 1977.

Ferguson, Sinclair, B. *Daniel: The Communicator's Commentary*. Nashville: Thomas Nelson, 1988.

Ford, J. Massyngberde. *Revelation: The Anchor Bible Commentary*. New Haven, CT: Yale University Press, 2007.

France, R. T. *The Gospel of Matthew*. Grand Rapids: Eerdmans, 2007.

Galli, Mark, and Andy Crouch. "The Future of Today's Christianity." *Christianity Today*, March 2013, 45.

Gillquist, Peter. "A Marathon We Are Meant to Win." *Christianity Today*, October 1981, 22–23.

Goetz, David L. *Death by Suburb: How to Keep the Suburbs from Killing Your Soul.* San Francisco: Harper, 2006.

Grounds, Vernon. "Faith for Failure: A Meditation on Motivation for Ministry." *TSF Bulletin* (March–April, 1986): 4.

Hann, H. C. *Dictionary on New Testament Theology,* vol. 3. Grand Rapids: Zondervan, 1978.

Harink, Douglas. *1 & 2 Peter: The Brazos Theological Commentary.* Grand Rapids: Brazos, 2009.

Henzel, Ronald M. *Darby, Dualism and the Decline of Dispensationalism.* Tucson: Fenestra, 2003.

Highfield, Roger, and Paul Carter. *The Private Lives of Albert Einstein.* New York: St. Martin's Griffen, 1993.

Hitchcock, Mark. *The End: A Complete Overview of Bible Prophecy and the End of Days.* Carol Stream, IL: Tyndale House, 2012.

Hughes, Philip Edgcumbe. *The Book of The Revelation.* Grand Rapids: Eerdmans, 1990.

Huntemann, George. *The Other Bonhoeffer.* Grand Rapids: Baker, 1993.

Hunter, James Davison. *To Change the World: The Irony, Tragedy, and Possibility of Christianity in the Late Modern World.* New York: Oxford University Press, 2010.

Hybels, Bill. *Courageous Leadership.* Grand Rapids: Zondervan, 2009.

Isaacson, Walter. *Steve Jobs.* New York: Simon & Schuster, 2011.

Jacobs, Alan. *The Narnian: The Life and Imagination of C. S. Lewis.* San Francisco: HarperCollins, 2005.

Johnson, Darrell W. *Discipleship on the Edge: An Expository Journey Through The Book of Revelation.* Vancouver, BC: Regent College Publishing, 2004.

Kapolyo, Joseph. "Matthew." In *Africa Bible Commentary,* edited by Tokunboh Adeyemo, 1105–70. Grand Rapids: Zondervan, 2006.

Keener, Craig S. *Revelation: The NIV Application Commentary.* Grand Rapids: Zondervan, 2000.

Keller, Timothy. *Center Church: Doing Balanced, Gospel-Centered Ministry in Your City.* Grand Rapids: Zondervan, 2012.

———. *Counterfeit Gods: The Empty Promises of Money, Sex, and Power, and the Only Hope That Matters.* New York: Dutton, 2009.

Kidner, Derek. *Psalms 73–150.* Downers Grove, IL: InterVarsity, 1975.

Kierkegaard, Soren, *Training in Christianity.* Princeton, NJ: Princeton University Press, 1957.

———. *Works of Love.* New York: Harper & Row, 1962.

Lawrence, D. H. *Apocalypse and the Writings of Revelation.* Edited by Mara Kalnins. Cambridge: Cambridge University Press, 1980.

Lewis, C. S. *The Four Loves.* New York: Harcourt Brace, 1960.

———. *God In The Dock.* Grand Rapids: Eerdmans, 1970.

———. *Mere Christianity.* New York: Collier, 1960.

———. *Miracles.* London: Fontana, 1972.

———. *The Problem of Pain.* New York: MacMillan, 1962.

———. *Screwtape Letters.* New York: HarperOne, 2001.

———. *Surprised by Joy.* London: Fontana, 1972.

———. *The Weight of Glory.* New York: Collier, 1965.

Liefeld, Walter L. "The Nature of Authority in the New Testament." In *Discovering Biblical Equality*, edited by Ronald W. Pierce and Rebecca Merrill Groothius, 260–70. Downers Grove, IL: InterVarsity, 2004.

Lincoln, Andrew T. *Ephesians: Word Biblical Commentary*. Dallas: Word, 1990.

Lloyd-Jones, D. M. *Faith on Trial*. London: Inter-Varsity, 1965.

Lofton, Kathryn. *Oprah: The Gospel of an Icon*. Berkeley, CA: University of California Press, 2011.

Lovelace, Richard. "Evangelicalism: Recovering a Tradition of Spiritual Depth." *The Reformed Journal* (September 1990): 25–26.

Luther, Martin. *The Bondage of the Will*. Grand Rapids: Revell, 1957.

———. "A Mighty Fortress is Our God" (1529) in *Hymns for the Living Church* (Carol Stream, IL: Hope Publishing, 1974), 11.

Lyotard, Jean-François. *Differend: Phrases in Dispute*. Minneapolis: University of Minnesota Press, 1989.

———. *The Postmodern Condition: A Report on Knowledge*. Translated by Geoff Bennington and Brian Massumi. Minneapolis: University of Minnesota Press, 1984.

Mangina, Joseph L. *Revelation: The Brazos Theological Commentary*. Grand Rapids: Brazos, 2010.

Marshall, Paul, Lela Gilbert, and Nina Shea. *Persecuted: The Global Assault On Christians*. Nashville: Thomas Nelson, 2013.

Marshall, Paul. *Their Blood Cries Out*. Nashville: Thomas Nelson, 1997.

Milton, John. *Complete Poems and Major Prose*. Edited by Merritt Y. Hughes. New York: Odyssey, 1957.

Mounce, Robert. *Revelation: New International Commentary*. Grand Rapids: Eerdmans, 1994.

Mouw, Richard. "The Life of Bondage in the Light of Grace." *Christianity Today*, December 9, 1988, 41–42.

Newbigin, Lesslie. *The Gospel in a Pluralistic Society*. Grand Rapids: Eerdmans, 1989.

Nietzsche, Friedrich. *Basic Writings of Nietzsche*. Translated and edited by Walter Kaufmann. New York: The Modern Library, 2000.

Olson, Bruce. *For This Cross I'll Kill You*. Carol Stream, IL: Creation House, 1973.

Osborne, Grant R. *Revelation: Baker Exegetical Commentary on the New Testament*. Grand Rapids: Baker Academic, 2002.

Osteen, Joel, *Your Best Life Now*. New York: FaithWords, 2007.

Pagels, Elaine. *Revelations: Visions, Prophecy, and Politics in the Book of Revelation*. New York: Penguin, 2012.

Peterson, Eugene, H. *Christ Plays in Ten Thousand Places*. Grand Rapids: Eerdmans, 2009.

———. *Eat This Book*. Grand Rapids: Eerdmans, 2005.

———. *The Jesus Way*. Grand Rapids: Eerdmans, 2007.

———. *The Pastor: A Memoir*. New York: HarperOne, 2011.

———. *Reversed Thunder: The Revelation of John and the Praying Imagination*. San Francisco: Harper & Row, 1988.

———. "Spirituality for All the Wrong Reasons." *Christianity Today*, March 4, 2005, 44–45.

Postman, Neil. *Amusing Ourselves to Death: Public Discourse in the Age of Show Business*. New York: Penguin, 1985.

Robertson, E. H. *Christians Against Hitler*. London: SCM, 1962.

Rohr, Richard. *Falling Upward: A Spirituality for the Two Halves of Life*. San Francisco: Jossey-Bass, 2011.

Rushdie, Salman. Wikiquote. https://en.wikiquote.org/wiki/Salman_Rushdie.

Rutledge, Fleming. *The Battle for Middle Earth: Tolken's Divine Design in the Lord of the Rings*. Grand Rapids: Eerdmans, 2004.

Samuel, Vinay. "Religion: Cause or Cure for Terrorism? The Christian Church and a World of Religiously Inspired Violence." *SPU Response*, Spring 2003, 9–10.

Sauer, Mark. "Drawing From Experience." *The San Diego Union-Tribune*, October 8, 2000.

Sheets, Dwight. "Something Old, Something New: Revelation and Empire." In *Jesus Is Lord, Caesar Is Not: Evaluating Empire in New Testament Studies*, edited by Scot McKnight and Joseph B. Modica, 197–210. Downers Grove, IL: InterVarsity, 2013.

Sittser, Gerald L. *A Grace Disguised: How the Soul Grows Through Loss*. Grand Rapids: Zondervan, 1996.

Snodgrass, Klyne. *Ephesians: The NIV Application Commentary*. Grand Rapids: Zondervan, 1996.

Stafford, Tim. "The Joy of Suffering in Sri Lanka." *Christianity Today*, October 1, 2003, 55–57.

Steiner, George. *Language & Silence: Essays on Language, Literature, and the Inhuman*. New Haven, CT: Yale University Press, 1998.

Stott, John R. W. *Christ the Controversialist*. Downers Grove, IL.: Inter-Varsity, 1970.

———. *The Christian Counter Culture: The Message of the Sermon on the Mount*. Downers Grove, IL: InterVarsity, 1978.

———. *God's New Society: The Message of Ephesians*. Downers Grove, IL: InterVarsity, 1979.

———. *What Christ Thinks of the Church: An Exposition of Revelation 1–3*. Wheaton, IL: Harold Shaw, 1990.

Sullivan, Andrew. "When Not Seeing Is Believing." *Time*, October 6, 2006, 59–60.

Tapper, Jake. *The Outpost: An Untold Story of American Valor*. New York: Little, Brown and Company, 2012.

Ten Boom, Corrie, with Elizabeth Sherrill and John Sherrill. *The Hiding Place*. Grand Rapids: Baker, 2006.

Tennent, Timothy C. *Invitation To World Missions: A Trinitarian Missiology for the Twenty-first Century*. Grand Rapids: Kregel, 2010.

Thielicke, Helmut. *Life Can Begin Again: Sermons on the Sermon on the Mount*. Translated by John W. Doberstein. Philadelphia: Fortress, 1963.

Volf, Miroslav. *A Public Faith: How Followers of Christ Should Serve the Common Good*. Grand Rapids: Brazos, 2011.

———. *The End of Memory: Remembering Rightly in a Violent World*. Grand Rapids: Eerdmans, 2006.

———. *Exclusion and Embrace: A Theological Exploration of Identity, Otherness, and Reconciliation*. Nashville: Abingdon, 1996.

Wallace, David Foster. "Federer As Religious Experience." *New York Times Magazine*, September, 2006, 46–51, 80–83.

Walvoord, John F. *The Millennial Kingdom*. Grand Rapids: Zondervan, 1959.

———. *The Revelation of Jesus Christ*. Chicago: Moody, 1966.

Weinberg, Steven. *The First Three Minutes: A Modern View of the Origin of the Universe*. New York: Basic, 1977.

Wells, David. *No Place For Truth*. Grand Rapids: Eerdmans, 1993.

Wenham, John W. *The Goodness of God*. Downers Grove, IL: InterVarsity, 1974.

Wiker, Benjamin and Jonathan Witt. *A Meaningful World: How the Arts and Sciences Reveal the Genius of Nature*. Downers Grove, IL: InterVarsity, 2006.

Wilcock, Michael. *The Message of Revelation*. Downers Grove, IL: InterVarsity, 2006.

Willard, Dallas. *The Spirit of the Disciplines*. New York: HarperOne, 1990.

Wood, Ralph. *Flannery O'Connor and the Christ-Haunted South*. Grand Rapids: Eerdmans, 2005.

Wright, Christopher J. H. *The Mission of God: Unlocking the Bible's Grand Narrative*. Downers Grove, IL: InterVarsity, 2006.

Wright, N. T. *After You Believe: Why Christian Character Matters*. New York: HarperOne, 2010.

Wuthnow, Robert. *After the Baby Boomers: How Twenty- and Thirty-Somethings Are Shaping The Future of American Religion*. Princeton, NJ: Princeton University Press, 2007.

Yeats, W. B. "The Second Coming." In *The Collected Poems*, edited by Richard J. Finneran, 187. New York: Scribner, 1996.

Yoder, John Howard. *The Politics of Jesus*. Grand Rapids: Eerdmans, 1972.